EURIPIDES OUR CONTEMPORARY

J. Michael Walton is Emeritus Professor of Drama at the University of Hull. He studied Greek under Kenneth Dover and Douglas Young at the University of St Andrews, where he directed the first of over fifty subsequent productions with professional or student casts. At Hull he was founder-director of the Performance Translation Centre and he has been a Getty Visiting Scholar. He was General Editor of the sixteen volumes of Methuen Drama's Classical Greek Dramatists series, to which he also contributed nine translations. His books include *Greek Theatre Practice*, *The Greek Sense of Theatre: Tragedy Reviewed*, *Living Greek Theatre: A Handbook of Classical Performance and Modern Production*, *Menander and the Making of Comedy* (with Peter D. Arnott) and *Found in Translation: Greek Drama in English*. He edited *Craig on Theatre* and, with Marianne McDonald, *Amid Our Troubles: Irish Versions of Greek Tragedy* and *The Cambridge Companion to Greek and Roman Theatre*.

EURIPIDES OUR CONTEMPORARY

J. Michael Walton

UNIVERSITY OF CALIFORNIA PRESS

Berkeley   Los Angeles

University of California Press, one of the most distinguished university presses in the
United States, enriches lives around the world by advancing scholarship in the humanities,
social sciences, and natural sciences. Its activities are supported by the UC Press
Foundation and by philanthropic contributions from individuals and institutions.
For more information, visit www.ucpress.edu.

University of California Press
Berkeley and Los Angeles, California

This edition first published in the United Kingdom in 2009 by
Methuen Drama
A & C Black Publishers Ltd
36 Soho Square
London W1D 3QY
www.methuendrama.com

University of California Press edition 2010

Cataloging-in-Publication data for this title is on file with the Library of Congress.

ISBN 978-0-520-26179-2 (cloth : alk. paper)
ISBN 978-0-520-26182-2 (pbk. : alk. paper)

19 18 17 16 15 14 13 12 11 10
10 9 8 7 6 5 4 3 2 1

Typeset by SX Composing DTP, Rayleigh, Essex, United Kingdom
Printed by MPG Books, Bodmin, Cornwall, United Kingdom

CONTENTS

ACKNOWLEDGMENTS

I have greatly appreciated the constructive criticism of readers of the manuscript, among them Mary-Kay Gamel and Herbert Golder. I also wish to thank my frequent co-translator and co-editor Marianne McDonald for her always valuable and supportive suggestions at every stage. I exonerate her completely from any responsibility for the more idiosyncratic interpretations of individual plays.

INTRODUCTION

In 1964, the Polish critic Jan Kott's book on Shakespeare was published in England as *Shakespeare Our Contemporary*.[1] It was in the form of a series of essays, eight on various of Shakespeare's tragedies, three on his comedies. Peter Brook wrote a brief foreword in which he described meeting Kott at a nightclub in Warsaw and spending half the night with him trying to secure the release of one of Kott's students who had been arrested by the police. Brook was surprised that, at the police station, the police called Kott 'Professor' and asked him what he was a professor of. 'Of drama,' replied Kott. This seemed a revelation to Brook and not without reason. In 1964 there were only three independent Drama departments in British universities, at Bristol, Manchester and Hull – a fourth was about to open at Birmingham – and only two professors of Drama.

Kott's book was greeted with enthusiasm by numerous critics and practitioners for combining serious study of the texts with an awareness, derived from his own political situation and circumstances, of the historical and social climate that spawned them – 'scholarly without what we associate with scholarship' was Brook's verdict. The essays were accessible and informative to actors and directors as well as to students and teachers. To put it another way, this was an academic book with a minimum of footnotes. The other factor that made Kott's study unusual among books on Shakespeare was that it looked forwards as well as backwards, the index including references to the major European theatrical influences of the 1960s, Adamov, Artaud, Brecht, Dürrenmatt, Genet, Ionesco, Sartre and, above all, Beckett, as well Camus, Kafka and Malraux.

Two years later, in 1966, Kott began work on a further volume, this time about Greek tragedy, which was published in 1970 as *The Eating of the Gods: An Interpretation of Greek Tragedy*.[2] This second book, a series of essays on Aeschylus' *Prometheus*, Sophocles' *Ajax* and *Philoctetes* and Euripides' *Alcestis*, *Bacchae* and related topics, proved less influential than the first, perhaps because Kott needed recourse to

[1] Jan Kott, *szekspirze wspólczesny* (1965), trans. Bolesaw Taborski, published as *Shakespeare Our Contemporary*, London: Methuen, 1964, revised 1967.
[2] Published by Random House (1973) and subsequently in Great Britain by Eyre Methuen (1974). Taborski was again the translator, this time in collaboration with Edward J. Czerwinski.

1

scholars of ancient Greek. Though he turned to the work of major luminaries in the field, among them Richard Jebb, A. W. Verrall, Gilbert Murray, George D. Thomson, Maurice Bowra, T. B. L. Webster, E. R. Dodds, Humphrey Kitto, Bernard Knox and Peter D. Arnott, never mind philosophers and anthropologists, Heidegger, Lévi-Strauss, Graves and Auerbach, the work of such giants on the classical world is not always compatible. The resultant essays vary from provocative insight, worthy of the author of *Shakespeare Our Contemporary*, to awkward generalisation[1] and actual inaccuracy.[2] Nonetheless, it is in appreciation of Kott that the present book acquired its title. *Euripides Our Contemporary* is intended both as an acknowledgment of the need for Drama professors from time to time to re-investigate the earliest manifestations of the world's theatre repertoire and a strong belief that the kind of interrogation that has been applied to Shakespeare may be just as appropriate for Euripides.

As far as Greek tragedy is concerned, a far greater influence than Kott has been William Arrowsmith, a formidable scholar and translator of Greek drama. His 'Euripides and the Dramaturgy of Crisis' was initially a lecture delivered at Columbia University in 1984.[3] This reassessment of Euripides as a playmaker, in the light of his conglomeration of styles, his scepticism and sheer theatricality, went a long way to identifying Euripides' significance for a twentieth-century world. This is not to suggest that there has been any dearth, either before or after 1984, of books and articles on Euripides and his nineteen plays which have survived, in close to six hundred English translations since Lady Jane Lumley's Elizabethan *Iphigeneia*. Two thousand four hundred years after his death, it might not be unreasonable to wonder what sort of book can any longer be written about Euripides. The linguistic details and textual peculiarities which formed the basis of school and university study for longer than bear thinking about are surely an exhausted seam; too little is known for a biography; individual plays have received the closest and

---

[1] For example 'Alcestis is a heroine of tragedy, but has a husband taken from comedy', p. 83; 'Of all Greek plays, *The Bacchae* seems to be most pervaded by eroticism', p. 224. What of *Hippolytus*?

[2] '*Prometheus Bound* is the only Greek tragedy in which the Chorus perishes with the hero', p. 36 – neither dies; 'Medea does not address the gods. They do not exist for her, just as the world does not exist, as her children do not exist', p. 237 – she invokes Hecate, Themis, Artemis, Hera and Zeus, never mind her grandfather, Helios.

[3] Arrowsmith delivered the four Bampton lectures at Columbia in 1984, in the first of which he explored the notion of 'anachronization' in Euripides. This first lecture was published posthumously in 1999, but at the time of writing the other three remain unpublished, his premature death in 1992 having prevented revision.

most ingenious of scrutinies; locating the playwright within the social and political context of his time is a well-trodden path, if still a contentious one. Less explored has been Euripides' impact on later generations. It is in this kind of territory that the present study is to be located. The aim is specific. What Euripides was in his own time is less important here than why he should still have something to say about our hectic contemporary world when concerns such as global warming, nuclear proliferation, terrorist infiltration and bank failures dominate the headlines. How, in short, and why may Euripides still resonate?

If this were to be simply a book listing topics to show how 'contemporary' the plays of Euripides may prove, it could be short indeed. What are the subjects of this ancient Greek playwright? War, its causes and conduct; morality and power; the influence of oligarchy in a notional democracy; domestic strife; old age, illness and bereavement; sickness within society; personal responsibility; refugees and immigration; religion and ideology; sacrifice and self-sacrifice. No difficulty finding comment on such themes in Euripides. His plays are filled with people who constantly fiddle with the truth, gods, heroes, soldiers, politicians, even messengers. At a symposium on 'Contemporary Performance of Greek and Roman Drama' held at the J. Paul Getty Museum in June, 2002, the American director, Peter Sellars, told his audience he had just returned to America after two years away: 'and I'm shocked at the absence of dissent in this country. The absence of public voice over things that absolutely must be spoken of. So, of course, I am now working with Euripides. That's simple . . . and the reason I'm working on *The Children of Heracles*, it's about refugees and immigration.' To give his words their full political context, they were delivered almost exactly at midpoint between the destruction of the Twin Towers and the second invasion of Iraq.

This book takes Sellars' position as a starting point and aims further. Comment on their own time was filtered by the Greek tragedians in a way that transcends period. Euripides may have no knowledge of the specific problems of our age, but any comment on his own age was strictly deflected. He and his contemporaries set their tragedies, with minor exceptions, in the world of myth. The advantage of myth is that its stories are basic but malleable. Entrenched in an unspecific Greek past as nebulous as that of Shakespeare's *Troilus and Cressida*, *Timon of Athens* or *A Midsummer Night's Dream*, the plots of all three Greek tragedians engaged topical issues from an oblique perspective. The Trojan War served as a means of viewing any war, its avoidability or unavoidability, its heroics and mock-heroics, its consequences, its futility and its misery.

3

It still can. Euripides wrote most of his plays during the Peloponnesian War between Athens and Sparta (431–04 BC). His investigations of the causes, conduct and aftermath of that war must all have reverberated at a dramatic festival, one of whose opening ceremonies included a parade of the sons of those who had died in battle during the previous year. There have still been few more potent statements in any age about the effect of war on winners, never mind losers, than *Trojan Women* and *Hecuba*, both of which have received major productions in recent years: English-language *Hecuba*s were performed in at least four new translations, all published, in 2004–5 alone.

Euripides' comparative lack of tangible success in his own time – only four competitive victories at the Great Dionysia in a career that lasted fifty years – reflected both the novelty of his approach and the challenges, often seemingly ironic, jaundiced or simply flippant, that he offered to received wisdom on all manner of topics. Like the innovative artist in any era he risked derision and gossip. Undependable later biographies say he worked in a cave on Salamis; could not control his wife or wives; had funny foreign friends, several of whom were dangerous. There was Protagoras, for instance, deported from Athens after reading a book at Euripides' house which was then publicly burnt, and the natural philosopher (scientist), Anaxagoras, who suggested that the sun was not a god but a large mass of hot stone, as big as the Peloponnese. Euripides was a freethinker. His plays were full of popular music and unpopular opinions. Remarks made by his characters were taken, perhaps inevitably, as representing his own attitudes.

At the same time we have tales like the one about the Athenian survivors of the Sicilian expedition, seven thousand of whom were condemned to working in the Syracusan stone quarries. Some of these, the story goes, secured their freedom by being able to recite (or sing?) Euripidean choruses, this making them a desirable after-dinner cabaret at Syracusan soirées. The reasons for the playwright's leaving Athens for Macedon in the final years of his life are uncertain and contradictory. If Aristophanes knew the true version, he chose to ignore it in his *Frogs* (405 BC, the year after Euripides' death) where Euripides and Aeschylus compete for the right to return from the dead to save Athens.

In the century after his death Euripides' popularity grew, but subsequently has gone up and down like a yo-yo, varying from ecstatic endorsement to rank dismissal. Many of the most distinguished scholars of the nineteenth and twentieth centuries rated him a poor third after Aeschylus and Sophocles. Aristotle had not been over-keen on him either, but rigid formulae for what constitutes 'tragedy', debated as they have been over centuries, tend to fracture and collapse when faced with the realities of a playwright of genius. Shakespeare simply refuses to submit to any kind of literary rules or single interpretations. The same is true of Euripides, as I hope this study of all his surviving dramas may show. The word 'drama' rather than 'tragedy' is used advisedly. Though in his nineteen surviving plays we have enough to recognise Aristotle's description of him as *tragikôtatos*, we probably have too few to work out precisely what meaning 'most tragic' may have had, either for Aristotle or for Euripides himself. Among that nineteen, we have one farcical satyr play, at least four without the death of one of the characters, and two more where an apparent death is put in doubt. Nearly half have what may seem like a happy ending and the range of sentiment and mood is far greater than in any other ancient playwright.

It was tempting to look at the plays in some sort of chronological order, despite the glaring objection of there being firm dates for only eight of the nineteen and its being anyone's guess for most of the others. An alternative might have been to group them by genres, pointing to the different moods they parade from deepest despair to unforeseen jauntiness; by recurrent characters in comparison with their Aeschylean and Sophoclean counterparts (Electra, Clytemnestra, Menelaus, Heracles, Theseus); or again by broad political sentiment, whether the politics be theological, military, gender or domestic. It would be feasible to sort them into premier league (*Medea*, *Hippolytus*, *Trojan Women*, *Bacchae*) and lower division (*Suppliants*, *Children of Heracles*, *Rhesus*, *Iphigeneia Among the Taurians*).

In the end it seemed more important to pick themes for each chapter and range across the whole canon, if appropriate, with certain plays accentuated.[1] It has been a priority that every surviving play should feature in at least one chapter: several crop up more than once. Fragmentary plays are for the most part discounted, their overall structure being largely conjectural. Some plays are discussed with which many readers may be unfamiliar, the price to pay if Euripides' place in the contemporary repertoire is to be fully espoused and celebrated. Accordingly, though commentary is accompanied by the immediate context, there is a reference Appendix at the end, with a short summary of the plots of all nineteen plays.

The biggest difficulty has been whittling down the possible approaches to the compass of a single book when subjects as diverse as 'Euripides and

---

[1] This is the favoured method of several of the whole-book studies of Euripides to which I am indebted for the insights of their authors, including Bates (1930); Grube (1941); Conacher (1967); Barlow (1971); Vellacott (1975).

the Afterlife', 'Euripides and Discrimination' or 'Euripides and Democracy' might all claim a place. Thematic links tend to be inflicted by critic rather than by playwright, but organisation of some sort is unavoidable. My interest here is less in interpreting the plays of Euripides than suggesting how and why they are still amenable to interpretation. The chapter on 'The Family Saga', for example, does not consider the family in classical Athens, only what still recognisable aspects of family relationships surface within certain plays. A similar approach is taken to his treatment of women, the comic, war and the military, revenge, the gods, sanity, madness and responsibility, and theatre and illusion. The first chapter is an introduction to Euripides and his working method which those familiar with his work can skip with equanimity. The final chapters involve Euripides' approach to theatre and how this relates to individual roles within his plays. This serves as a bridge to identifying a selection of playwrights from the last hundred or so years who might most seem to have returned Euripides to the modern theatre through dramatic and theatrical approaches, first found in his work, which they have chosen to develop and transcend.

This is not, in other words, except incidentally, any sort of consideration of ancient Greek life or of Greek plays within the context of their own time. There are already numbers of fine studies to which the reader may turn if that is what they are looking for. Too many others, I fear, have been written by those determined to make Euripides conform with their personal idea of Greek tragedy and who have taken it as a personal affront when he insists on proving himself a playwright first, a poet second and a theorist last.

Still less is this book an evaluation of contemporary reception of Euripides' plays or a reflection on the nature of adaptation and its relationship to translation.[1] The history of the production of Euripides' plays belongs in another and different book, written with the authority of someone who has spent more time as a member of an audience than in the rehearsal room. Least of all is *Euripides Our Contemporary* intended as advice to would-be directors on how to handle a chorus or digest the nature of a masked drama. If it proves helpful in informing such decisions, well and good. What I do hope is that any director who wishes to take on the challenge of Greek tragedy, and even those who have previously considered Euripides as mired in the deep past, may find a stimulus in these pages: actors too and anyone with a broad interest in the

---

[1] This is a subject that I have already dealt with in some detail elsewhere (Walton 2006 and 2007 b).

history of the drama who may have been wary of searching any further back than Shakespeare.

Many of my interpretations and explanations have been absorbed from previous scholars – and indeed practitioners – or stimulated by them. For their not always being given due acknowledgment I offer apologies, under the defence that this was to be more a book for the theatre professional and the general reader than the classical scholar for whom chapter, verse and cross-reference are *de rigueur*. The select bibliography points to previous studies which have been influential in encouraging or forming my own sense of the playwright and his plays, though for the most part that has been inspired by my work as director, actor and translator. If all the ideas are not necessarily new, I hope they are presented in a fresh kind of way. The job here, as I see it, is less to dictate parallels than to invite them.

Greek words have been reduced to a minimum and are transliterated in italics, bearing in mind that the Greek alphabet differs considerably from the Roman. The titles of the Greek plays are in their most familiar form to the modern reader, accessibility triumphing over the preferences of many current classical scholars. Plays written in French, Italian or German referred to in Chapter 11 are under their translated title unless they have not been performed in English. Translation of various passages, unless otherwise acknowledged, is my own. Some examples can be found in published translations from the Methuen Drama series 'Classical Greek Dramatists' (*Alcestis*, *Bacchae*, *Cyclops*, *Medea*, *Rhesus*); others were prepared in collaboration with Marianne McDonald for publication and/or performance (*Andromache* and *Electra* for Nick Hern Books, *Helen*, *Iphigeneia Among the Taurians* and *Frogs*). Lyric passages have an initial capital for each line; iambic dialogue in the Greek is in a much freer verse, or prose, form. I have tried to suit the English versions to the mood of scenes in the original, which may vary from the savage to the farcical. Line-numberings refer to the Greek text, usually the Oxford text of James Diggle.

I. DOMESTICATING TRAGEDY

1 PLAYMAKER AND IMAGE-BREAKER

In 1913, as the First World War was looming, but still seemed preventable, Gilbert Murray published his *Euripides and His Age*.[1] It quickly became a classic study which sealed his reputation; and so it remains, with some reservations over his enthusiasm for the ritual nature of tragedy. Not that Murray's reputation needed much cementing by 1913. Twenty-four years earlier, at the absurdly young age of twenty-three, he had accepted the Chair of Greek at the University of Glasgow. Before long he was a major, if occasionally erratic, editor of Euripides, and a produced playwright who had become closely associated with the innovative Court Theatre in London. By the time he was appointed as Regius Professor of Greek at the University of Oxford in 1908, he was a theatrical celebrity, a translator whose versions of Euripides' *Hippolytus*, *The Trojan Women*, *Electra* and *Medea* had introduced Euripides to the West End stage for the first time since *Hecuba* was booed off at Drury Lane in 1726.[2] He was a friend and associate of playwright and director Harley Granville Barker and had featured, in affectionate caricature, as Professor Adolphus Cusins in George Bernard Shaw's *Major Barbara* of 1905. He was to become one of the founders of the League of Nations at the conclusion of the First World War and a Joint President of the United Nations Association after the Second until his death in 1955.

Within the bounds of such a remarkable career, one modest volume might seem but another small feather in an extravagantly large cap. *Euripides and His Age* was more than that. It was an account which helped to liberate the most versatile of the Athenian tragedians from the exclusive enclave of classical scholarship and place him in the consciousness of those with no background in Greek and Latin. More significantly, while still considering the plays within the context of their own time, Murray made a powerful case for treating them as

---

[1] *Euripides and His Age* is still a seminal assessment of the background to the playwright's career. Murray's translations may have gone out of fashion and, indeed, seem at this remove to merit the derision heaped upon them by critics from Edith Hamilton to T. S. Eliot to Peter Green, but his insights into the classical world and its writers can be as cogent as ever.

[2] Translator Richard West had anticipated a hostile reception from the audience at Drury Lane, if not the 'rout of vandals in the gallerie' which put paid to his enterprise.

performance, rather than simply literary, pieces. He may not have been the first to attempt this, as the history of nineteenth-century scholarship shows: he was the first to have much real understanding of the requirements of the stage. Murray's translations of the Greeks, comedy as well as tragedy, are indeed dated, but he laid the foundation of all more recent studies when he pronounced in his Presidential Address to the Classical Association in January 1918 that, 'The Scholar's special duty is to turn the written signs in which old poetry or philosophy is now enshrined back into living thought or feeling. He must so understand as to relive.' For Murray, as E. R. Dodds wrote in his Introduction to *Gilbert Murray: An Unfinished Autobiography*, 'A play was first and foremost a piece of theatre to be enjoyed and criticised as such, and only secondarily a document to be analysed in the study.'[1]

Artists are a product of their own time, culture and environment. Whatever case may be made for ignoring this in the novelist, to deny its significance for the playwright reveals a serious confusion over how drama functions. The extent to which that should affect an appreciation of a play is more equivocal. The focus of this book is not on the Athens in which Euripides lived and worked, but how and why he can 'relive', to use Murray's word, in today's theatre. One factor is especially helpful in this, if not always fully appreciated: the plays that the first audiences in Athens witnessed in the Theatre of Dionysus did not offer, except covertly, a picture of life in Euripides' Athens. If theatre offered a mirror to nature for the Athenians it was a distorting mirror and hence an oblique one. The political systems on which the plays are structured are hardly Athenian. It is this quality that Arrowsmith identified as 'anachronization'. The notion of kingship in classical Athens had been swept away with the removal of Hippias in 510 BC. The democracy that took its place had its flaws, being based on slavery and on an exclusively male participation in the decision-making process. It was nevertheless more enlightened than anything in other Greek cities and, as George McDonald Fraser wrote in a slightly different context, 'You cannot, you must not, judge the past by the present; you must try to see it in its own terms, if you are to have any inkling of it.'[2]

The aristocratic families survived in Athens and from time to time made a bid for power, but that democracy was never seriously undermined in Euripides' lifetime. In tragedy, decisions are made by kings, though they are frequently guided by, or sensibly take note of,

---

[1] Smith and Toynbee, eds. (1960), p. 16. See also Stray (2007).
[2] George McDonald Fraser, *Quartered Safe Out Here*, first pb. London: HarperCollins, 2000, p. xxiv.

public opinion as revealed in state assemblies. What Euripides' own political preferences were is hard to gauge, especially so when he resets his regime according to each play. Individual characters may reveal serious doubts on the influence of the rabble-rouser, but it is rash to look for Euripides himself in his own characters.[1] All that can be suggested with any confidence is that he became more cynical about the nature of heroes the longer he wrote, though telltale signs of such an attitude can be found in all his surviving plays.

Murray chose to scrutinise Euripides' life and work more or less chronologically, insofar as that is possible. Properly, in a full study of Euripides as a playwright, he considered the major political and social changes of fifth-century BC Athens as influential on what Euripides wrote. Most of Euripides' work was produced when Athens was engaged in the Peloponnesian War with Sparta which continued, if sporadically, from 431 BC until 404 BC, two years after his death in Macedon where he spent his last years at the court of King Archelaus. The gradual decline that the war signalled for his home city seems reflected by a growing disillusion in the playwright. Classical Athens was at the centre of an intellectual ferment, matched by extraordinary developments in the arts, art, architecture, sculpture, pottery, dance and music: and theatre in which all these manifestations became crystallised. Euripides was a dramatic and theatrical innovator. Of that we can be sure, if only through the comedies of Aristophanes, where he is pilloried for his advanced music, his realistic effects and stage mechanics, his situations and his characters.

Aristophanes' *Frogs* opens in the contemporary Athens of 405 BC, after the death of both Euripides and Sophocles in the previous year. So upset is Dionysus that he finds his way down to Hades to try and resurrect Euripides without whom he, as god of the theatre, feels utterly desolate. When he gets to Hades he discovers that Pluto, god of the underworld, has instituted a competition between Euripides and Aeschylus who is upset at finding his position as dramatist laureate threatened. Each will be given the opportunity to extol his own virtues and criticise the dramatic skills of his rival. Though distilled through the requirements of a stage fantasy-comedy, *Frogs* proves to be an illuminating insight into the working and dramatic structures of the two tragedians. It is the

---

[1] Aristophanes exercises his comedian's prerogative by using the sentiments of Euripides' characters in his own comedies on a number of occasions. One of the more celebrated was Hippolytus' 'It was my tongue that swore: my heart remained unsworn' (*Hippolytus*, l. 612), turned against the playwright by the stage Dionysus as an excuse for rejecting the stage Euripides' claims to victory in the dramatic contest with Aeschylus in *Frogs* (l. 1471).

nearest we have to dramatic criticism from the whole of the classical period up to Aristotle; and from a working playwright, however exaggerated his two dead mouthpieces. What is especially valuable about the competition in which the two caricatures mock one another's stage devices, language and music, as well as their morality and beliefs, is that it gives licence to us today to use a similar critical vocabulary as Aristophanes in making our own evaluations of the tragedians' work. Dionysus ends up in part judging farcically between the two playwrights by which can utter the weightier lines when spoken on to a set of scales, but the clinching aspect is their level of advice on how to save Athens. By this time the Spartans were almost at their doorstep. In Aristophanes serious points underpin the comedy, whether addressed to dramatic criticism or political stance.

Such features, including the satire, do and should affect our understanding of all Athenian drama, though Peter Burian, when analysing Arrowsmith's Bampton lecture, did wonder if there had been too much such speculation over Euripides in recent years, suggesting (in 1999) that Euripidean criticism in the first half of our century abounded with:

> attempts to 'explain' Euripides with a single idea or trope: Euripides the Realist, the Idealist, the Rationalist – all these and more have come and gone and we are not much closer to consensus than we were before about either the meaning or the merit of the plays.[1]

This verdict is a little harsh. Plays are by their very nature flexible in meaning, depending, as they do, on hands other than their author's for consummation. They are bound to be open to more than one interpretation. Numbers of critics over the last hundred years have dissected and illuminated the work of all the Greek tragedians and our understanding is the greater for the breadth of readings.[2] When the purpose is, as here, to throw light, less on how Euripides may best be served in a modern production, than on how the texts may be read to make their revival justifiable in the first place, the search is on for something more elusive that will give them new life.

One starting-place might be to identify what is different about this

---

[1] Burian (1999): pp. 24–5.
[2] See especially among the most accessible, F. L. Lucas (1924); D. W. Lucas (1950); Greenwood (1953); Kitto (1961); Conacher (1967); Winnington-Ingram (1969); Knox (1979); Foley (1985 and 2001); Heath (1987); Kovacs (1987); Michelini, ed. (1987); P. D. Arnott (1989); Powell, ed. (1990); McDonald (1992, 2002 and 2003); Croally (1994); Macintosh (1994); the various contributors to Easterling, ed. (1997), Goldhill and Osborne, eds. (1999); Rehm (2003); Mossman, ed. (2003); Hall, Macintosh and Wrigley, eds. (2004).

playwright's playmaking, both in and out of his own time, and how he subjects the mythic past to reappraisal in the light of commonplace experience. When the original Athenian audience saw and heard his plays they did so through the perspective of their own lives and expectations. The same is true for us today, but in the time of Euripides this involved an intricate cultural complex only part of which we can still hope to understand. An element within that context entailed both the function of theatre and the history of an art form that was a bare seventy-five years old when Euripides first presented a production. From this early period at most nine tragedies survive, seven by Aeschylus, who had died in 456 BC, and probably no more than two by Sophocles, who was to remain a rival of Euripides for the rest of both their lives. Unearthing Euripides' persistent striving for innovation in his extant work is not difficult. He wanted his plays to be different from those of previous playwrights and to achieve this he would forge new dramatic weapons and use them to challenge previous ideas about tragedy and tragic form.

Three aspects of this iconoclasm exemplify his purpose: surprise, parody and a reappraisal of the expectation of familiar characters. It is on these that the remainder of this first chapter will focus, as a stepping-stone to the central themes which link the playwright's output and make his plays so receptive to modern readings and modern performance.

Alcestis from 438 BC, and the first Euripides we have, is a play whose tone has always raised the blood pressure of those wedded to compartmentalising drama. It was, apart from anything else, apparently a 'fourth' play, at a time when this was customarily a farcical satyr drama. Euripides had first presented a group of four plays at the Great Dionysia of 455 BC, less than a year after the death of Aeschylus. The likelihood has to be that Euripides was present at several Aeschylean 'first nights', including the *Oresteia*, his later reaction to which has often come under scrutiny and will do so again below. In 438 BC Euripides was comfortably past forty and, if *Alcestis* is anything to go by, already an innovator in both form and content. One of the plays in the same group which failed to survive, except by reputation, was *Telephus*. Telephus in myth was a son of Heracles, injured in battle by Achilles when his land of Mysia was invaded by the Greek forces on their way to Troy. He subsequently disguised himself as a beggar and arrived at the Greek camp, having been told by the oracle at Delphi that only Achilles could cure his wound. He then had to save his own skin by taking hostage the infant Orestes and threatening to kill him. Exactly when, where and how all this took place is far from clear, but the scene of Telephus threatening the baby was to become a celebrated one, familiar enough to be parodied in

Aristophanes' *Women at the Thesmophoria* and celebrated on a famous vase.[1] As renowned, or perhaps infamous, was the fact that Euripides apparently dressed the beggar king as a beggar rather than as a king. If this does not in hindsight seem to be sufficiently revolutionary to represent a major turning point in the presentation of Greek tragedy, it is perhaps worth bearing in mind that realism within a masked theatre tradition is strictly a relative term and that Euripides made his reputation by flouting the familiar.

Many of his most powerful dramatic situations arise out of the contradictions that are thrown up between received myth and possible human reactions to such events. 438 BC was an experimental year for Euripides and the central issue raised by any contemporary approach to the myth of Alcestis was part of the experiment. The plot, in brief, homes in on Admetus, king of Pherae, granted the favour by Apollo that, when his time comes to die, he may offer a substitute (see also Chapter 3, pp. 46–51 and Appendix, pp. 213–14). His wife Alcestis agrees to take his place. Eventually Heracles wrestles with Death and restores her to her husband. Euripides' play centres on the nature of Apollo's good turn and appears to raise uncomfortable questions about the domestic consequences. Such an interpretation may amount to no more than raising the sort of issue which should never be queried in a fairy-tale. In a world of godmothers with magic wands and glass slippers, why seek the reason for Cinderella's passive acceptance of her plight, or for her having a unique size of foot? No more do you enquire why Oedipus has never got round to asking Jocasta about the death of her former husband when they have been married long enough to have four children together. But Euripides does habitually, as we shall see, ask all sorts of awkward questions. That is his trademark. His characters are far enough divorced from their origins to resemble people with a real life beyond the confines of the play. They remain only close enough to their mythical situation for the plots still to function at the level of parable, and then, frequently, only by the timely intervention of a god. In *Alcestis*, Euripides sets up circumstances in which it is difficult not to speculate on the relationship between husband and wife that permits Admetus to accept Alcestis dying instead of him. For us today, whether or not for the Athenians of Euripides' time, *Alcestis* sets a pattern of dramatic interrogation about motive and purpose which the rest of his work will perpetuate.

A further unifying theme of his work is the manipulation of dramatic

---

[1] The Apulian bell-crater is held in the Martin von Wagner Museen der Universität, Würzburg (H. 5696), and widely reproduced, including McDonald and Walton, eds. (2007).

surprise, what Aristotle will later identify as *peripeteia*, 'reversal of expectation', which the philosopher links with *anagnorisis*, 'recognition of the truth'. Four of Euripides' plays (*Alcestis*, *Andromache*, *Helen* and *Bacchae*) end with the same five lines, always spoken by the Chorus who have witnessed events unfold: another, *Medea*, has a variation on the first line of the five but is otherwise the same. Here is a literal translation of the lines in question:

Many are the forms of divine beings,
[in *Medea*, 'Zeus is the overseer of many things on Olympus']
and the gods arrange many things unexpectedly:
what has been expected has not been accomplished,
and the god finds an unexpected path.
Such a thing has happened here.

In the Oxford text in Greek, the most detailed and reliable appraisal of the various manuscripts, fragments and quotations, these final lines are placed in square brackets in *Medea*, *Helen* and *Bacchae*, indicating that the editor, James Diggle, has some reservation about their authenticity. The coincidence of similar endings, even if it were to apply to only two of the five, is such that these curtain comments read like an author's flourish, a declaration by Euripides of what his plays are about, their spine, or moral signature if you wish. A central requirement for Euripidean drama, it would seem, is that it will reflect, rather than account for, the unpredictable in life. A comparison with earlier Greek tragedy is revealing.

Aeschylus, as the first of the three great tragedians, is inevitably credited with discovering the basic rules of both tragedy and the theatrical art. There had been other playwrights, several known by name, though by little else, who had presented tragedies at the Great Dionysia before him, or in competition with him, but their plays disappeared into that limbo which was the usual destination of what is, after all, still primarily a throwaway art. All the Greek playwrights who passed the scrutiny of the archon responsible for selecting the bill for the Dionysiac festivals could have expectation of no more than a single performance, whatever the health of the cast on the day, the political situation or the weather. From Aeschylus' considerable output we have the bare seven plays, none of those complete. He wrote for the most part in connected tetralogies, the fourth play being the comic satyr piece which dealt with some peripheral aspect of the myth already subjected to serious treatment in the previous three tragedies. The nearest we have to a whole tetralogy is his *Oresteia*: *Agamemnon*, *Libation-Bearers* (*Choephori*) and *Eumenides*.

That certainly works on stage as complete in itself, or even as three separate individual plays, but the loss of the satyr play *Proteus*, known only from its title and some minimal fragments, cannot but leave a sneaking feeling that our *Oresteia* may not be quite the whole *Oresteia*. At any rate, from these three plays and the other four (as well as Aristophanes' *Frogs*), we can see that the theatre for Aeschylus was a forum for ideas, but couched in a highly stylised form.

Euripides by contrast sets up a world where human action requires plausible motive. He reminds the audience of how his approach to playwriting differs from Aeschylus. Certain scenes play on an assumed knowledge of earlier tragedies. Three examples are especially striking. In *Phoenician Women*, Euripides' Theban civil war play, he seems to scorn Aeschylus' handling of plot and character in *Seven Against Thebes*. The Aeschylus play opens in Thebes, with the enemy forces at the very gates of the city. It is an exciting call to arms from Eteocles, king of Thebes, against his brother Polyneices who is determined to replace him. A scout brings news that the invaders plan to send a champion to each of the seven gates. In a subsequent scene, which lasts for almost a third of the play, he identifies each of the formidable seven and Eteocles selects his own defending hero. Aeschylus' countdown to the seventh gate is slow, deliberate and dramatically calculated, the tension mounting as the opposition of the two brothers becomes more and more inevitable.

Euripides' no-nonsense approach ensures that Eteocles has no truck with this sort of ceremony. An early scene from the ramparts between Antigone and an old Servant has already introduced the enemy hard men. Jocasta, hoping for a reconciliation, engineers a meeting between her two sons. 'Where will you be in the field?' demands Polyneices. 'Why do you want to know?' responds his brother. 'So I can stand opposite and kill you,' comes the unambiguous reply (ll. 621-2). Later, when Creon suggests posting one of their own best men at each of the seven gates, Eteocles' response is blunt:

ETEOCLES. Right. I'll go round the city's seven stations,
and, as you recommend, post a captain at each.
To name them all would be a complete waste of time,
with the enemy at the gates. (ll. 748-50)

This is not just a different, more realistic approach to the situation. It is, if not a parody of Aeschylus, at the very least a flagging-up of how drama has changed in the sixty-odd years between Aeschylus' *Seven Against Thebes* and Euripides' *Phoenician Women*.

The question has to be asked how any audience could be expected to have picked up such references when very few could have seen both first productions. Published books were a rarity in Athens and, as has already been pointed out, playwrights expected their plays to be performed on a single occasion only. There is an answer. After Aeschylus' death, a special dispensation was introduced which made it permissible for a producer (*chorêgos*) to offer a revival of Aeschylus' plays at the Great Dionysia, or other dramatic festivals, instead of original work.[1] It is possible, in consequence, that the Oedipus tetralogy which included *Seven Against Thebes* had been performed in or near Athens quite recently before Euripides presented his own *Phoenician Women*. As possible, though no less conjecture, is that the ground-breaking Euripides was so exasperated by seeing *Seven Against Thebes* when he was hardly more than a boy that, as he sat fuming in the auditorium, he was already planning to create a more believable version of the story.

There can be no doubt whatsoever that a conscious debunking permeates Euripides' version of the Electra story. *Libation-Bearers*, the second play of Aeschylus' *Oresteia*, opens with the arrival back from exile of Orestes, son of Agamemnon and Clytemnestra, with his companion, Pylades. After the murder of Agamemnon, hacked to death in his bath, Electra had remained in the palace, longing for revenge. At his father's tomb Orestes now cuts a lock of his hair and places it as an offering. The two men are disturbed and hide when a procession arrives from the palace, which turns out to consist of Electra and the Chorus of palace slaves. They have come, at Clytemnestra's insistence, after the queen has been frightened by a dream.

Electra pours her libations and suddenly catches sight of the hair which Orestes has placed on the tomb. She wonders whether it could belong to her brother, as no one else in Argos would be likely to make such a presentation. Then she sees two pairs of footprints and finds her own feet match one set. Orestes steps forward and identifies himself, suggesting she compare the cut lock with her own. Electra has sudden doubts, but he convinces her by showing a piece of embroidery which she had woven for him when he was little. Brother and sister are reunited. That is Aeschylus in 458 BC.

Some forty or more years later Sophocles and Euripides both wrote an *Electra*. The dates are unsure and there is wide disagreement about

---

[1] Though this practice is referred to in one of the unreliable later *Lives*, it seems to be born out by Aristophanes' assumption that the Athenians of his time were familiar with the plays of Aeschylus. *Seven Against Thebes* is one of the plays the stage character Aeschylus invokes in his defence in *Frogs* (405 BC), claiming that, 'Every proper man who saw that decided to become a war hero' (l. 722).

whether the Sophocles came first, or the Euripides. All that can be said with any certainty is that both were exercising their ingenuity as playwrights in offering highly charged, and widely divergent, accounts from that of Aeschylus, most especially in how the recognition between Orestes and Electra is handled. Sophocles has a complicated plot with a story of Orestes' death in a chariot race, to lower the guard of Clytemnestra and Aegisthus. Orestes confesses who he is only when moved by Electra's reaction to an urn which he claims contains Orestes' ashes.

Euripides, however, does a Euripides. Orestes encounters Electra soon after he arrives with his comrade-in-arms Pylades. But what an Electra! She has been married off to a peasant farmer and lives far from the palace, in a state of deprivation that is at least partly self-imposed. Orestes seems aghast at the ragged and self-pitying creature who confronts him and spends most of the first half of the play trying to prevent her finding out who he is (see also Chapter 4, pp. 70–2 and Appendix, pp. 219–20). Their relationship is revealed by a relentless and intractable old man, but not before the following necessarily extended exchange between the Old Man and Electra while Orestes and Pylades are indoors:

> OLD MAN. I took a side path to your father's tomb
> and, since I was alone, I dissolved in tears.
> I opened the wineskin I was bringing for the guests,
> poured some on the tomb, and adorned it with myrtle.
> Then I happened to see a black-fleeced lamb,
> its blood shed in sacrifice,
> and, alongside, this lock of blond hair.
> I was astonished, child, that anyone had dared
> go to the tomb. No Argive would.
> Maybe your brother came in secret
> and paid his respects to the pitiful tomb.
> Hold the lock up to your own hair
> and see if the colour matches.
> It's not unusual for those born of the same father
> to share physical characteristics.
> ELECTRA. You insult him, old man, if you suggest
> that my brave brother would return
> to this land by stealth, for fear of Aegisthus.
> Anyway, why should our hair match,
> he, of high birth, groomed in the wrestling ring,
> I, a woman with hair fine-combed? It's absurd!
> You can find lots of people with similar hair,
> old man, who are in no way related.

OLD MAN. You could try putting your foot into his print
    and see if that matches, child.
ELECTRA. A footprint on the stones?
    But let's say there were one,
    how would a brother's footprint match his sister's?
    I'm a woman. He's a man, with bigger feet.
OLD MAN. If your brother does come,
    isn't there something woven he was wearing
    when I stole him away and saved his life?
ELECTRA. I was a child, you realise, when the Orestes left this land.
    Even if I had woven something,
    it wouldn't have grown bigger as he grew. No!
    Some stranger must have come in secret to the tomb
    and out of pity cut a lock of his own hair. (ll. 509–47)

The echo from Aeschylus is unequivocal, though over the last hundred
and fifty years critical response to Euripides' choosing to write such a
scene has varied from delight to dismay.

Orestes and Pylades duly enter and a reluctant Orestes is at last
identified by a scar which the Old Man recognises:

ORESTES. Why is he staring so closely at me?
    For some distinguishing sign, like a hallmark?
    Does he think he knows me?
ELECTRA. Perhaps he is happy to see someone of Orestes' age.
ORESTES. Orestes whom we both love. Why is he walking round me?
ELECTRA . His behaviour is peculiar.
OLD MAN. Lady Electra, my child, thank the gods! [...]
    This is Orestes, son of Agamemnon.
ELECTRA. What gives you that impression? What proof do you have?
OLD MAN. The scar on his brow. (ll. 558–73)

Orestes turns out to be a hesitant and reluctant avenger, a far cry from
the knight in shining armour of Electra's dreams (and indeed of the
Orestes of Aeschylus and Sophocles). Neither is what the other expected
or hoped for.

In Euripides' *Orestes*, set a mere six days after the murder of
Clytemnestra, the contrast to a similar situation in Aeschylus'
Eumenides is just as marked. A deranged Orestes is being looked after
by his sister. He is tormented by visions of the Furies but, when
Menelaus asks about the nature of his sickness, he blames 'Conscience:
I'm aware of the terrible things I have done' (l. 396). The people of
Argos are about to bring brother and sister to court on a charge of
matricide. Argos, as Tyndareus will later point out, has a perfectly good

21

legal system if Orestes and Electra felt they had been wronged. At the trial the siblings only escape the penalty of being stoned to death by agreeing to commit suicide. To Clytemnestra's father, Tyndareus, Orestes offers a specious version of the defence that Apollo offers for Orestes in Aeschylus' *Eumenides*:

> ORESTES. What was I to do? Two choices. My father planted the seed.
> My mother gave birth to me. There can be no child without a father,
> so I reckoned it was my duty to take his part, not hers:
> that daughter of yours! I won't deign to call her 'Mother'. (ll. 552–7)

The Argive jury promptly find him guilty.

If the shaking up of expectations through echoes from his predecessors is one means of Euripides homing in on the human aspects of a mythological past, a different, or complementary, approach is in revisions of character. The malleability of individuals within myth was one of its advantages for the playwright, both in terms of short cuts and in springing surprises. The Creons of Sophocles' *Antigone*, *Oedipus Tyrannus* and *Oedipus at Colonus* have characters dictated more by circumstance than continuity, but then the three plays were composed over at least thirty-five years, and not as a sequence. Such a tendency is more obvious in Euripides where the volume of plays offers that much more opportunity for recurring individuals. Menelaus and Odysseus are prime examples of the versatility of character within the mythic canon, but neither more so than in the case of what today's media would have to describe as the 'iconic' Helen.

Helen, the most beautiful woman in the world, left Sparta, where she was married to Menelaus, with Paris, one of the sons of Priam and Hecuba, king and queen of Troy. The result was that, directly or indirectly, she became the cause of the Trojan War. These events form the outlines of her story. In any of the plays situated around that war and its aftermath, with the exception of *Rhesus*, she is part of the fabric. For Euripides the revisionist this offers golden opportunities. Alongside the three Euripides plays where she appears in person, *Helen*, *Orestes* and *Trojan Women*, there are another five, *Iphigeneia at Aulis*, *Hecuba*, *Iphigeneia Among the Taurians*, *Andromache* and *Electra* where she is mentioned, usually with contempt or revulsion.[1] There are considerable variations over the details of the beauty contest between Hera, Athena and Aphrodite which Paris was invited to judge. Aphrodite's superior

---

[1] Vellacott (1975) devotes a whole chapter to the attitude to Helen within these plays.

bribe of the most beautiful woman in the world is almost glossed over in *Iphigeneia at Aulis*. There, Agamemnon reduces the whole matter to an adulterous marriage when he says brusquely to his brother:

> AGAMEMNON. You lost a rotten wife and want her back again.
> You should be thanking the gods for doing you a favour. (ll. 389–90)

When Clytemnestra finally beards her husband over his decision to sacrifice their daughter Iphigeneia she is equally forthright:

> CLYTEMNESTRA. And, if someone asks you why you killed her,
> what are you going to say? How about
> 'So Menelaus could get his Helen back'? Fine.
> You pay with your daughter's life to get back an evil woman. (ll. 1166–9)

In *Hecuba* Helen gets off quite lightly, with a shared curse on her and Paris from the Chorus, and an oblique death threat. *Iphigeneia Among the Taurians* has Iphigeneia regretting she has never had the chance to take revenge for the position in which she finds herself, and the Chorus singing a charming song willing 'Leda's daughter, dear Helen' (l. 440) to come to their land to get her throat slit by Iphigeneia. Orestes later reveals, aggrievedly, that Helen is back home in Sparta, living with Menelaus.

Andromache is a bit closer to home because it features Hermione, Helen's daughter, and her father Menelaus, a thoroughly unpleasant pair. Helen is primarily a target for vilification, at least when invoked by Andromache to Hermione:

> ANDROMACHE. When it comes to having it off with men,
> don't try and compete with your mother, Helen.
> The sensible child shuns the mother's vice. (ll. 229–31)

In an equally spiteful interchange between Peleus and Menelaus (with more than a touch of the *Daily Mail* about it) Peleus has this to say about her to Menelaus:

> PELEUS. Call yourself a man, do you? You left your house wide open,
> unprotected, and some Trojan ran off with your wife.
> Thought you had a demure little bride, did you?
> Pity she was a whore. A Spartan woman couldn't be chaste
> if she wanted! She wouldn't know how! Gadabouts! Off with the men,
> skirts round their necks, showing everything they've got . . .
> naked thighs and all the rest. They share the same running tracks!
> They wrestle with the men! Intolerable! Can you be surprised
> there's not a chaste one among them? Try asking Helen!
> She left house and home to run off with some young foreigner.

And you raised a massive army of Greeks and led them to Troy for *that*?
Once you'd realised what she was, you should have written her off
and not lifted a single spear. Leave her in Troy,
that's what you should have done, and paid them to keep her.
    (ll. 591–609)

In *Electra* so much flak is aimed at Helen's sister, Clytemnestra, that there is not a lot left for Helen. Clytemnestra does describe her as *margos* (l. 1027) which can mean a lot of things from 'crazy' to 'greedy' to 'randy', and in the mouth of a sister probably all three. Her brother, the demi-god Castor, on the other hand, lets her off the hook by suggesting that she never went to Troy at all. Such a possibility is too good to miss and Euripides turns to it in his *Helen*.[1]

Helen may be a notional tragedy but it is for the most part imbued by delightful comedy based on this version of her story that first crops up a hundred years before Euripides, in the work of the Sicilian lyric poet Stesichorus. His take on Helen, and that of Euripides here, is that she never went to Troy at all. Instead, Paris was fooled by a replica as a 'breathing image' (*eidôlon*), made by a Hera, piqued at losing out to Aphrodite in the Judgement of Paris. However insubstantial, this flimsy substitute managed to fulfil everyone's requirements of Helen for seventeen years while the real Helen languished in Egypt, chaste and faithful, though latterly hotly pursued by the local pharaoh. The play revolves around the arrival of a shipwrecked Menelaus and the plot, mainly Helen's, to free the two of them and sail home to Sparta. Though the first Greek she encounters remembers her as do most Greeks, the reality is a dewy-eyed creature if a little touched by middle-age (see Chapter 4, pp. 75–8).

The Helens of *Orestes* and *Trojan Women* can provide no such alibi. She is the first character to appear in *Orestes* after a prologue from Electra, but she has only the one scene during which she gives a fairly sympathetic account of herself and her trip to Troy, 'I blame Apollo actually' (l. 76). Nor does she appear over-critical of Orestes for killing her sister, Clytemnestra, even if she was his mother. Orestes responds to this charity by cheerfully going along with Pylades' suggestion of murdering her to upset Menelaus. They think they have succeeded too, urged on by the Chorus, until the belated appearance of Apollo who informs all present that 'As for Helen whom you were so keen to kill, you failed. There she is, translated to the stars' (ll. 1629–31). She is, after all,

---

[1] There is evidence, though largely circumstantial, that *Electra* and *Helen* might have been performed in the same submission, perhaps even with *Iphigeneia Among the Taurians*.

a daughter of Zeus and, as Helen herself indicated (ll. 39–40), Zeus wanted a major war to reduce the population.[1]

However bizarre, this does seem to be exoneration of a kind. There is little such charity on view in *Trojan Women*. Helen's entrance is delayed, 900 lines into a 1300 line play, until after the effects of the Trojan War have been laid out with awful clarity. There is no mention of her in the prologue between the gods Poseidon and Athena, beyond a passing reference from Poseidon that she is being kept as a prisoner. Early scenes contain the odd disparaging allusion, but concentrate on the fate of Hecuba, ex-queen of Troy, her children and grandson. Only after the murder of Andromache's baby does the spotlight move from the defeated Trojans to the victorious Greeks. Menelaus has been 'awarded' Helen to kill. He has decided instead to take her back to Sparta to finish her there. Helen's single scene is quite short, consisting of an admission of complicity over her abduction but a defence of her subsequent behaviour, most of it refuted by Hecuba, the living witness to her time in Troy. The scene ends with Helen begging forgiveness and a distinct impression that the long voyage home will prove less a spell in the condemned cell than a second honeymoon.

The point is, of course, that Helen is useful as a target for all manner of grievance and amounts, as does any creature of myth, to little more than a conglomeration of all versions. A similar exercise could just as easily be mounted over Heracles and with just as erratic results. Helen regularly receives a bad press, whether from Greeks or Trojans, but then Euripides' fondness for the contrary opinion surfaces at almost any time when he introduces a standard hero, frequently with a savage touch of invective. The dressing-down of Menelaus by Peleus in *Andromache* concludes with a wonderfully derisive slur:

PELEUS. You were the only one to come home without a scratch on you. Your
armour went to Troy and came back without being unpacked – still in
mint condition! (ll. 616–18)

Such a tirade has the smack of the Athenian lawcourt about it and is especially pleasing when aimed at a character whose vindictiveness and cowardice have already been established. The playwright works a similar trick in *Medea* when Jason is subjected to Medea's spleen:

MEDEA. I'm glad you came, though. It gives me the pleasure
of telling you what I think of you. Enjoy it.

---

[1] The possibility that *Orestes* is a genuine parody of the whole form of Greek tragedy will be considered further in Chapter 4.

Where to begin, that's the problem.
I saved your life. There's not a single Greek
of those who crewed the *Argo* would deny that,
when you were sent off to tame fire-breathing bulls,
to yoke them and sow that deadly field.
Then there was the dragon, guardian of the Golden Fleece,
with all its massive coils, never sleeping.
Who killed it? I killed it, and saved your reputation in the process.
   (ll. 473–83)

Jason is fair game, at least at this point in the play when the bad
behaviour of men towards women is on the agenda: an easy target,
after making his first entrance full of recrimination for the threats
Medea has issued against the royal family, his new bride among them.
As a means of empathising with Medea it is effective, but there will be
a sting in the tail.

As interesting is the usurper Lycus in *Heracles*, villain through and
through, who, in the long-term absence of Heracles, is set on massacring
the hero's wife and children. Lycus starts with some character
assassination:

LYCUS. What was so special about what your husband did?
   Polishing off some water snake; or that creature in Nemea
   which he caught in a net and then claimed he'd
   killed with his bare hands. Is that what you're pinning your hopes on?
   His children deserve a reprieve for achievements like those?
   He may have some sort of a reputation for slaughtering animals,
   but that's as brave as it gets. He's never drawn a shield on his left arm,
   or put himself within reach of a spear. He used a bow.
   A bow! The coward's weapon. Shoot and run away! (ll. 151–61)

The gibe meets a quick response. Heracles arrives and promptly deals
with the scornful Lycus. The returning hero himself falls victim to
madness which turns him into the killer of his entire family.

More subtle, perhaps, is *Electra* where Aegisthus is demonised by
Electra as someone who, she has heard, 'dances on the grave [of
Agamemnon] and throws stones at his monument' (ll. 326–8). Her
catalogue of accusations in a tirade of hate over his dead body seems at
odds with the hospitable and friendly man who unwittingly invites his
killer to a solemn feast. The audience may expect the worst of Aegisthus,
and Clytemnestra too, but they are shown in a much better light than
Electra portrays them.

Rhesus, which is still written off by a few critics as spuriously
attributed to Euripides, certainly uses this Euripidean device in depicting

Hector as impetuous and none too bright, confronted with a subordinate who pulls no punches:

> AENEAS. I wish you had brains to match your brawn.
>   One man can't have everything, I suppose.
>   We all have different talents.
>   Yours is fighting. Leave the thinking to others, eh? (ll. 105–8)

Straight talking from forthright soldiers. No reputation is spared. Very Euripidean.[1]

There is one other place in Euripides where heroes are cut down to size. That is in the satyr play, *Cyclops*. Satyr plays, as fourth in a group submission, may have been comic in tone but they were a fundamental aspect of tragedy, not of comedy, as much in Aeschylus or Sophocles as in Euripides. *Cyclops* is the only complete play of its kind to survive. Odysseus and his crew arrive in Sicily on their way home from the Trojan War and the somewhat pompous Odysseus finds out the hard way that the one-eyed giant, Polyphemus, is a cannibal. The Greek hero eventually succeeds in blinding the monster, but only after the death of some of his comrades-in-arms. The Chorus of satyrs, semi-human followers of the god Dionysus, are intrigued by Odysseus' involvement in the recapture of Helen:

> CHORUS. Here, Odysseus. Can we have a word?
> ODYSSEUS. Fire away. We're all friends here.
> CHORUS. Did you really capture Troy?
> ODYSSEUS. Certainly.
> CHORUS. And get Helen back?
> ODYSSEUS. We sacked Priam's entire domain.
> CHORUS. And when you got her, did you all give her a bang? Did you? Give
>   her what she wanted? I bet she enjoyed it, did she? The bitch. One look at
>   some fancy trousers and a medallion and, phht! Bye, bye, Menelaus. Poor
>   little chap. They ought to abolish women, the whole lot of them.
>   But leave a few for me. (ll. 175–87)

Apart from the singular misogyny, which was probably not untypical of the satyrs (and most of Euripides' audience), to which Odysseus does not deign to respond, Odysseus himself meets with a minimum of respect. The comic aspects of Euripides will be considered more fully later (Chapter 4), but the approach to mythological plotlines as though they were set in a recognisable world, and to heroic figures as fallible, is applicable to all kinds of Euripidean play. When Gilbert Murray turned

---

[1] See also Ritchie (1964) and Walton (2000).

to *Cyclops* in *Euripides and His Age* he wrote of it as 'a gay and grotesque piece', suggesting that the light-hearted tone identified the play as early Euripides: 'The later Euripides would probably have made it horrible and swung our sympathies violently round to the side of the victim' (p. 33). This seems precisely where over-contextualising can freeze a play into its own period. Euripides is more than simply an example of a past civilisation, as I hope the rest of this book will show. The purpose of the satyr play was serious, I believe, to have a place where the horrors of living could be to some extent disarmed, or at least balanced against a view of life that could mock the most monstrous and the most feared. Today's media equivalents to the satyr plays range widely over a culture unimaginable forty years ago, never mind two thousand four hundred years. No less than the Athenians, we need our own antidotes to despair.

2 THE FAMILY SAGA

Phoenician Women, Bacchae, Iphigeneia at Aulis

Phoenician Women is Euripides' Oedipus play, seldom read and not often seen, though a production was directed by Katie Mitchell for the Royal Shakespeare Company at The Other Place in Stratford in 1994, and subsequently transferred to the Pit at the Barbican. That production inspired a critic on the *Didaskalia* website to describe the play as 'rambling to the point of picaresque'. It may seem odd to begin the study of a dramatist's output with a play that hardly anyone knows, and that is unpopular with some of those who do, but *Phoenician Women* happens to be a prime example of a Euripides piece which starts out looking as though it is one thing and turns out to be something rather different.

The story of Oedipus was familiar enough to any educated Athenian.[1] The whole story is a long one, the saga of a dynasty. It begins with the curse on Laius for kidnapping and raping Chrysippus, the son of Pelops, passes through his marriage to Jocasta (or Epicaste) and the oracle that leads to Laius exposing his baby, fearing that a son of his would kill him. The child survives, as exposed children in drama invariably do, and is brought up in Corinth with the name Oedipus ('swollen-foot'), in ignorance of his true parentage. Warned in his turn by the oracle that he will kill his father and marry his mother, and despite trying to avoid his fate, Oedipus does both. The story continues into the next generation with the death of Oedipus, and Oedipus and Jocasta's sons engaging in civil strife. Both are killed and their sister, Antigone, defying a decree from Creon to leave one of the two exposed, buries her brother, an act that results in her own death. Even then it is not all over and Euripides returns to the aftermath in his *Suppliants* (see Chapter 5).

Any play about these events might open at any point in the chronicle and contain whatever version of the past and the present happened to suit the playwright's purpose. The only absolute requirement was some sort of originality within a frame of certain 'givens'. What is given in the Oedipus story is that Oedipus will kill his father and marry his mother. What is not given is the extent to which he, or anybody else, will be

---

[1] Odysseus meets Oedipus' wife/mother, there named Epicaste, among the dead during a visit to Hades in the eleventh book of Homer's *Odyssey*.

culpable for the fracturing of two of the great taboos of the Greek moral code (at least for mortals), parricide and incest. Nor is it a given how Oedipus or Jocasta will react to the discovery of their true relationship. Sophocles' *Oedipus Tyrannus* ends with Jocasta hanging herself, after which Oedipus puts out his own eyes and returns to the palace, prior to exile.[1] Some fifteen years on, at the opening of Euripides' *Phoenician Women*, the children of Oedipus and Jocasta are grown up. Oedipus is still in the palace and Jocasta is very much alive, striving in any way she may to prevent a war which, when it boils down to it, is an escalated vendetta between two brothers who cannot stand the sight of one another.

Aeschylus in his *Seven Against Thebes* chose to concentrate on the threat of civil war when succession is not secured. Sophocles in his three Theban plays, *Antigone*, *Oedipus Tyrannus* and *Oedipus at Colonus* (the first two produced before *Phoenician Women*, the last after it) concentrates on the nature of oracles, on the conflict between civil and natural law and the personal reactions of the central characters to each new twist and revelation. All of this is present, or implied, in Euripides but is largely overtaken by what is essentially a matter of blood ties.

In the prologue Jocasta describes dispassionately how her son Oedipus came to be born, how he killed Laius when Laius was on his way to consult the oracle (not on his way back from Delphi as in Sophocles). He then defeated the Sphinx, as a result of which the now widowed Jocasta was 'awarded' to the young man for saving Thebes. She bore him four children, Eteocles and Polyneices, Antigone and Ismene. When Oedipus discovered what he had done he blinded himself (as per Sophocles), but stayed on in Thebes. As soon as the boys were grown up they locked their father in the attic, like some first Mrs Rochester, 'so that what he had done might be forgotten, though it took some covering up' (ll. 64–5). This is a wonderfully succinct phrase in the Greek, almost impossible to translate, but it brings the whole play down to the level of a royal scandal.

While Jocasta is speaking, Oedipus is up there in his garret, having roundly cursed his sons who had agreed to rule the city, turn and turn about. Eteocles, the elder brother (in Sophocles he is the younger), has now refused to relinquish power: and so the story picks up again, with Jocasta trying to prevent bloodshed.

The former queen leaves the scene and the play proper begins. In a review of the enemy troops from the palace battlements, which brings to

---

[1] The play is also known in translation as *Oedipus the King*, or by its Latinised title *Oedipus Rex*, but neither conveys the irony of the original.

mind both something similar in the third book of Homer's *Iliad* and Act One, Scene Two, of Shakespeare's *Troilus and Cressida*, an old Tutor identifies to Antigone each of seven Argive heroes who are about to lay siege to Thebes, among them her own favourite brother, Polyneices: 'If only I could fly through the misty sky to my own dear brother and, after his lengthy time in exile, wrap my arms around his neck and hug him tight' (ll. 163–6). She never has a good word to say about her other brother, Eteocles, for all he is king of Thebes: nor, as it turns out, does anyone else.

Jocasta has engineered a meeting between her two sons to try and resolve their dispute, but it is plain that she is not impartial either. Polyneices, the 'illustrious' Polyneices, is his mother's darling. Clearly it is he that has the charm, though to the reader there is not a lot to choose between them, a bloodthirsty pair who seem to debate the politics of what position each takes, but in reality welcome the chance to get at one another's throats. Rebuffed by Eteocles, Polyneices quickly changes his tune, 'Let the whole house be destroyed,' he declares. 'Blood is what my sword is after' (ll. 624–5). The play proceeds, interrupted by the arrival of the prophet Teiresias who tells Creon he must sacrifice his son, Menoeceus, if the city is to survive.[1] The noble Menoeceus volunteers his own life, standing on the battlements and stabbing himself through the neck. How far this contributes to 'saving' the city is unclear. The city is saved, so perhaps it is more than a futile gesture, but Euripides never seems comfortable with the notion of the young sacrificed for the sake of the old. Eteocles and Polyneices have still decided to engage in single combat. Jocasta and Antigone head for the battlefield as soon as they hear, but arrive too late and Jocasta stabs herself to death over the bodies of her sons.

Here is no tragedy of fate or 'Fate'. It is all about personal relationships. This is a family with such a history that nobody could expect it to be exactly functional, but Euripides chooses to concentrate on the family more than on the history. Jocasta and her sons, Eteocles and Polyneices, plus one of her daughters, Antigone, all have their part to play. So do Creon and his son, Menoeceus. Only when four of them are dead, Menoeceus and Jocasta by their own hand, does Antigone summon Oedipus, her wretched father, from the palace to hear the outcome of his curse. He arrives at a moment when an audience might expect a *deus ex machina* (or rather *theos ek mêchanês*), a 'god from the machine' to sort

---

[1] Creon is Jocasta's brother, Menoeceus Jocasta's nephew. Complications of the family history make it difficult to identify how Jocasta's children are related to Creon's, but they are some sort of cousin. Haemon and Ismene, major characters in Sophocles' *Antigone*, do not appear.

things out and restore the myth. Oedipus appears as a kind of 'anti-deus', incapable of assisting anyone, a peripheral figure, not that old in terms of years, but more like some bilious but pathetic grandparent who has outlived both children and grandchildren. Seven of this, the largest cast in a Greek tragedy, are members of the same family. That is more than the total number of characters in any play of Aeschylus.

But that is not all. Who are these Phoenician women who give the play its title, happen in on such havoc and find themselves stranded? They are, they say, from Phoenicia and are heading for Delphi to become votaries of Apollo. Stopping off to pay their respects to Oedipus, they find themselves in the middle of a political and military crisis. There is some question of their claiming a family connection.[1] At the very least they have been dispatched to Delphi by the sons of Agenor. Agenor was the father of Cadmus, founder of Thebes, great-grandfather of Laius. This is another family connection, if distant. They are swept into the mayhem without being in any way involved in what has happened, and is now happening, in Thebes, but tied in by blood. No wholly convincing reason has been advanced for the play's being named after them, but a stronger possibility than most is that they demonstrate how a small cause may evolve into a disaster that affects an entire family, at whatever remove in time or place. Laius' crime, as it is related within Jocasta's prologue, does not reach back any further than his failure to father a child, the warning from the oracle that a son of his will kill him, and a drunken moment when he begets the boy which the parents subsequently try to get rid of. Consultations with oracles over childlessness play a major part in other Euripides plays, *Ion* and *Medea*, though with different consequences. In *Phoenician Women* Euripides shows how the great questions of politics, philosophy and theology may always be presented in the light of individual cases and close relationships. These are the driving forces behind much of his drama.

Euripides' two last plays offer a similar outcome suggesting that this remained a preoccupation for him in old age. The Chorus of neither *Bacchae* nor *Iphigeneia at Aulis*, Euripides' two posthumous pieces, may claim even the tenuous connection with the ruling families that the Phoenician visitors do, but the central characters view major issues primarily through the perspective of the family unit. The family situation in *Bacchae*, performed first in 405 BC in the same group as *Iphigeneia at*

---

[1] 'Blood in common, children in common, descended from the horned Io' (ll. 247–8). Io was regarded as the mother of both the Ionian Greeks around Tyre and the Argives of the Peloponnese. She is a character in Aeschylus' *Prometheus Bound*, turned into a cow and tormented by a gadfly sent by Hera after she had been pursued by Zeus.

Aulis, is precarious. The death here is simply the result of an act of revenge. The god Dionysus arrives in Thebes and in his opening speech describes exactly what he intends to do and why:

> DIONYSUS. Here, in Thebes, I have first excited women's cries –
> these women of Thebes the first to dress in fawnskin –
> placed in their hands my thyrsus, the ivy-covered shaft.
> Why these? Because these sisters of my mother,
> these aunts of mine, denied that I was born of Zeus.
> The last who should have done so, they defamed my mother,
> Semele, proclaiming my god-like birth a trick
> devised by Cadmus to save a harlot-daughter's face.
> That was why, they said, Zeus incinerated my mother,
> for her presumption. I have driven them mad.
> Homes abandoned, they roam the mountains,
> out of their senses, deranged: every last woman in Thebes,
> up there amongst the rocks and the trees,
> witless and homeless. Cadmus' daughters too.
> Thebes will have to learn to appreciate me
> and my rituals. My mother will receive her recognition
> when all acknowledge my divinity.
> Cadmus has grown old and abdicated his throne
> to his grandson Pentheus. This Pentheus wages holy war
> on me, offers no libations, ignores me in his prayers.
> I am going to have to show this Pentheus, show all of Thebes,
> what kind of god I am. (ll. 23–49)

This is the same Thebes which provides the setting for *Phoenician Women,* but several generations earlier. Semele was one of the four daughters of Cadmus, founder of Thebes. Zeus took a fancy to her. If this sounds like a familiar trope it becomes more so. When Semele became pregnant Hera maliciously suggested to the gullible girl that she invite Zeus to reveal himself to her in his true form. Picking her moment judiciously Semele exacted a promise from the reluctant king of the gods and, his true form being a thunderbolt, she was promptly reduced to a pile of ashes. But the embryo was rescued by Zeus and sealed in his thigh from which Dionysus was in due time born. Dionysus in his prologue refers to the incineration of his mother, but keeps off the details of Zeus' rescue (see also Chapter 7, pp. 137–8).

Euripides' dramatic method with such material was not so much to reduce myth to human proportions as to create a stage world in which the characters, faced with a situation from received myth, would react in a recognisable way. This particular play has a special theatrical quality which will be investigated later (see Chapter 9, pp. 164–7). The reason for considering it here is in Dionysus' reaction to being both human and divine. Living within his myth, his father was Zeus, which makes him immortal and the possessor of special powers. His mother was part of the mortal family of Cadmus, but that family have rejected him: for this rejection, as he asserts in the prologue, he wants revenge. The awesome, or rather, awful aspect of the story is that the human part of Dionysus makes him resentful of being an outcast, while the superhuman part gives him the power to exact a particularly terrible vengeance. Of the four main characters in the play, Cadmus is Dionysus' grandfather, Agave his aunt and Pentheus his cousin.

Agave, as Dionysus tells us, and her sisters Ino and Autonoe (more aunts of Dionysus) are roaming the mountains, out of their senses. Cadmus, who has abdicated in favour of Pentheus, has his own doubts about the old story, as Dionysus knows, but is persuaded by the prophet Teiresias to go up to the mountains and worship the god. Teiresias' rational explanation of the birth of Dionysus queries the detail of the myth while recognising the power of the religion. Cadmus, on the other hand, faced with the cynicism of his grandson, now the king, takes him to one side and suggests, even more cynically:

CADMUS. Even if this god is not really a god
    as you believe, you could at least say that he is.
    It's just a little white lie. Semele gives birth to a god
    and our family gets the credit. (ll. 333–6)

This somewhat seedy justification for religious observance and, indeed, social significance, is one of the more comic aspects of Cadmus in his first scene. Pentheus' angry response is aimed less at his grandfather than at Teiresias for making the old man look foolish in public. The next time Cadmus makes an appearance it is after Pentheus' death at the hands of his mother and his aunts – Cadmus' remaining daughters, that is. No loss of dignity this time. When Agave enters brandishing her son's head in the belief it is a lion's, Cadmus brings her back to her senses as gently as he may. His lament over Pentheus' remains reveals the extent of real affection between grandfather and grandson:

CADMUS. The family is destroyed.
    This house looked up to you, my boy.
    My grandson, my support.
    They went in awe of you in Thebes.
    No one could insult the old man with you around.
    Or else you made him pay [...]
    I loved you most, in death I love you still.

Never again to hug you,
To feel your touch on my cheek, or hear your voice:
'Is something the matter, grandfather?
Is someone upsetting you?
Tell me. I'll soon put a stop to it.' (ll. 1306–21)

Dionysus, the destructive Dionysus, demolishes the very family unit to which his human half had seemed so to want to belong, using the divine power that excluded him from it.

Iphigeneia at Aulis deals with the other major dynasty around which dramatic myth developed, that of the House of Atreus, an epic that goes back through a bloody history to Tantalus, yet another illegitimate son of Zeus, who had incurred the wrath of the gods by, according to one version, stealing the gods' nectar and ambrosia, in another, serving them up his own son in a stew. The ramifications usually spread over several blood-tarnished generations, but in *Iphigeneia at Aulis* Tantalus turns out to have been not a figure from the dense and deep past, but Clytemnestra's previous husband, murdered by Agamemnon, along with their child, for no declared reason. This play picks up the story before the beginning of the Trojan War when the massive Greek fleet is about to set sail for Troy. The allies are made up, for the most part, of forces raised by former suitors of the beautiful Helen, who had sworn an oath, while they were still in the running, to support the successful wooer should he ever find it necessary to ask for help in maintaining his marriage. This he did when she ran off (or did not, as we have already seen may have been the case) with Paris, prince of Troy. The cuckolded husband, Menelaus of Sparta, asked his brother, Agamemnon, king of Mycenae and married to Helen's sister Clytemnestra, to be commander-in-chief. The fleet got no further than their assembly point at Aulis on the coast of Boeotia, opposite the island of Euboea, where they found themselves unable to proceed because of a contrary wind. The army's seer, Calchas, has told Agamemnon that the wind will not relent until and unless he sacrifice to Artemis his own daughter Iphigeneia, safely at home in Mycenae with her mother, Clytemnestra (see also Chapter 5, pp. 93–6 for the effects of this prophecy on the army as a whole).

The play that we have is unrevised, or, perhaps, completed by a different hand, not so surprising in a piece which had to wait for production until after the author's death. There appear to be two separate expositions, one in the form of a prologue: in addition scholars are almost unanimous in disregarding the final scene in which it is reported that Iphigeneia has, at the last moment, been miraculously rescued and a deer substituted. The grounds on which such doubts about authenticity are based are not, it has to be said, necessarily dramatic. The play's ending on a question-mark may be unusual, but it is not the first such to be found in Euripides, for whom the timely arrival of a *deus ex machina* to sort everything (*Orestes*, *Ion*, *Electra*) usually needs taking with a pinch of salt. Though characters of the same name, with markedly different personalities, may appear in more than one play of the same author (Heracles, Helen, Orestes), this is not what is happening here. The story of Iphigeneia's rescue and subsequent career as a priestess was well known at the time. Euripides' own earlier play *Iphigeneia Among the Taurians* was used as a reference point on several occasions by Aristotle in the *Poetics*.

Iphigeneia's survival in a different play placed no obligation on Euripides in this play either to opt for the execution of the human sacrifice or to suggest divine intervention to prevent it. What we actually have is a rousing messenger speech delivered to the victim's mother about how the priest prepared for the execution, then:

> MESSENGER. All of a sudden something extraordinary. We heard, every one of us, the sound of the blow, but no one could see what in the world had happened to the girl [...] there on the ground was a deer, its blood all over the altar of the goddess. (ll. 1581–7)

Divine intervention is not unusual in Euripides, but this is different. No god appears. There is simply a report of a miracle. It implies either a complete *volte-face* on the part of Artemis or an elaborate con trick to keep both the army and Clytemnestra happy. 'I saw everything,' says the Messenger. 'I was there' (l. 1607). Yes, he was, though most messengers do not have to protest so much, until, that is, Sophocles and Euripides introduced the idea of messengers who lie, or embroider the truth (in their respective *Electra*s, for example, *Women of Trachis* or *Children of Heracles*). Clytemnestra is unconvinced: 'How can I not say that all this is some make-believe, to alleviate my grief?' (ll. 1616–18). Or, as Don Taylor put it in his Methuen translation, succinctly, if slightly gilding the lily, 'Do you expect me to believe this story?' In Euripides, especially late Euripides, we find ourselves in a world of sceptics and the circumstances of the expedition setting out for Troy is as much a place for the sceptic as most.

Few, if any, of the first audience for *Iphigeneia at Aulis* could have failed to pick up the resonances here. The next time Clytemnestra sees her husband is when he returns from the war ten years later to a hot bath and cold steel. Homer may have suggested that it was Aegisthus struck Agamemnon down, but in Aeschylus the hand on the axe was

Clytemnestra's. This great war between Greeks and Trojans which lasted for ten years begins and ends in a family affair: so does Euripides' play. Despite the uncertain beginning in the surviving script, Agamemnon's letter to his wife makes a powerful opening statement. Convinced by Calchas that he must sacrifice his daughter if the expedition is ever to get going, Agamemnon has earlier sent word to Clytemnestra to bring Iphigeneia to Aulis because he has arranged a marriage to Achilles, the Greek fighting machine. Menelaus is one of only three other people to know about this deception. Unwisely, Agamemnon has neglected to consult Achilles at all. Now, after a sleepless night, Agamemnon has decided he cannot go through with it and has written another letter, telling Clytemnestra that under no circumstances should she bring Iphigeneia to Aulis. The opening scene gives him the opportunity to rehearse the background to the marriage of Helen and his brother. In this version it was Helen who chose Menelaus over her other suitors. No mention of the gods here. No Zeus; no egg. Helen and Clytemnestra are simply sisters (there is reference to another called Phoebe): Tyndareus and Leda are their father and mother. No heavenly beauty contest between Aphrodite, Athena and Hera: just Paris, a flamboyant gigolo from Troy who seduced Helen during the absence of Menelaus, and carried her off to his 'cowshed on Mount Ida'. That's what this war is all about.

Agamemnon gives his replacement letter, with his seal upon it, to a family servant to deliver and off they go, the old man to fulfil his mission, Agamemnon to consider how to get out of the hole he has dug for himself. A long choral entry follows from a group of local young women who have nothing to do with the plot, but just want to get a look at the ships and heroes: and suitably impressed they are, but the next person to enter is a furious Menelaus who has intercepted the letter and opened it. In the ensuing row between the two brothers no punches are pulled. Agamemnon tells Menelaus he should be relieved to have got rid of such a bad lot of a wife with so little difficulty, and Menelaus heads off to spill the beans to the army. Agamemnon is close to panic when a messenger enters to say that Clytemnestra and Iphigeneia have already turned up. Almost immediately Menelaus returns. He has had a change of heart and realises that, of course, sacrificing Iphigeneia is out of the question. He is even happy to murder Calchas so nobody finds out the truth.

Things are spiralling out of control. Clytemnestra and Iphigeneia now arrive, all ready for a wedding.[1] They are excited when Agamemnon enters:

---

[1] In Katie Mitchell's production for the National Theatre Company in 2004 the family had brought dozens of pieces of luggage with them.

IPHIGENEIA. Mother, don't mind me running ahead. Don't be cross.
 I just want to squeeze my father to my breast [...]
CLYTEMNESTRA. Of course you must. You always loved your father best,
 more than any of my other children.
IPHIGENEIA. Oh, I'm so happy to see you, Father. It's been ages.
AGAMEMNON. And your father is pleased to see you. Same for both of us.
IPHIGENEIA. Well, here I am. I'm so glad you sent for me.
AGAMEMNON. I'm not sure whether to agree or not.
IPHIGENEIA. You don't seem pleased to see me. Not the way you used to be.
AGAMEMNON. A lot of things on my mind as king. As general too.
 (ll. 635–44)

There can be no other scene in Greek tragedy which so tenderly depicts the
love of a child for a father, or of a father for a child, for that matter, as
when Iphigeneia asks her father not to go to war but stay at home with
her: or, if he has to go, to take her along. And so the tragedy develops. The
extraordinary feature of all this is not so much the reactions of
Clytemnestra, Agamemnon and Iphigeneia, or the various fringe witnesses
(including the Chorus who know perfectly well what is happening), as the
other character present during the scene. Clytemnestra has brought with
her the baby Orestes who is specifically mentioned in her first speech and
invited to wake up for his sister's wedding.

Mother and daughter leave when Clytemnestra discovers, inevitably as
she must, the trick that has been played on her and on Achilles. The next
time Iphigeneia is summoned Clytemnestra expressly tells her to bring in
Orestes. In her pathetic plea for her life Iphigeneia appeals to the infant
Orestes to intercede for her. He remains present in the mind for the rest of
the play. The audience who, like the Chorus, have turned up to see off the
expedition to Troy, find themselves witnesses to a family publicly
disintegrating before their eyes. This is not a tragedy that began with a
dispute between goddesses, but a story that starts here, in one family
where Agamemnon has made a terrible decision and, in trying to right the
lunacy that has exposed his own daughter to death, finds that his authority
as general is ineffective. And always, there is the baby, easy for the reader
to overlook, to remind the audience that, ten years hence, Agamemnon
will return to his wife and, a further ten years after that, this baby, now
grown up, will murder the mother who has brought him to Aulis.

The introduction of young children is a regular feature of Euripides and
always for a calculated purpose. Apart from the significance of Orestes in
Iphigeneia at Aulis, in *Alcestis*, the two children, Eumelus and an
unnamed daughter, accompany their mother when she is brought in on
her deathbed. Their future is the central, if not the sole, subject of Alcestis'

farewell to her husband: it is Eumelus who sings the dirge immediately after her death. The sons of Heracles in *Heracles* are silent, but their affectionate welcome makes his subsequent murder of them all the more terrible. In another play, set many years after Heracles' death, *The Children of Heracles*, others of the hero's children comprise the suppliant group. The sons of the seven who fell attacking Thebes form a separate Chorus in *Suppliants*. In *Andromache*, Hector's former wife, now a slave, has had a child by Neoptolemus whose wife, Hermione, cannot conceive. The boy becomes a pawn in the encounter between the two women. Hecuba, the former queen of Troy, tells Polymestor to bring his two boys when she invites him to hear about her secret treasure. The treacherous Polymestor is unaware that Hecuba knows he has murdered her son. He arrives with the children and enters the women's tent where the boys are killed and he is blinded.

The two most wrenching appearances by children are the baby Astyanax in *Trojan Women*, introduced with his mother Andromache, before being seized from her to be hurled from the walls of Troy; and the two boys in *Medea*. Medea's sons are given exceptional prominence by appearing on so many separate occasions. They make their first entrance before Medea makes hers (l. 45); they are summoned to meet their father, Jason, and carry the poisoned robe to the palace (l. 896); they return after their deadly mission and are sent indoors (l. 1002); they re-enter, exit and then re-enter again half way through Medea's farewell speech to them (l. 1069) – the whole of which is included later (Chapter 10, pp. 169–71); their desperate voices are heard offstage as they try to escape their implacable mother (from l. 1271); and finally they can be seen in Medea's epiphany, where their bodies are draped over the dragon-chariot in which she will escape to Athens (l. 1316).

The baby Orestes appears at least three times in *Iphigeneia at Aulis*, but is as much stage property as individual. He is no longer onstage when the unsuspecting Achilles arrives and, in a scene of acute embarrassment, is warmly greeted by Clytemnestra. When Achilles discovers that this woman treating him in so familiar a fashion has been led to believe he is about to become her son-in-law, offended dignity notwithstanding, he is drawn almost unwittingly into the family circle and vows to persuade the blood-lusting army to back down.

The revelation of the whole truth results in Clytemnestra confronting Agamemnon. Her lengthy response to her husband's shamed admission is startling for what it reveals about the family history, so far glossed over. Clytemnestra reminds Agamemnon what a faithful wife she has been: that he murdered her first husband, Tantalus, dashed out her baby's brains and raped her, after which her brothers were only prevented from exacting revenge by the intervention of Tyndareus who forced her into marriage instead (see Chapter 10, pp. 180–2 for her entire speech). This is a shocking revelation to start with, but the remainder of the speech ('after I became reconciled') is more familial. 'Think of her empty chair'; 'Do you imagine the other children will even look at you again?'; and, perhaps most cogently, for its sheer logic 'Why Iphigeneia? Why doesn't Menelaus kill his and Helen's daughter, Hermione?' The introduction of Agamemnon's barbaric earlier conduct is a timely reminder, among other reasoned argument, of what action has been contemplated here, as well as what sort of man becomes commander-in-chief of such an army. The questions being asked are those of a dramatist determined to scrutinise motivation in myth, not just causes and effects.

This is the moment where another Greek tragedian, or a younger Euripides, might have offered a riposte or an apologia, even one as specious as Jason's rejoinder to Medea's tirade (*Medea*, l. 522ff.). Here it is Iphigeneia who replies, in a desperate and moving plea for life. It ends, in a passage whose authenticity has been challenged, with a dozen lines addressed to the baby Orestes (ll. 1241–52). Whatever the linguistic arguments, in the context, such a speech can be dramatically stunning. Agamemnon's own response to both wife and daughter rings all the more hollow. What it amounts to is a declaration of love for his family, but the belief that, if he tries to withdraw now, the entire family will be murdered.

An extended lament from Iphigeneia ends abruptly with the arrival of Achilles. So hot are the army for a sacrifice that they have stoned him when he tries to face them down. It is at this point that Iphigeneia intervenes. Many critics have found her change of heart too abrupt, but, whether the cause is filial duty or blind terror, it is dramatically and psychologically sound. Her decision comes in the wake of a scene where powerful grown-ups, the great hero Achilles and her formidable mother, have found themselves completely at a loss. She demonstrates an unexpected but dramatically effective resolution from her first words, 'Mother, listen to me. There's no point in being angry with your husband' (ll. 1369–70) to her last, 'Greeks have to control barbarians, not the other way round' (ll. 1400–1), followed by a sentiment expressed in the first ever translation of a Greek tragedy into English, 'for the grecians bi [*sic*] nature are free, like as the barbarians are borne to bondage'.[1] The sentiment may have a jingoistic ring to it, but the Greeks' belief in their

[1] *The Tragedie of Euripides called Iphigenia translated out of Greake into Englisshe by Lady Jane Lumley* (c. 1555), first published as *Iphigenia at Aulis translated by Lady Lumley*, ed. Harold Child (London, 1909).

superiority seems to be acceptable to Euripides, or at least recognised by him as a motive in moments of crisis. Iphigeneia may begin the play as an excited child, but in the end she shows more strength than any of her elders, deciding to die for what she believes to be right, for her father and for her country. It is not a comfortable decision for a modern audience, though there are precedents or parallels with Menoeceus in *Phoenician Women*, Macaria in *Children of Heracles* and Alcestis in *Alcestis*: all for the general good, but predominantly for the good of the family.

Euripides has already dealt with aspects of this dynasty in three previous plays, though all from the latter years of his career, *Iphigeneia Among the Taurians*, *Electra* and *Orestes*. *Iphigeneia Among the Taurians* takes as its premise that Iphigeneia was indeed miraculously preserved from sacrifice and relocated in the Crimea where she is serving as a priestess to King Thoas, with the specific task of sacrificing to Artemis any stranger rash enough to turn up in his kingdom. After a prologue she reveals what happened at Aulis. She has recently had a dream which she interprets as a sign that her brother Orestes is dead. She then retreats into the palace. Orestes and Pylades promptly appear, on a mission from Apollo to steal an image of Artemis and take it to Athens. Successful completion of the task will conclude his rehabilitation after the murder of his mother Clytemnestra. After setting their part of the scene for the audience they discuss plans for recovering the statue before exiting.

This is a strange play, more of an adventure story than a tragedy. It bears a resemblance both in plotline and in tone to Euripides' *Helen*, where Menelaus is threatened with death when he turns up in Egypt and discovers his wife who never really went to Troy. Orestes, it soon emerges, is still beset by the Furies and in no time at all both he and Pylades have been captured and hauled in front of the Priestess – Orestes' sister, though only the audience know this. Everything depends on brother and sister discovering their relationship in time, which, as they are both Greeks, might seem to be delayed only briefly. Recognition takes the best part of four hundred lines, much of it a cross-examination of the prisoners by Iphigeneia absurdly prolonged to the point of parody: which, of course, it may well be. Whenever either sibling asks a straight question about the other, each manages to find some devious means to avoid giving away who they are. Iphigeneia milks her brother for all the family news, about Helen, Menelaus, even Agamemnon and Electra. Eventually Iphigeneia resorts to writing a letter to be taken back to Mycenae. Only when she reads it out loud to Pylades in case he loses it on the way (and for the benefit of the audience) does the penny finally drop.

Affectionate as is their reunion, the overall drive of the play seems curious. A joint plan to hoodwink Thoas, make off with the wooden Artemis and hightail it back to Greece is effected in a manner not dissimilar to the escape of Helen and Menelaus from Egypt in *Helen*. All will end happily ever after. What can be going on here? Or, at least, what may appear to be going on here that could make a difference to received ideas about the nature of Greek tragedy?

Dating of this group of Euripides' post-Trojan War plays is uncertain. *Orestes* is reliably fixed at 408 BC, the others, the posthumous *Iphigeneia at Aulis* apart, within a short span of time within the previous five years. It is possible, indeed, that *Iphigeneia Among the Taurians* and *Helen* formed part of the same submission, maybe, even, with *Electra* as a third. If there were such a link, speculation about Euripides' purpose is tempting. Are these unexpected versions and subtly differing balances of relationship a means of providing, not so much aspects of dramatic paradox, as a versatility of behaviour pattern according to perspective? Orestes and Iphigeneia, Helen and Menelaus, Orestes and Electra may all be dramatic juggling as character and motive, action and consequence take on new dimensions, from the broadly comic to the virtually manic, among these frantic and public lives. This public nature is often a contributory factor in disaster as will later happen so often in Shakespeare's tragedies, *Hamlet*, *Othello*, *Lear* or *Antony and Cleopatra*. *Macbeth* is unusual in taking place largely behind closed doors, either literally or metaphorically. With the Greeks the action is conducted in the open air and usually within the range of a Chorus who must, by their act of witness, become complicit in affairs of state.

Electra and *Orestes*, as do the Iphigeneia plays, show the children of Agamemnon and Clytemnestra in two more deliberate variations on the family tie, both firmly at the darker range of the sibling spectrum. The end of *Electra* has both of them linked in the murder of Clytemnestra, Orestes appalled at what he has had to do, Electra reduced to the point of collapse by the realisation of her obsession. The arrival *ex machina* of their cousins, Castor and Pollux, sorts things out so that Orestes and Electra will never have to meet again, he heading for Athens pursued by the Furies, she parcelled off as a 'proper' wife to the accommodating Pylades, and to the considerable relief, it is difficult not to feel, of the long-suffering Farmer who has had to put up with her in recent years.

Orestes opens in front of the palace of Mycenae, with Orestes lying on the couch where he has been ever since the murder of Clytemnestra, alternating between periods of delirium and coma. When he finally comes round he proves every bit as bloodthirsty as his sister. They are soon joined by an even more ruthless Pylades. Between them they try to murder Helen and kidnap her daughter, Hermione. In a terrific climax, more like the final scene in a disaster movie than a Greek tragedy, Orestes, Pylades, Electra and Hermione, a knife at her throat, appear on the roof of the palace, Orestes threatening to set it on fire if Menelaus and his men try to break in and rescue the girl. Only the arrival of Apollo sorts out the stalemate.

In 1966 John Hopkins wrote a series of plays under the title *Talking to a Stranger*, which the television critic of the *Observer* described as 'the first authentic masterpiece written directly for television'. They were shown over four successive weeks on BBC 2. What was so innovatory about them was that all four had the same plot, but each was seen through the point of view of a different character. Some scenes were duplicated, others included offering exclusive insights to which only selected characters were privy: and, of course, as each play developed, audience perception of previous events was subtly and sometimes drastically altered. The device was further explored by Alan Ayckbourn in the three stage plays that make up *The Norman Conquests* (1973). It would be going too far to suggest that such an idea was rooted in Euripides, but in the Greek playwright's revisiting of well-known characters came a similar opportunity to adjust perspective. There is every reason to believe that the variations on the theme of Agamemnon and Clytemnestra's family was much more extensive than the ten or so surviving plays. The same would be true for the Theban cycle. What it does explain is why the Greeks should so often resort to familiar as well as familial outlines: and why so many playwrights since the Renaissance have returned to such sources. This is not to suggest that all the plays mentioned above do not have further dimensions to them. It is to suggest that what is exciting in Euripides is how he will engage with the manners of living alongside the processes of dying. Beyond that is the dramatic truth that within any stratum of society or culture, good stories will have a dimension of family relationship.

Of the nineteen Euripides plays all but two deal with issues within the family, whatever the external circumstances. The only two that do not are *Cyclops*, about Odysseus and his crew on their travels home from Troy, and *Rhesus*, another Trojan War play, but one whose authorship by Euripides is still disputed by some authorities. One which deals, ultimately, with a closer picture of family life is *Alcestis*. It might deserve analysis here but works better as a fitting transition to a chapter on the battle of the sexes.

3 WOMEN AND MEN

Alcestis, Medea, Hippolytus

After Dionysus goes down to Hades in Aristophanes' *Frogs*, driven by 'an absolutely huge lust' for Euripides, the competition between the long-dead Aeschylus and the recently-dead Euripides over which should return to Athens includes the following exchange:

> AESCHYLUS. Anyway, none of your damned Phaedras and Sthenoboeas, or whores like that. You won't find any lascivious women in a play of mine.[1]
>
> EURIPIDES. I don't doubt it with Aphrodite conspicuously missing in your life.
>
> AESCHYLUS. Praise the gods. Aphrodite spent enough time in your house, though, as I recall.
>
> DIONYSUS. True enough. Your writing about nymphomaniac wives was from personal experience.
>
> EURIPIDES. What harm did my *Sthenoboea* do to the state, confound you?
>
> AESCHYLUS. Respectable wives of respectable men were so appalled by a married woman propositioning a house-guest, they committed suicide.
>
> EURIPIDES. I never invented Phaedra, did I?
>
> AESCHYLUS. Maybe not. Same thing. The job of the dramatist is to draw a veil over indecency, not to give lessons in it. Children have schoolteachers; grown-ups have playwrights. We should be preaching morality. (ll.1043–53)

Interesting as it is that the two tragedians, albeit through the mouthpiece of a third party, should agree about the moral purpose of drama, there is another issue here. Euripides' treatment of female characters has over the years been one of the most hotly debated of subjects relating to classical theatre.[2] From classical times the idea has been widely disseminated that he was a misogynist. There is little sign of that in the *Frogs* passage above, but Aristophanes' earlier *Women at the Thesmophoria* certainly does broach the topic. The Thesmophoria was one of the women-only festivals in Athens and, consequently, a source of both fascination and misgiving to Athenian men. That play opens with another stage version of

---

[1] Phaedra in *Hippolytus,* one of Euripides' most popular plays: his *Sthenoboea* has not survived.

[2] A side issue in the present study is whether or not this should be seen as evidence of the attendance of women at the Athenian dramatic festivals. 'Respectable wives' committing suicide through outrage may fall into the realm of comic licence, but the joke has no point if women could not have attended such a play in the first place.

Euripides, this time desperately looking for help because, as he reveals to one of his male relations, he has heard that the women are gunning for him:

EURIPIDES. Something nasty is brewing.
KEDESTES. Such as?
EURIPIDES. Today means life or death for me.
KEDESTES. How can that be? It's the Thesmophoria. The courts don't sit today.
EURIPIDES. That's just the point: that's why I fear for my life. The women are plotting against me. I'm at the top of their agenda. They want to condemn me to death.
KEDESTES. Whatever for?
EURIPIDES. Because I give such a bad impression of them. In my plays.
KEDESTES. No more than you deserve. (ll. 75–86)

Euripides turns up as a character in Aristophanes' *Acharnians* too, and gets a mention in most of the other plays of his that we have. Though all this shows is that he was well-enough known to be a recognisable comic target, part of his celebrity may well be his portrayal onstage of strong females.

For the record, four women commit murder in Euripides' nineteen plays: Electra (in collaboration with her brother, in *Electra*), Agave (unwittingly, in *Bacchae*), Hecuba and Medea (in both cases, children). In addition, there are a couple of suicides, Jocasta (*Phoenician Women*) and Phaedra (*Hippolytus*), a certain amount of murderous intent: Phaedra again and Creusa (*Ion*). There is Alcmena in *Children of Heracles*, which is anyway something of a special case because of the self-sacrifice (suicide?) of Macaria; and by the end of *Iphigeneia at Aulis* Clytemnestra is feeling pretty homicidal.

Compared with Aeschylus' or Sophocles' Clytemnestra, or the latter's Antigone or Jocasta, there is no denying that Euripides' Hecuba, Helen, Electra, Iphigeneia and Clytemnestra (all in more than one incarnation), Medea, Alcestis, Alcmena, Evadne, Creusa, Hermione and Andromache are formidable creations, a few more cameo than lead, but several among the longest roles in all Greek tragedy. And, like Shakespeare's Portia, Beatrice, Lady Macbeth, Juliet, Cleopatra, or the three daughters of Lear, all were created to be played by male actors, but have, in more recent years, provided the kind of meaty part that few living writers seem to create for the female actor (see also Chapter 10).

This perception of Euripides as hostile to women has a lengthy history. The first biography of Euripides may be principally anecdotal, but it does include the categorical statement that 'He hated laughter and

45

he hated women'.[1] The reason offered is that he had two wives, both of whom were unfaithful to him and that this gave him a jaundiced view of the whole sex. As this story is followed immediately by another about the women's condemnation of him at the Thesmophoria, which is clearly rooted in the comic situation in the Aristophanes play, it is hard to accept that much, if any, of this account is reliable. Unfortunately, there is little alternative evidence against which a check can be made and biographers seem to treat comic playwrights as their best primary source.

That critics in subsequent centuries, especially the nineteenth, should have almost universally confirmed that Euripides was a misogynist may well be more revealing about the critics than about the playwright. It is certainly enlightening about the restricted way in which his plays were read and perceived in other centuries. Equally possible is that, never mind women, Euripides was a man who did not like anybody very much. There are indications in his plays that he felt hostility towards politicians, soldiers, prophets, and indeed democracy. On the other hand, there are just as many suggestions that he felt sympathy towards ethnic minorities, slaves, children and, yes, women.

Alcestis is a good starting point, if only because so much of the play is devoted to the respect and affection that other characters feel for the eponymous heroine, both before and after her death. The play has always provoked strong reactions and contrary interpretations, controversy compounded by its having apparently been presented in fourth place in a submission, a slot usually reserved for a satyr play. As the issue here is not to decide what might account for this or how it was manifest, we may comfortably take it as we find it, a domestic piece where the focus is on the family unit, but with special emphasis on the nature and personality of a wife, Alcestis, and her relationship with her husband, Admetus. Apollo has granted to Admetus, king of Pherae, the boon that, when his time comes to die, he may find a substitute. This proves harder than he had appreciated. As the god bluntly puts it:

> APOLLO. He tried everyone, his family in turn,
> his father, even his aged mother.
> No one could he find willing to leave this life,
> and pass from dark to light for him –
> save one, his wife, Alcestis.
> Now she lies propped up in his arms,
> gasping out her last remaining breath.

[1] Lefkowitz (1981), p. 166.

This is the day when he was doomed to die,
the very day when she must face the grave instead. (ll. 16–22)

This portrait of a king doing the rounds of his family, looking for anyone
to take his place, is hardly dignified. It cannot help inviting some misgiving about the appeal of Apollo's boon in the first place (see also
Chapter 7, pp. 46–51). That this is not simply a perverse reading of a
mythical situation becomes abundantly clear soon after Alcestis' death
when Admetus' father, Pheres, arrives to praise Alcestis while claiming to
offer his condolences:

PHERES. We should pay proper respects to the body of someone
    prepared to save your skin, eh son,
    and preserve me from a childless and miserable
    old age? Her life's a shining example to any woman. (ll. 619–22)

Admetus turns on Pheres with a ferocity that has few parallels anywhere
in Greek drama, especially when it is a son addressing a father:

ADMETUS. Sympathise! You should have sympathised when I was dying.
    You stood aside then, sure enough, old man,
    to let a young man die instead. Crocodile tears!
    Were you really my father?
    And what about my so-called mother?
    Son of a servant, am I, a behind-closed-doors child
    transferred to your wife's breast in secret?
    Put to the test you showed your colours soon enough.
    I disown you as a father. (ll. 633–41)

Pheres gives as good as he gets in an exchange that is all the more terrible
for being conducted over the body of Alcestis on its way to burial:

PHERES. It's a clever scheme you've worked out, I must admit.
    How to cheat death permanently. All you have to do is marry
    another wife and she'll do your dying for you. (ll. 699–701)

As a comment on marriage and what Admetus sees as a wife's duty, this
can be devastating, not least for the guilt it reveals. It may be the first
example we have of Euripides' taking a received myth and populating it
with characters whose reactions are true-to-life. It is certainly not the last.
The implications of the situation still resonate today, perhaps more so, in
today's world of transplant surgery. The myth pictures Admetus as a man
of outstanding nobility, both in his benign treatment of the subservient
god and in his hospitality. By the time that Pheres enters, we have seen a
notable example of the latter in the king's invitation to Heracles to stay

in the palace as his guest, and his decision to lie to Heracles about the family circumstances.

Heracles, as Apollo has already hinted, will eventually rescue Alcestis, as he has rescued Admetus, but none of the mortal characters knows this, least of all Alcestis herself. When the question has been raised as to the benefit of Apollo's gift, it is impossible not to wonder what sort of law of friendship is being upheld when Admetus informs Heracles that the death in the family is only that of some fringe relative and of no importance. The Chorus express doubt over the wisdom of his decision at the time. Later, when all is revealed, Heracles roundly reproves him for it.

Alcestis' own two scenes are comparatively short, though we get a wonderful description of her bidding farewell to her house and home from an old servant before we actually see her, a sort of pre-messenger speech. In her death scene she has a mere seventy-seven lines, on her return from death, none at all: not that this in any way makes the naming of the play after her puzzling. Onstage or off, it is her situation and the whole household's warmth towards her that dominate the action. This universal affection makes it that much harder to justify Admetus' decisions, as many a classical critic has attempted, on the grounds that survival of the king is more important to the state than any mere personal matter. That would seem a much more Sophoclean concern. Euripides is seldom preoccupied with the great issues of state as such, but rather with the impact they have on the lives of individuals. All his examples of self-sacrifice, Menoeceus (*Phoenician Women*), Iphigeneia (*Iphigeneia at Aulis*) and Macaria (*Children of Heracles*) fit into a similar mould. Alcestis is different, principally because neither she nor her country is involved in a war. Euripides elsewhere shows himself at best sceptical about the sacrifice of the individual in the general good, especially on the advice of a prophet. No prophet urges on Alcestis, one might think, except that the person who should be answerable for the situation is Apollo himself, the god of prophecy, patron of the Delphic oracle and deliverer of the prologue.

Apart from asking stern questions about the nature of Apollo's gift, the play is directed precisely at the domestic effect of the loss of a wife and mother. Alcestis' entry is delayed until after the arrival of the Chorus, who initially find themselves in a nice Euripidean quandary. They are local men of Pherae who have come to pay their respects. Their problem is that they know the queen is destined to die, but they are unsure whether or not she is already dead. This gives them an entry song not so much comic as embarrassed, while they look for signs of mourning, spring water or a lock of hair on the step, and go so far as to listen at the palace doors for sounds of weeping. When a servant does enter she has the saddest of tales about Alcestis' preparations, ceremonial bath, special clothes and prayers to Hestia, patron of the hearth, ironically the goddess who was supplanted by Dionysus as one of the twelve Olympians. Alcestis then bids farewell to her marriage bed and to her children. There is no quiet acquiescence here but full-blooded grief in which the whole household joins.

The Chorus are so appalled that they are speculating on whether such an experience might not drive a man to suicide at the very moment when Admetus and Alcestis enter. So far, an audience's impression of Admetus is hardly flattering and his reactions as the scene progresses do little to polish an already tarnished halo. Alcestis has to be wheeled in on a couch: the two children are with her. Already in a delirium she has a vision of Charon approaching in his boat to ferry her to Hades and Death himself standing by her couch. Her chilling account is counterpointed by Admetus telling her not to desert him – a bit late for that, it is difficult not to reflect – and then declaring how tough it is for those who are left behind, the children and, especially, Admetus himself. This bizarre though lyrical exchange (almost certainly sung in the original) comes to an abrupt end when Alcestis suddenly embarks on a lucid speech of some forty lines addressed to her husband. This speech is most notable in the first instance for what she does not say. She lays claim to respect, to a sense of duty, to the fact of her decision in part being from her not wanting to have to bring up the children without him: but that is the closest she gets to any declaration of love. Instead, she tells her husband, with surprisingly little tact, that as a widow she could have married anyone else in Thessaly.

What she is really concerned about are the children. She requires from her husband an assurance, a promise that he will not marry again. Such a demand is not born out of a misplaced jealousy, but out of concern over the way her son and daughter might fare having to grow up with a stepmother: 'Promise me you won't do that. Stepmothers always hate a first wife's family. Like poison' (ll. 308–10). The rest of what she says is aimed exclusively at the children. Admetus is left to make effusive promises about faithfulness to her memory and a lifetime of mourning with music and parties forbidden.[1] At the end of her husband's extended speech she turns to son and daughter:

ALCESTIS. You heard all that, children?

---

[1] When music is such an important aspect of the plays it is tempting to wonder whether the choral odes after Alcestis' death might not have been played unaccompanied.

Your father's promise never to remarry,
never to supplant you or replace me? (ll. 371–3)

Only when he has given his word, does Alcestis hand over her children to him: 'On those terms, receive them from my hand' (l. 375). For the brief remainder of the scene until her death it is Alcestis who comforts the distraught Admetus.[1]

This is an extraordinary scene by any dramatic standard, just three hundred lines into the first Euripides play we have. To the unwary, brought up to think of Greek tragedy as being the stuff of the *Oresteia* or *Oedipus Tyrannus*, it provides a shock to the system. *Alcestis* is not, of course, a tragedy, and this is not the final act of the play. Heracles arrives, is persuaded to stay as a guest by Admetus for reasons best left to a director. He finds out when drunk what has really happened and leaves to repair the damage. Admetus comes back from the funeral feeling very sorry for himself. So genuine does his grief seem by this point it is easy to wonder whether it was not until Alcestis actually died that the reality of what has happened gets through to him. The recollections Euripides gives him of his wedding day, and now her empty chair and cobwebs under the eaves may still bear an element of self-pity, but the detail rings true. Perhaps the most telling touch at this point is that some of what his father said has struck home: people will point to him as 'the man who's still alive, the coward without the nerve to die' (ll. 953–4).

Heracles returns, in the company of a veiled woman he claims to have won at the local games and whom he is now offering to Admetus, on loan till he comes back from the mission which brought him to Pherae in the first place. And so the play proceeds to its bitter-sweet end, so reminiscent of Shakespeare's glorious celebration of redemption in *The Winter's Tale* when the 'statue' of Hermione comes to life. Hermione speaks only to her daughter in that scene, not to Leontes. The unveiled Alcestis, for whom Heracles has wrestled with Death, does not speak at all throughout the last scene.

The question is not why Euripides does not let Alcestis speak – Heracles offers a technical reason, later commentators several alternatives – but what impression is left in the reading of the play and what interpretations are open.[2] Alcestis tends to be seen as a paragon of virtue, 'the noblest wife', as Chorus and Servant agree, but any devotion to Admetus seems at best tempered by concerns for her (rather than their) children. It is

---

[1] The popular belief that death was not permitted on the stage in Athens is given the lie by the end of this scene. Hippolytus too will die in front of the audience, though the goddess Artemis removes herself before it happens. In Sophocles' *Ajax* the hero commits suicide, apparently in full view of the audience.

[2] See Walton (2007 b), pp. 104–10.

Admetus who falls apart. It is Admetus who envies his wife because she is now free from her troubles while 'It is I who should not be alive, I who live on time less borrowed than ransacked' (ll. 938–9). It is Admetus who breaks his oath and accepts another woman into his home. Alcestis has her moment of despair in private, or, out of the presence of the audience, which here amounts to the same thing. Her last speech suggests a steely strength, a quality acknowledged by almost everyone else in the play. *Alcestis* does seem to offer a reappraisal of a marriage in the light of what happens to Alcestis herself. The myth ends here, but the drama invites you to speculate on what happens next. Of course there are other issues within this complex and beautiful fable where the presence of Death in person invokes the whole question of mortality and how we face it, but what lingers in the mind is the portrait of a wife who is distinguished not by some blazing passion, but through personal qualities which outshine those of her husband in every facet of her life.

The same might be argued for Medea, demonised throughout history as the wickedest of all women for the murder of her children, but rehabilitated or reassessed in some modern versions.[1] The nineteenth-century theatre in France and England saw variations on her story including burlesques, from several of which she emerged as a woman more sinned against than sinning.[2] These versions coincided with a rash of new translations of the Euripides, more than a dozen in the last half of the century. All this can be put down to Euripides' original play which may have introduced the idea of Medea as an infanticide, but somehow accords her considerable sympathy. If *Medea* is perhaps the best known of all Euripides' work on the modern stage it is certainly not because it introduces as its leading character a psychopath who has already murdered at least two other people, one her own brother, and proceeds to do away with the king of Corinth and his daughter, followed closely by her own two sons. What is more, as has often been pointed out, she not only kills all these people, she gets away with it, escaping in a winged chariot supplied by her grandfather, the Sun, to go and cause more trouble in Athens, if tales of her subsequent career can be trusted. Euripides goes no further than her escape, taking her dead boys with her and leaving Jason, their father, a broken man.

Despite the baggage it carries, this is at heart a story of marital infidelity and revenge of the kind you may find almost daily in the more sensational

[1] Franca Rame and Dario Fo's *Medea* (1977) and novels by Henry Treece (*Jason*, Bodley Head, 1961), Christa Wolf (*Medea*, Virago, 1998) and Robert Holdstock's *Merlin Codex* trilogy (Simon and Schuster, 2001, 2002, 2007).
[2] See especially Hall, Macintosh and Taplin, eds. (2000); Hall and Macintosh (2005).

press. Reduced to its bare bones, and removing both the mythical and the Athenian context, here is the situation. A man settles in a foreign city (Jason is not from Corinth) with an even more foreign wife (Medea has accompanied him from Georgia at the far end of the Black Sea) who has helped him in a business enterprise. They have children, two of them, but after a while he decides to ditch her for a more advantageous match which will help both his career and his social standing. She gets her own back in the only way she can envisage which will affect him. Whose side do you take?

In fifth-century BC Athens it was simple for a man to divorce his wife. He made the announcement before witnesses and she was sent off home to her father. In Athens a Jason, even a Jason who was an Athenian citizen, could not legally have married a non-Athenian, never mind a non-Greek, a barbarian. It is conspicuously not fifth-century BC Athens in which the play is set. Euripides' Corinth, like the settings of all his plays, is a mythical place in a mythical period whose culture and morality are as removed from that of the very first audience as they are from an audience today. The circumstances of the play have to be taken on trust, and in that sense the myth serves as a kind of prism from which the story may be viewed as much of today as it is of classical Athens. Medea and the other characters are products of the circumstances we hear about, mostly in the prologue delivered by the children's Nurse. Medea has discovered about Jason's new marriage and the Nurse is apprehensive about her reaction. The children are introduced early, the first of four scenes in which they appear, so that no one may forget what Medea's plans will entail. As the play proper begins Medea can be heard offstage, ranting and threatening suicide. The boys are sent indoors with the Tutor for their own protection.

It is now that the Chorus enter, a group of local women who hear her off-stage weeping but react in individual ways. The lines as written suggest a series of voices, one sympathetic, one shocked at the suggestion of suicide, one fatalistic, another hardly concerned. What Medea will do is forge them into a unified group of women who will condone four murders. This is the real source of Medea's strength in forming a plot and making all manner of people complicit. She is a step ahead of everyone she deals with. By the time she makes her entrance, the hair-tearing is over. She appears quite calm, dangerously calm. Her first requirement is to win over the Chorus, including the doubters. This she does in a remarkable speech, woman to woman, that is worth quoting in its entirety:

MEDEA. There now. I've come outside.
  I wouldn't want to be reproached, my Corinthian friends,
    for being high and mighty, indoors and aloof.
  If you like a quiet life they'll call you antisocial.

But when were first impressions reliable?
One man will hate another for no reason,
the moment he claps eyes on him.
A gut reaction, but where's the justice in that?
If you're a foreigner, well, it's best to conform.
Even a citizen can't make the rules
simply to suit himself. That would be bad manners.
But I . . . I was not expecting this.
It pierces me to the soul.
You are my friends. I've lost the will to live.
My life was centred on one man, my husband.
A hollow man.
Poor women.
No living, breathing creature feels as we do.
We want a husband? It's an auction
where we pay to give away our bodies.
That's not the half of it. A good man or a bad?
By the time you find that out it's too late.
Divorce for a woman means disgrace.
And once she's married, there's no saying 'no'.
It's she who has to change the patterns of her life.
You'd need to be clairvoyant
to predict how he'll behave in bed.
If you do strike lucky
and this husband turns out bearable,
submits gracefully, then fine. Congratulations.
If not, you might as well be dead.
When a man starts to get bored at home
he can visit a friend, some kindred spirit,
look for consolation elsewhere.
We have a single focus, him.
'You've a nice, easy life,' that's what they say,
safe at home when they're off fighting.
Good thinking, that is, isn't it?
I'd fight three wars rather than give birth once.
Our situations are different, of course.
This is your city. Your father's house was here.
Life at its best with your friends around you.
But I'm alone, stateless, abused
by a husband like something picked up abroad.
No mother. No brother. No relation
to turn to in a time of trouble.
That's why I'd like to ask for your support.
If I hit upon some means, some stratagem

to pay my husband back for what he's done,
the bride and giver of the bride he means to marry,
say nothing.
A woman's always full of fears, of course,
petrified by the mere sight of steel.
But scorn her, cross her in love,
and savour the colour of her vengeance.
CHORUS. Of course. Pay him back, Medea.
That's only fair. You suffer. Why shouldn't you? (ll. 212–68)

And this playwright is a misogynist?

The Chorus are certainly won over, a united force behind her, turning all others into enemies. Creon, the king, who now enters, is met with several tactics by Medea for getting her way – innocence, debate, hysterics. He sees through them all, but admits that he is frightened of her because she is clever:

MEDEA. 'Clever'? I've been called that before, Creon.
I've a reputation, haven't I, for causing trouble?
No man in his right mind
should teach his children to be clever . . .
People don't like it. (ll. 292–5)

But clever is exactly what Medea is, adjusting her reactions to every circumstance. Eventually it is an appeal on behalf of the children which gains her the twenty-four hours she wants. 'You can't get up to much mischief in one day' is Creon's ominous exit line. Off the back of this victory of words, Medea suddenly reveals to the Chorus that she plans three murders in that twenty-four hours, Creon, his daughter and her husband: no mention yet of the children. Late in the speech she unexpectedly summons the assistance of Hecate:

MEDEA. To the task then.
Conjure, Medea, conjure all your craft.
Ooze into evil. Hold hard like a limpet.
Concentrate on grievance. (ll. 402–5)

This is the same Hecate who appears twice in Shakespeare's *Macbeth*, once to chide the witches, later to commend them. For Euripides, the call is less to summon her powers of witchcraft than as a goddess of transformation: Medea acknowledging that success depends on dressing herself in whatever identity the moment requires.[1]

---

[1] In Sumerian legend, much of which was absorbed into Greek culture, Hecate and Circe were the two principal goddesses of transformation. Circe, best remembered as the sorceress who turned Odysseus' men into pigs in Homer's *Odyssey*, was Medea's aunt.

Passing over the first of her three scenes with Jason, Medea similarly manipulates Aegeus, the king of Athens, who arrives just when she needs to find a bolthole. He has been to Delphi to consult the oracle about his childlessness. Medea is supportive. She can help, though her husband is throwing her out. Will he give her sanctuary in Athens? Aegeus agrees, as long as she can get there under her own steam. She makes him swear a surprisingly powerful oath. Immediately after Aegeus has left, Medea reveals – lets slip almost – that she will use her children to help kill the Princess:

> MEDEA. When that is done, it's done.
> But what comes next, ah, there are the tears.
> I have to kill the children. My children.
> No one shall take them from me. (ll. 790–3)

The Chorus suddenly find that the silence they signed up to through female solidarity is about to make them accomplices in a terrifying sequence of destruction. Medea certainly does not embark on the murder of her boys with equanimity. She is close to relenting when she tries to say goodbye to them but, after taking the fatal step of setting in train the death of the Princess, she cannot weaken. When a Messenger confirms that this has happened, and that Creon is dead too, she faces up to what she must do:

> MEDEA. I gave them life. I'll take it away again.
> Steel yourself, my heart. Why wait?
> Awful, but this you have to do.
> Grasp the sword, vile hand.
> The slow, short walk. To a life sentence.
> Don't weaken. Don't think of them as children,
> your children. Ignore love. For one short day
> make believe they are not your boys.
> Then there will be a time for grief.
> You kill them. Poor Medea. But I love them. (ll. 1242–50)

The three scenes which Medea shares with Jason encompass all her moods and confirm her as a consummate actress. Initially, she is simply incensed by her husband's specious excuses for his behaviour: 'the best thing really, for you and the boys' (ll. 549–50) and his descriptions of the benefits of civilisation she has reaped from the time she spent married to him, followed by his sneering:

> JASON. You women, you're fixated. You've convinced yourselves,
> if you're happy in bed, nothing else matters.
> If you're not, then everything's a disaster.

I wish there were some other way to father children.
No women! That would solve everything. (ll. 569–73)

She does, at least, succeed in knocking some of his heroic pretensions
down to size (see Chapter 1, pp. 25–6).

By the time of his second entrance, her resolution has firmed up and the
dissembling Medea takes over. Jason's misgivings are undermined as he
patronises her apparent conciliation:

JASON. That's my girl. I don't blame you.
A woman's likely to get a bit emotional
with her husband marrying again. (ll. 908–10)

In their last scene, Jason stands shattered in front of the palace while
Medea in her chariot, the corpses of their children on display, forecasts
the rest of his life for him, as she takes off for hers. These three
confrontations between Medea and Jason present a remarkable portrait
of the decline of a marriage into the crossfire of blame (see also Chapter
6, pp. 108–13). At the last Medea is aloof, located on the stage physically
above her former husband as she prepares to move on to a new life. It is
the most haunting of images for a disastrously fractured relationship.

Can any crime be worse than the murder of your own children?
Perhaps not, and Euripides offers no apology for Medea's revenge. What
he does do is demonstrate the circumstances which might contribute to a
woman taking such a step. The Chorus at one point pray never to suffer
'passion, too much passion' (l. 627). They at least recognise by this time
to what they are becoming witnesses. It may be impossible to justify
Medea's actions, or even sympathise with them. Euripides does account
for them in terms of how she has been treated, both as a woman and as a
non-Greek. If the play made uncomfortable viewing for its first Athenian
audience (and the set of plays which included Medea was placed last at
the Great Dionysia of 431 BC), then it still has much the same effect in
modern society and within some modern relationships.

The same may appear true in the tragedy that, more than any other,
was felt to parade Euripides' decadence, Hippolytus. The play we have is
believed to be a rewrite, after an earlier version proved too near the
knuckle, with a scene where Phaedra declared her love in person to her
stepson, Hippolytus. Instead, in this second version, the information is
made at second hand through the mediation of the Nurse. This device
works best dramatically in the scene where Phaedra confides to the
Nurse the identity of the man with whom she has fallen in love.
The Nurse's disastrous advice to yield to temptation and her subsequent

revelation to Hippolytus are almost as effective.

The term 'fallen in love' would have presented shades of meaning, and some mystification, in classical times. Men tended to fall in lust, rather than in love, and the line that is drawn, if at all, between seduction and rape is a fine one. Mythology is packed with illegitimate children, many of them spawned by gods in strange disguises. Usually the result of the male pursuit of a desired female is that he catches up with her, resistance often proving more oppressive than submission. The unfortunate women suffer the consequences, which may vary simply from bastard offspring, to bastard offspring with some superhuman power, or bastard offspring delivered in an egg or some other eccentric form. If or when women feel lustfully inclined it is regarded as an aberration. In Crete Phaedra's mother, Pasiphae, fancied a bull so much that she had a mechanical cow made, so that she could climb inside to be serviced by the creature. The result was the Minotaur, half bull, half man, which Theseus eventually killed. The whiff of something unnatural in Phaedra's past pervades *Hippolytus*, though Aphrodite's personal involvement will be considered later (see Chapter 7, pp. 125–8).

The Greeks identified a difference between *erôs*, carnal love, and *philia*, loving friendship, though Plato, especially in *The Symposium*, was to treat them as complementary or interdependent. Both were different again from love for children which in a man was based in part on the need for protection in old age, driven by a desire for survival of the bloodline. Within Greek tragedy there is a variety of irregular relationships, the most significant of which are those that threaten a marriage. Aegisthus and Clytemnestra in Aeschylus' *Oresteia* are one such couple, though Agamemnon's return with Cassandra from the war is considered more equivocally. In Sophocles, the only lovers seen in one another's company are the ill-starred Oedipus and Jocasta and, in *Ajax*, Ajax himself and his concubine, Tecmessa. Heracles never meets on stage either his wife or the woman he has fallen for in *Women of Trachis* and, rather more strangely, Antigone and Haemon, though betrothed, have no scene together in *Antigone*. Bearing in mind that the cause of the Trojan War was the seduction and/or abduction of Helen, wife of Menelaus, staging of love affairs is a rarity. The triangular relationship Euripides portrays in *Hippolytus* involves a father, a son and a stepmother. Phaedra is dead by the time that Theseus returns from consulting the oracle and this throws a strong emphasis of the tragedy on to the relationship between Theseus and Hippolytus. With so much known about Theseus and Phaedra from other sources, it is important to trace their relationship here only in terms of what is contained within the play.

Apart from what is said by Aphrodite in the prologue, and the roles of Aphrodite and Artemis are a subject to return to later, we find out little about the past or the present. Theseus, son of Aegeus (though not by Medea), is a ubiquitous character in myth, and especially drama, as the noble king of Athens and friend of Heracles. In *Hippolytus* he is in exile for a year at Trozen, this having the effect of divorcing him from his Athenian past and reputation. Hippolytus is Theseus' illegitimate son by Hippolyta, queen of the Amazons and, according to the Nurse, if Phaedra kills herself, his heir in preference to Phaedra's children (ll. 304–9), whose age and gender, indeed whereabouts, are not revealed. Phaedra at one point invokes both her mother, Pasiphae, and her sister, Ariadne, unceremoniously ditched on Naxos after helping Theseus to kill the Minotaur, and sees herself as the family's third victim of *erôs*.

The less emphasis there is on the background to the characters – and there is virtually nothing about Hippolytus beyond his devotion to Artemis – the more the play becomes a marital tragedy, where a desperate situation is made worse by the way people react to it.[1] The Nurse's decision to sound out Hippolytus is a dreadful one. No possible response could improve the situation. Hippolytus himself may respond with disgust and in an over-prudish fashion, but two of his remarks sound curiously like Jason's when rebuking Medea:

HIPPOLYTUS. Zeus, [...] if the human race has to be reproduced
    there ought to be some way of doing it without women.
    Make a deposit at a temple, whatever you can afford,
    and buy a child. (ll. 616–21)

    The most trouble-free household is where a woman is nothing.
    Though, if she's stupid, just sitting at home is trouble enough.
    I can't stand a clever woman. In my house
    I want no woman cleverer than she should be.
    It's amongst the clever ones that sex [Cypris, 'the Cypriot', an
      epithet of Aphrodite] causes most trouble. (ll. 638–43)

When Theseus returns to find his wife hanged and his son accused of attempted rape, he will hear no defence for Hippolytus and calls down a curse which Poseidon fulfils with disastrous consequences. It takes the goddess Artemis in person to convince him that he was wrong about his son.

All these three, the Nurse, Hippolytus and Theseus, make at least one disastrous error of judgement (*hamartia*) and contribute to the tragedy.

---

[1] It is a theme that was used by, among others, Eugene O'Neill in *Desire Under the Elms* (1924) and Brian Friel in *Living Quarters: After Hippolytus* (1977).

Then there is Phaedra herself. The initial impression of her is of someone who struggles against something utterly beyond her control. When she finally confesses her passion for Hippolytus to both Nurse and Chorus, she reveals how much she has tried to resist:

> PHAEDRA. I am going to tell what track my thoughts took,
>   when I found myself smitten by this passion [*erôs*],
>   I set my mind to how to manage, how to cope with it.
>   My first thought was simply to say nothing,
>   to suffer in silence this sickness of mine.
>   The tongue is dangerous when criticising others:
>   secondly, willpower to overcome my addiction.
>   When I found I simply could not control this desire,
>   suicide seemed the only answer. (ll. 391–401)

But how can there be any defence for what Theseus finds on his return? His wife has taken her third option and committed suicide. She has left behind a suicide note in which she accuses Hippolytus of assaulting her. Is his disgust at what she confessed sufficient to justify an accusation of attempted rape? It is a question that the play asks, but to which it offers no definitive answer. She can hardly be unaware of the havoc she will cause. One possible excuse might be to safeguard the position of her children, but she chooses to make it as much to keep her own reputation intact as to ensure their future:

> I have made a discovery: a way out for all of us,
>   preserving a reputation for my boys
>   and some advantage for myself from what has happened. (ll. 716–18)

In her last speech she tells the Chorus:

> By my death I will at least bring ruin on one person.
>   That will teach him not to express such disdain
>   for my unhappiness. Perhaps from this sickness of mine
>   he'll learn the meaning of self-control. (ll. 728–31)

Quite the reverse, you may be tempted to think – self-control is not one of Hippolytus' problems – but off she goes to write the fatal letter for her husband to find in her dead hand. It is hard not to find this simply a vindictive act, one all of Phaedra's own creation, whatever the cause of her infatuation. Any of the possible outcomes after she departs from the scene are not going to cure Hippolytus' misogyny. He may priggishly claim the moral high-ground in his devotion to chastity, but he is never shown to be a hypocrite as is the fate of most of drama's puritans. He simply follows his inclinations, as Phaedra tries not to follow hers. It is a largely blameless Theseus, at least as far as Phaedra is concerned, who is left alive to grieve.

In the post-Trojan War plays women more often than not have the central roles. They are the most prominent victims of war, largely as commodities, with apparently no control over their destiny. Yet Hecuba acquires a strength, in *Hecuba*, if not in *Trojan Women*. *Andromache* is, perhaps, the most dramatically versatile play in this respect. Widow of Hector and allocated to Neoptolemus, son of Achilles, she is prominent in *Trojan Women* and *Hecuba* mostly as the mother of the baby Astyanax, ruthlessly dispatched by the Greeks. In the play where she is the title character she and another son are under threat from Helen's daughter, Hermione. Neoptolemus is the father of this child of hers, Hermione the legitimate wife who blames Andromache for her failure to conceive. The head-to-head between the two women offers some of the most ferocious and realistic dialogue in all Greek tragedy (see Chapter 6, pp. 106–8), and their hostility is brilliantly observed. They are still both dependent on men. The threatened Andromache finds a defender in old Peleus, Neoptolemus' grandfather, while the poisonous Hermione is unceremoniously dumped by her own father, Menelaus, only to escape with Orestes, who turns up out of the blue claiming to have engineered the death of Neoptolemus. At the end of *Orestes* too Orestes and Hermione sail off into the sunset together, though their previous encounter in the play does not suggest much of a recipe for wedded bliss. But then, nor does the union of Electra and Pylades bode well if the characters in *Orestes* or in *Electra* offer a foretaste. As for Andromache, in *Andromache* she again finds herself reallocated, this time by Thetis to marry Helenus in Molossia.

Best off by far, in this world of convoluted and unbalanced relationships between women and men, is the lovely Helen, not the unfaithful wife who caused the Trojan War, and subject of almost universal condemnation thereafter, but the one who is revealed in *Helen* as having lived in respectable celibacy in Egypt for seventeen years waiting for the arrival of her affable, if none too bright, and fondly remembered Menelaus.

The treatment of women as disposables is given such uncomfortable prominence by Euripides that it is difficult not to attribute it far more to the playwright's very real sympathy for women as victims than to any broad condemnation of their more savage responses. The resonances are pervasive. Play after play is dominated by its female characters: all but five have a female Chorus, which makes their cast more female than male: four Euripides Choruses give a play its title. Eight more plays take their from a female character. What do these eight women, and other central female characters have in common? Nothing: nothing, beyond a certain depth and a certain status. They are all highly individual, including the two Iphigeneias, Electra and another Electra in *Orestes*, Hecuba and another Hecuba in *Trojan Women*, Helen and the other Helens in both *Orestes* and *Trojan Women*. All offer fine roles for actors, male or female (see also Chapter 10). What is beyond dispute is that Euripides took women seriously, whatever the circumstances and influences of his own private life, more seriously, it would seem, than did most of his fellow-Athenians. He created women whose strength, for good or bad, should guarantee their survival on the modern stage.

4 THE COMIC TOUCH

Cyclops, Ion, Orestes, Electra, Bacchae, Children of Heracles, Helen

In the grim and relentless *Trojan Women*, set in the immediate aftermath of the sack of Troy, with the women allocated and about to confront whatever fate the Greeks have in store for them, there is a moment when Helen is dragged in to face Menelaus. Hecuba tells him not to travel home on the same ship as his wife and Menelaus replies, 'Why so? Is she carrying more weight than she used to?' (l. 1050). It is a feeble joke. It is probably the feeblest joke in Greek tragedy; or comedy for that matter. By the beginning of the play Hecuba has lost her husband Priam, her son Hector and many of her other children, her home and her status. By the time of this exchange with Menelaus, she has discovered she is to serve as a slave to the hated Odysseus. She has seen her demented daughter Cassandra dragged off to become Agamemnon's concubine. Another daughter, Polyxena, has been sacrificed to appease the ghost of Achilles. A daughter-in-law, Andromache, has been wheeled in on a cart full of booty, with her baby son Astyanax, who is then dragged from his mother's arms to be thrown over the battlements in case he grows up to exact vengeance on the Greeks. Andromache too is taken away, to become the slave of Neoptolemus. Then Menelaus enters, and soon after, Helen. It is hardly the time for jokes.

In the situation, how funny the remark may be is not, of course, the point. The scene does offer a momentary change of mood, but Euripides is doing much more than create some light relief after unremitting anguish. Following a prologue conducted by the unholy alliance of two gods, the entirety of the play proper has been dominated by the wretched Trojans, all of whom are women. The only other character has been Talthybius, the male Greek herald, who comes and goes, because that is his job and that is what his position makes possible. Suddenly two Greeks who have been the central cause of all this ten years of misery arrive on the scene. Menelaus' opening line 'Ah, the sun is shining, and today I'll get my wife back' (ll. 860–1) leaves no doubt about his frame of mind. It may jar for an audience, but it does work as an extraordinary jolt to the system, especially when, immediately after this scene, Euripides has the dead baby carried in on Hector's shield to be bathed and mourned in whatever pathetic way the women may.

Behind this extreme example lies Euripides' instinctive and musical sense of modulation of mood. Would that all modern directors were sensitive to such structures. Every Euripides play contains its moments of comedy, if comedy is to be equated with the smile of recognition, incongruity, humanity, or bathos, as well as the laughter of wit, buffoonery, satire or burlesque. In other chapters plenty of examples can be found of such moments, in *Phoenician Women*, *Electra*, *Alcestis*, *Andromache*, *Helen*, *Medea*, *Heracles*, *Ion* or *Bacchae*. For Euripides the laughing moment becomes a stock-in-trade.[1]

The rest of this chapter will consider not what might have made the Greeks laugh, but what might still seem to touch the dramatic nerve where an audience is in that dangerous territory between comic and tragic, wondering at what point the licence to laugh runs out. Humour in Euripides comes in a variety of forms and is derived from several sources. This is, in part, a translation issue and there is no doubt that there are lines in the original Greek that may be given an ironic or sarcastic nuance, or not, according to the mindset of the individual translator, or, indeed, post-translator, by director and actor. What translators perceive as humour will inevitably be relocated in the colloquial language of their own cultures. That Euripides is a playwright who often walks the tightrope between the tragic and the comic gives a certain licence, as translation of all comedy invites more freedom of interpretation than does tragedy. His work has often appeared out of kilter with formula-driven tragedy, as for centuries after his death Shakespeare was castigated, and even edited, so that no Porter should be first on the scene after the murder of Duncan, no clownish Gravedigger herald the burial of Ophelia. Ours is an era that, more than any in history, seems aware of how close tragedy is to farce, farce to tragedy. We are ready for Euripides.

Cyclops, as a satyr play, is full of gags. Choruses in Euripides sometimes function primarily as witnesses to events (*Iphigeneia at Aulis*, *Ion*), sometimes as accomplices (*Medea*, *Hecuba*). Many are sympathetic (*Helen*, *Hippolytus*), others have a major role within the action (five give their play its title). The Chorus of satyrs in *Cyclops* tend to dictate the comic impetus by the way they react to events. This includes routines where they are central. They enter, apparently, driving a flock of unruly sheep which will not do what they are told. Late in the plays, after their leader Silenus has effectively sold Odysseus down the river, resulting in the death of some of his companions, Odysseus makes his plans to get the

---

[1] Locating comic elements in Euripides can be traced back comfortably into the nineteenth century, but it was often considered a mark of poor dramaturgy.

Cyclops drunk and put out his single eye. The Chorus are enthusiastic about assisting: 'Is there any way I could give a hand, especially with the red-hot gouging? I would like to give a hand with the gouging' (ll. 469–70). They even sing a song about it:

CHORUS (*variously*). After me. Me first, not you.
  Don't push. What's the rush? Form a queue,
  To grasp the flaming flagpole
  And shove it in his eyehole
  And twiddle till his brains come seeping through. (ll. 483–7)

When it comes to action, they all take one pace backwards:

Do you think you should tell us the batting order? Who holds the stake and where for the eye-burning? So we all get a share. Because some of us are a bit of a long way from the door for actually pushing the flame into his eye. And I've just turned my ankle. Funny you should say that. I think it's broken. I was standing over there and I just felt it go. Me too.
ODYSSEUS. Just felt it go!
CHORUS. Oh, dust in my eye. Ash, probably.
ODYSSEUS. You pifflers! A fine help you turned out to be.
CHORUS. Just because I don't want to damage my back – I've got a bad back – and have my teeth knocked out of my head. Suddenly I'm a coward!
  (ll. 631–47)

Much of the play's impetus comes from Homer, the plot being based on an incident in the *Odyssey*. The cunning Odysseus conceals his real name from the Cyclops, Polyphemus, by calling himself 'Nobody'. After the blinding, Polyphemus calls for help from the Chorus because Nobody has blinded him. In that case . . . Yes, well, maybe there is a worse joke than that of Menelaus about Helen's weight.

A lot of the comedy derives from the Chorus and is, probably originally was, predictable. What is more unexpected is that the Cyclops has a declaration of his philosophy when responding to Odysseus' asking for the customary respect for the traveller. The Cyclops' reply, somewhat edited, is close to a manifesto for today's drinking culture:

CYCLOPS. Listen, Pygmy. The clever man's god is money. Everything else is wind and words [...] I'm not afraid of any thunderbolt from Zeus, friend, 'cos I've got no reason to believe he's any bigger a god than I am. And I don't care. About anything. If it's raining, I go indoors where it's nice and sheltered. If I've an appetite, I serve it, a little bit of tasty, wild or tame. I lounge about massaging my belly, drinking by the gallon. And, if Zeus thunders at me, I outfart him [...] I don't make a sacrifice to anybody –

except me. The biggest of my gods is my stomach [...] Now creep off in there and show a little respect to my household god. Reverence the altar of me. (ll. 316–46)

There is a similar scene in *Alcestis*, where a drunken Heracles, unaware of the death of the mistress of the household, rings a bell for many a victim of the pub bore when he buttonholes one of the servants:

HERACLES. Oy, you. Why the long face?
   A servant shouldn't go all sulky in front of the guests.
   You need to be a bit more friendly.
   Smile a bit can't you?
   What are you looking like that for?
   One of your master's friends and you look at me
   like something the cat brought in.
   It's not your funeral, you know. Here!
   Come over here! I want to tell you something.
   Listen. Life, eh? What's it all about?
   Have you any idea? Have you any idea what life is?
   I haven't. I haven't a clue. And if I haven't a clue,
   what hope have you got? No, listen.
   Every single man and woman has got to die.
   That's their destiny. There's not one of them,
   not a single one of them, can say for sure
   that they will live through tomorrow. Not one. It's a fact.
   Because Fate moves in a mysterious way.
   No one can teach us about Fate.
   We can't learn about Fate from experience.
   So, think about that. I'm telling you.
   Here's my philosophy. Enjoy yourself.
   Have a drink. Live in the present.
   Live from day to day and let Fate take care of the rest.
   Have a bit of fun. A bit of passion.
   There's something you can worship.
   Aphrodite's your goddess. Forget everything else.
   Am I right? Of course I am. Take it from me.
   So cheer up! Don't be all upset.
   Have a little drink with me and forget about Fate.
   Why not go and get a garland or two?
   I tell you. A drink will take that scowl off your face.
   Splish-splash. Gurgle, gurgle. Down the hatch.
   You are human, aren't you? Then act human,
   for god's sake. You don't want to be one of those
   wet blankets, those po-faced puritans, do you?
   If you ask me, in my considered judgement,

that's no life. No life at all.
A calamity on legs, that's what you are. (ll. 773–802)

The rest of Euripides' output consists of tragedies proper, though they range from the starkest to several plays which are only 'potential tragedies' or 'tragedies avoided', like some late Shakespeare, and more suitably labelled as 'romances'. *Ion*, *Helen* and *Iphigeneia Among the Taurians* all involve deaths prevented. Fifth-century BC Athenians, for whom 'comedy' meant the freewheeling fantasies of Aristophanes and his fellows, would never have recognised them as comedies.[1] As has always been appreciated, these plays look forward in tone to the New Comedies of the century after Euripides' death when his reputation soared through revival and eclipsed that of either Aeschylus or Sophocles.

It is not only in their endings that these plays reveal themselves as a new form of tragedy. They regularly incorporate incidents which signal a happy ending. The Chorus, as in the satyr play, sometimes provides the pointer. *Ion* concerns the parentage of the name character. He is first discovered as a temple attendant in Delphi, performing his cleaning duties before the day's visitors arrive from Athens, trying to keep the birds from crapping on the pillars and building nests on the roof. Ion has been brought up as a foundling after being left at the temple steps by Hermes on the instructions of Apollo, the baby's father. Mundane enough an occupation to take an audience by surprise, Ion's daily chores are the prelude to the arrival of the Chorus, female attendants of Creusa, queen of Athens, who in due time will turn out to be Ion's mother. They swan in ahead of their mistress, like day-trippers off a coach from the metropolis, and wander about admiring the architecture:

CHORUS. So, it's not only in Athens
  You can find temples of the gods,
  With pillars so beautifully proportioned,
  In honour of Apollo of the roadside.
  Here too, as god of prophecy,
  Twin porticoes, shining bright.

  Look. Take a look at that!
  See? That's the hydra of Lernaea,
  Heracles killing it with his golden sword.
  I see. And someone else with a torch.
  Would that be – Oh, I heard the story once

[1] In his essay 'Euripidean Comedy' Bernard Knox identified this issue and picked out several of the same examples from *Electra* and *Ion* as will be singled out below (Knox, 1979, pp. 250–74).

While I was working at the loom –
Iolaus, that's it. With the shield.
Didn't he give Heracles a helping hand
With all those labours of his?

Here. Over here, the fire-breathing monster,
Part-snake, goat and lion, and Bellerophon,
Killing it, on Pegasus, his winged horse.

I don't know where to look next.
There, see? Carved on the stone,
The defeat of the Giants.
Yes, I see what you mean.
Oh, my dears!
And look at who that is,
Brandishing her Gorgon aegis
Over Enceladus. It's Athena!
Pallas Athena! Our goddess.
And isn't that a thunderbolt,
Covered in flame,
About to be hurled by Zeus?
Yes, it is. And Mimas is the target.
And Dionysus, our Bacchic god,
With his thyrsus, slaying
Another of the Sons of Earth. (ll. 184–219)

It is not the lines that are funny, though they could be made so in a freer translation. Nor are the mythological references (slightly clarified here) a barrier. It is the situation: a Chorus entering the *orchêstra* of the Theatre of Dionysus at Athens and admiring the set. Euripides is surely giving licence to look in the play for something other than high tragedy. We confirm it later in two scenes of comic misunderstanding. Creusa has arrived in Delphi with her husband, Xuthus, to ask for advice from the oracle about their childlessness. Xuthus rushes from the shrine while Ion is talking to the Chorus and the following exchange takes place (in a fairly literal translation):

XUTHUS. Greetings, my boy. That's the proper way for me to begin.
ION. And my greetings to you. Behave yourself and we'll both be happy.
XUTHUS. Let me kiss your hand and give you a hug.
ION. You are in your right mind, are you? Not maddened by a god?
XUTHUS. In my right mind? Of course I am! My heart's desire and I'm longing to stroke him?
ION. Get off. You'll damage my holy vestments.
XUTHUS. I just have to touch you. I'm not abducting you. I've found my love.

ION. Leave me alone unless you want an arrow in the ribs.
XUTHUS. Why are you avoiding me? Don't you recognise love?
ION. What I don't love is strangers behaving like lunatics. (ll. 517–26)

What Ion does not realise, and nor do the audience yet, is that Xuthus has been told by the Oracle, somewhat dubiously in the circumstances, that the first person he meets when he leaves the shrine will be his son. Ion – and it seems difficult to interpret the above scene in any other way – thinks he is being propositioned, an occupational hazard perhaps for a temple attendant at Delphi. When Xuthus explains the reasons for his behaviour, Ion still has his doubts about his background and these continue to the end of the play.

Later, after a series of improbable near-disasters, the Priestess emerges with the crib in which Ion was abandoned (though Ion finds it looks suspiciously new) and some clothes and trinkets which Creusa identifies. All looks set for the kind of reunion which was to become a popular way of resolving questions of paternity in the new comedies of the fourth century.[1] Ion, though, is not convinced that his father could possibly have been Apollo, who surely would never behave in such a way, and tells his mother so:

> ION. I'm extremely pleased we have found one another, Mother,
>   and am not blaming anyone for the circumstances of my birth.
>   But there is something I'd like to say to you in private.
>   Come over here. I don't want anyone else listening to this.
>   It's confidential. Might it not be, Mother, that you,
>   as young girls do, had a lover, a secret lover,
>   and that, to avoid the disgrace you are blaming a god
>   for what happened, when it was nothing to do with Apollo,
>   and there was nothing particularly godly about my father? (ll. 1518–27)

Creusa is dismayed, but fortunately Athena puts in an appearance to confirm the divine version of events. The joke, apart from being on Xuthus, is in the private conversation, away from any inquisitive ears – except the odd fifteen thousand who may have been in the audience. Like *Iphigeneia Among the Taurians* and *Helen*, *Ion* does reveal a level of real concern over human relationships and uncovers, as will the plays of Menander, a vein of seriousness and sentiment – not sentimentality – that encompasses various yearnings, from those of the childless to those who, as mother or child, have somehow forfeited the nurturing years.

---

[1] Menander's *The Arbitration* is the obvious example, though not all of the play has survived.

The story of Ion does involve a threat to his life, but is found in one of the less violent corners of myth. *Orestes* is plum in the middle of the bloodbath that is the House of Atreus, Euripides' version of what happened after the murder of Clytemnestra by her son and daughter, Orestes and Electra, and Orestes' friend Pylades. The choral entry here is more ambiguous but as defining. It is also uncharacteristically delayed until after a long prologue from Electra, explaining the situation, and a scene with Helen followed by the introduction of Helen's daughter, Hermione. Orestes has been raving on and off for six days and has at last fallen asleep, when in come the Chorus. Electra's first concern is that they will wake him up:

> ELECTRA. Dearest of friends, walk [literally] with a quiet foot,
>   keep quiet and no sudden noise. Your concern is well-meant,
>   I'm sure, but it would be dreadful to wake him up. (ll. 136–9)

She urges them to silence '*Siga! Siga!*' and then to back off from the couch on which Orestes lies. 'Back we go,' they sing. The scene continues in similar vein for thirty-five lines before Electra pleads with them to leave: which, being the Chorus, and having just arrived, they are unlikely to do. Electra explains to them over the next forty lines what has happened and they offer sympathy. They also take a look at Orestes and wonder if he might be dead without Electra having noticed: 'I don't like the look of him. He's too relaxed' (l. 210). In the process they do wake him.

This looks extremely like a parody of the tragic chorus and it would be difficult in a production not to make it seem so. The impression of pastiche is reinforced in the later messenger speeches. The first Messenger, who reports on Orestes' trial, turns out to have arrived purely by chance and only favours the family because they once gave him food when he was begging. That may be unusual, though not exactly parody. The second Messenger, however, with news of the murder of Helen, arrives apparently clambering over the roof of the palace, still wearing his 'barbarian slippers'. He is a Trojan slave, in such a panic he speaks pidgin Greek. He is even less fluent than the Scythian policeman in Aristophanes' *Women at the Thesmophoria* and he *is* meant to be a comic turn. The Chorus can barely understand what this Trojan is trying to say and he is later chased off stage by the sadistic Orestes.

As if this were not enough, Euripides concludes the play with the most eyebrow-raising of all *dei ex machina*. Condemned to death by the Argive court, Orestes and Electra have been persuaded by Pylades to kill Helen. Pylades, who is a more fearsome buccaneer than any of the others, does much of the initial planning and claims shared responsibility for the murder of Clytemnestra and Helen with all the enthusiasm of a para-military enforcer. The three of them now stand on the roof of the palace, along with Hermione, Helen's daughter, held hostage, a knife at her throat. Her father, Menelaus, is down below, trying to break in through the palace doors, while Orestes threatens to brain him with a piece of coping stone. Orestes is fully intent on murdering Hermione and getting Electra and Pylades to set the palace on fire, unless Menelaus goes back to the people of Argos and secures a pardon for the murder of Clytemnestra. Menelaus seems to have decided not to give in to black-mail, whatever the consequences. Sort that lot out, Apollo!

And so he does, appearing on the *mêchanê*, the stage crane. He takes one look at what is going on and tidies it all up in some sixty lines. This amounts to telling Menelaus to back off, and Orestes to let go of Hermione. Helen, whom they thought they had killed, has been rescued by Apollo and translated to heaven where she will spend eternity ministering to sailors! Orestes is to remove his sword from Hermione's throat and marry her instead. She happens to be betrothed to Neoptolemus, but Apollo will have him done away with in Delphi.[1] Orestes can stay and be king of Argos once he has got out of the way the small matter of a trial for matricide in Athens. Pylades and Electra will get married. Menelaus may return to Sparta and live off Helen's dowry. Everyone thinks this is a grand outcome.

It is difficult not to feel affection for this disorderly and unduly overlooked adventure story, sporting the most tongue-in-cheek of *ex machina* interventions. More black farce, perhaps, than parody, this is a suitable conclusion to a play that is like no other Greek tragedy. The style most resembles that of some of the Jacobean horror comics, Webster, perhaps, or *The Revenger's Tragedy*, attributed to Cyril Tourneur and described by Peter Thomson as 'sombrely ironic'. Euripides' 'happy-ever-after' ending has made generations of critics thoroughly unhappy, but it is the emerging extent of the depravity of the unholy trio which lies at its core. and gives it its savage, amoral tone. In the light of the apologies offered for the act of matricide and their subsequent behaviour, such an ending is the only one possible if any of the authorised future is to happen. A defence of acting outside the law on the grounds of divine guidance was clearly as open to question in Euripides' Athens as it is now.

If the comedy of *Orestes* is built on the situation, in *Electra* it is more derived from character. Aeschylus and Sophocles both offer instances of a play's tensions being modulated by the entrance of a figure of minor

---

[1] In *Andromache* Neoptolemus has already been married to Hermione for some time.

status, the Nurse in *Libation-Bearers*, for example, or the Guard in *Antigone*. The parody of Aeschylus' *Libation-Bearers* in Euripides' *Electra* has already been noted (Chapter 1, pp. 20–1), but it is prepared for by a climate of unexpected realism. The play opens with a prologue delivered by a Farmer. This Farmer reminds the audience of Agamemnon's death and the rescue of Orestes under threat from Aegisthus. As for Electra – and here is the novelty – she has been married off to him to prevent her having any noble children, and now lives with him on his farm by the border. Sufficiently independent to be his own master, he is a poor man, but as he says about his marriage:

> FARMER. I tell you this. The man you see here
> has never laid a hand on her.
> The goddess is my witness: she is still a virgin.
> I have too much respect for a lady of birth
> to take her by force. I'm not her equal [...]
> If anyone says I'm a fool
> to see a young girl in my house
> and keep my hands off her,
> then *he's* the fool –
> with a dirty mind at that. (ll. 40–53)

This aside to the audience, or afterthought, is very much a comic device and leads on to a broader picture of their life together than might be anticipated. When Electra arrives, she is on her way to fetch water. Her husband tells her there is no need, but that the spring is not so far away. When Orestes enters with Pylades he assumes that the woman he spots with short hair carrying a water-jar on her head must be some slave. It soon becomes clear to him who she is, but even at this stage her misery seems somewhat self-inflicted. She may look *like* a slave but she *has* a slave, to take the water indoors. A Chorus of friends turn up to invite her to a festival and offer her something to wear. She turns them down and in no time is telling her brother that she is friendless and forced to wear rags: and – somewhat unsuitably to a total stranger, as she believes – that she is still a virgin. Unsurprisingly, Orestes does not reveal himself at this juncture. A few minutes later her husband turns up from ploughing:

> FARMER. Now then, who are these strangers?
> Why have they come to our farm,
> so far from the city?
> What do they want? A woman
> shouldn't stand around talking to strangers. (ll. 341–5)

Informed that they have a message from Orestes he promptly invites them in. No sooner have they accepted his hospitality and gone indoors than Electra turns on the poor man:

> ELECTRA. Idiot! How could you invite
>   these noble guests into our poor home?
> FARMER. What's the matter?
>   If they are well born, as they seem,
>   won't they be satisfied
>   with what we can offer, however meagre?
> ELECTRA. So, you invited them: you do something about it.
>   Go to my dear father's old tutor . . .
>   Tell him we have guests. [...]
> FARMER. If that's what you want, I'll go and tell the old man.
>   You go straight into the house
>   and make what preparations you can.
>   A woman can always find something
>   to add to a meal, if she sets her mind to it.
>   There's enough in the house
>   to fill their bellies for one day at least. (ll. 404–25)

There seems an issue of class here, if only because Euripides shows this working man in a better light than any other character in the play, but it may be a different distinction, a familiar one in comedy from Shakespeare onwards, the difference between court and country morals. The Farmer departs, but is soon replaced by the Old Man who totters in complaining about his bad back and rickety legs. His attempt to persuade Electra that Orestes has returned is greeted with scorn (see Chapter 1, pp. 20–1), but the entrance of Orestes from the cottage dismisses any doubts about the comedy: 'Ah! Hello there. Electra, where did you find this decrepit old wreck?' (ll. 553–4). The trick here, though, is that the aged tutor is a man who is tarnished by the court and turns out to have few rustic virtues, but a viciousness to match that of Electra. Any potential for further comedy recedes swiftly with the death of Aegisthus and the entrance of Clytemnestra, summoned to assist her daughter after the claimed birth of a child: Electra's 'Go into my poor house, but take care not to get soot on your clothes' (ll. 1139–40) is one of those lines where the smile can freeze the blood.

This kind of gloating humour, which is not recognised by its target, gives a bloodcurdling dimension to *Bacchae* too. There, Dionysus, the unacknowledged son of Zeus and Semele, returns to the city of Thebes to avenge himself on his family for this slight. His various confrontations with Pentheus, the king of Thebes, are built around the audience's awareness that the 'stranger' is a god and that Pentheus has no chance of outwitting him. Eventually he falls under Dionysus' spell to the point where he is persuaded that, if he wants to witness what the Bacchants are up to on the mountain, he will have to disguise himself to look like one of them. Dionysus is exultant at having driven him out of his mind: 'I want Thebes helpless with laughter as he struts, ladylike, through the streets' (ll. 852–4).

Pentheus has departed into his palace and returns in drag, wondering about whether he looks more like his mother or his aunt, and concerned in case his seams are not straight. The exchange preceding his exit is as maliciously comic as any Euripides wrote:

PENTHEUS. Take me through the centre of Thebes
   as I am the only man with the nerve to go.
DIONYSUS. You bear responsibility for Thebes, all by yourself.
   You alone. Your trial awaits. Follow me.
   I will deliver you safely. Someone else will return you.
PENTHEUS.   My mother.
DIONYSUS. For everyone to see.
PENTHEUS.   That is why I am going.
DIONYSUS. You will be carried back . . .
PENTHEUS.   In triumph.
DIONYSUS. In your mother's arms.
PENTHEUS.   You will spoil me.
DIONYSUS. You could say that.
PENTHEUS.   Not that I don't deserve it. (ll. 961–70)

Cruel times create cruel humour, but not all Euripides' comic moments are so black. It sometimes seems as though his plays were written in the heat of the moment, which might account for their range. One with a happier outcome, though still hard-edged, is *Children of Heracles* in which the longest role belongs to Iolaus, an aged retainer and friend of the now dead Heracles, who has been trying to preserve Heracles' extended family (there seem to be at least ten of them) from falling victim to the vengeful Eurystheus. Eurystheus has harried them from country to country. They have ended up in Marathon and plead for protection from Demophon, a son of Theseus, now king of Athens. Iolaus is old but game. When a battle looms he is determined to go and fight. A servant makes strenuous attempts to dissuade him:

SERVANT. It'll take more than the sight of you to cause any damage without a
   bit of muscle.
IOLAUS. What are you talking about? I can still pierce a shield, can't I?
SERVANT. Yes, but you might fall over first. (ll. 684–6)

The Servant is prevailed upon to fetch arms and armour from inside the temple, but advises Iolaus not to put them on before reaching the field. Even getting off stage proves almost too much for him:

IOLAUS. Get a move on! It'll be dreadful if I arrive too late for the battle.
SERVANT. It's you that's slow, not me. Thinking's a bit different to doing.
IOLAUS. My feet are moving quickly enough. Look at them.
SERVANT. More ambition than speed. That's what I'm looking at.
IOLAUS. Just you wait till I get there. (ll. 732–6)

The distance someone has travelled in Greek plays, and their age, is often measured by the time it takes them to reach the centre of the action. The entry of the Old Man in *Electra* needs six lines at the least. It takes Iolaus and the Servant over twenty to reach the exit. A turning point in the play has been reached and doubts about the outcome are already neutralised. Better is to come. Not only is Eurystheus soundly thrashed but, as a Messenger tells Alcmena, Heracles' mother, Iolaus is the hero:

MESSENGER. Then old Iolaus, seeing Hyllus about to charge,
　　raised his right hand and begged for a place in the chariot.
He grabbed the reins and was off, after Eurystheus.
Now, what happened next was only reported to me.
I didn't actually see it. But, I'm told, as he was passing
the sacred hill of Athena, he caught sight of Eurystheus.
With a shouted appeal to Hebe and to Zeus,
he implored one day's return to his youthful self,
to teach his enemies the lesson they deserved.
A miracle! Two stars from heaven, above the horses,
covered the whole chariot in darkened shadow.
Your son Heracles and Hebe, the clever ones reckon.
And there in all that murk, a pair of young man's arms!
Iolaus, the magnificent, took Eurystheus prisoner
from his four-horse chariot, below the cliffs of Sciron.
He's bringing him back in fetters. (ll. 843–61)

Euripides is far too smart to bring Iolaus back onstage, though he is not yet finished with Eurystheus.

In most of these plays there are moments of frankness to startle an audience into laughter: the Nurse to Phaedra about her love for her stepson in *Hippolytus* 'Fine-sounding words are no use to you. It's the man you need: and the sooner the better' (ll. 490–1); the Theban Herald in *Suppliants* who says sourly 'When people vote for war, the death they anticipate is never their own' (ll. 481–2); Andromache protesting 'So much for fame. Fame! How many nonentities you elevate' (l. 319); Medea responding to Aegeus' confession of childlessness, with a loaded 'You are married?' (l. 672). Equally there are moments of gentle self-mockery: Admetus, viewing the restored Alcestis with 'Some phantom, maybe, stolen from the dead' and Heracles, who has wrestled Death himself for her, responding 'I'm not some necromancer, you know' (ll. 1127–8); the droll, long-drawn-out recognition scene in *Iphigeneia Among the Taurians* when Iphigeneia hands a letter to Pylades for him to take to Orestes who is standing beside him and Pylades replies 'Well, that shouldn't take long. Here, Orestes. This is a letter from your sister (ll. 789–91).

The reasons for such comic moments and, indeed, whole scenes may be in part parodic, in part self-referential. More, I think, they are an acknowledgment that tragedy has no rules, whatever Aristotle might later have been alleged to claim, beyond the requirement to function within a structure of dramatic rhythm and contrasting mood. It would anyway be wrong to assume that moments of light relief in Greek tragedy are a Euripidean invention. They can be found in any surviving play of Aeschylus or Sophocles, from a nurse's reflections on babies' excretory functions in *Libation-Bearers* to the discomforting of Odysseus threatened with being shot in *Philoctetes*, or the Messenger in *Antigone* having to tell his king how he and his mates missed seeing someone bury the body they were meant to be guarding.

The comic in Euripides has been shown to encompass situation, character, farce, romance, invective, parody and what for want of a better term can be called *shtick*. *Helen* has the lot. It is above all a sunny play, set seven years after the end of the Trojan War. Helen, in this version the innocent victim of Hera's grievance at only winning the silver medal in the beauty Olympics (though less a victim, one might think, than had Hera won it), has been languishing in Egypt while the phantom version was off with Paris in Troy. Ten years the Greeks fought before they took the city and got their synthetic Helen back: add another seven before Menelaus and the remnants of his crew find themselves washed up beside the Nile after their ship is wrecked.

Helen reveals the situation in a prologue. She is feeling thoroughly sorry for herself. Being gorgeous has proved more of a burden than a pleasure – the beauties of Greek myth customarily grumble about their looks, though not without reason. She is dubious about her mother's reputed seduction by Zeus in the form of a swan, and later will point out what a freak people think she is for having been born in an egg. She is fed up with everybody blaming her for the Trojan War. Worse, Proteus, the relatively benign former pharaoh has died and his successor fancies marrying her. She has had to take refuge at Proteus' tomb. The first character to arrive is Teucer, the pathetic surviving brother of Ajax who had committed suicide after the weapons of Achilles were awarded to Odysseus. As a result, their father Telamon has exiled him. Teucer does a 'take' as he thinks he recognises the detested Helen, but she is quick to avoid confessing who she is. He apologises for his error and, before leaving, gets her up to speed with what has been happening. Leda, Helen's mother, has committed suicide from shame and the news of her brothers, Castor and Pollux, is not promising. Menelaus is missing. By the time the Chorus of Greek slaves turn up Helen is on the verge of suicide herself, could she only find a dignified way of committing it.

No sooner have she and the Chorus returned to the palace than Menelaus puts in an appearance. His biggest immediate problem, apart from having lost his boat and most of his crew, is that all he has to cover his dignity is a scrap of sailcloth. The recollection of the rumpus caused when in Euripides' *Telephus* the eponymous hero appeared dressed in rags certainly makes Menelaus' embarrassment look like self-parody. No fewer than six subsequent references throughout the play to the skimpiness of his costume confirm it can hardly be more than minimal. His entrance triggers a string of comic routines. Initially he informs the audience about the difficult time he has had since leaving Troy, including the shipwreck that has landed him in Egypt. He has managed to save Helen, that Helen being the facsimile version, about whom he is far from complimentary. He needs help, so he knocks at the palace door. Out comes a doorkeeper, a female doorkeeper at that, who tells him in no uncertain terms to go away. When she threatens to hit him, he can only respond pathetically 'Where are all my military campaigns now?' (l. 453) before bursting into tears. Tears do not impress this *concièrge*, but she does tell him that Helen lives in the palace and has done since before the war started. Then she leaves, slamming the door behind her. Menelaus, who may be a hero of Troy, but is hardly the sharpest bayonet in the armoury, starts trying to work it all out, but a sound startles him into hiding in the shrine from which Helen had first emerged. It is the Chorus, back again and joined shortly by Helen. She is heading towards the sanctuary of Proteus' tomb when she runs into her husband:

HELEN. What a terrible-looking fellow!
MENELAUS. Stop! You, racing to the steps of the tomb, and
  the altar where offerings are burnt, stop!
  What are you running from?
  Good god! Your appearance has me at a loss for words!
  I'm truly amazed. (ll. 544–9)

What amazes Menelaus is how Helen has got from the cave, where he left her, up to the palace. But there is also the curious remark of the door-keeper about Helen. She takes a better look at the ragged figure before her. Their recognition is less of a take than a slow burn spread over the next thirty lines which read like an identity probe for internet banking. They end with Menelaus' 'My problem is I have another wife' to which Helen counters 'That was a fake one. I never went to Troy' (ll. 580–1). They have some catching up to do but are interrupted by the arrival of a Messenger from the beach and a delightful variation on the double take:

> MESSENGER. Ah! There you are, Menelaus!
>   I've been looking everywhere for you!
>   Wandering all over this godforsaken land.
>   The friends you left behind sent me to find you.
> MENELAUS. What is it? The barbarians aren't stealing our stuff, are they?
> MESSENGER. Amazing! Something very peculiar has happened.
>   You had to see it to believe it.
> MENELAUS. Out with it. If it's that urgent, it must be important. Strange, too.
> MESSENGER. All your countless exploits go for nothing now.
> MENELAUS. What's new about that? Tell me something I don't know.
> MESSENGER. It's your wife, sir. She's disappeared into thin air.
>   Her home's now in heaven. She vanished
>   from the cave where we were guarding her,
>   and announced to us: 'You poor Trojans [...]
>   and all the Greeks who died on my account
>   by the banks of the Scamander because you thought
>   that Paris had stole Helen, I'm here to tell you
>   he never had her. I've done what I had to do,
>   and now return to the sky that gave birth to me.
>   Poor Helen is blamed for what she never did.'
>   Oh, there you are, daughter of Leda. Good to see you.
>   I was just saying you upped and left the cave
>   to return to heaven! I didn't know you had wings.
>   Don't tease us like that. You caused enough trouble
>   in Troy for your husband and his allies. (ll. 597–621)

The implications of all this, that a war of ten years was fought for a phantom, are not lost on the bemused Messenger, but the significant seriousness never gets overtaken by, or submerged beneath, the candy-floss. It remains as the core throughout the rest of the play, which is largely taken up with plans to escape. Helen is the one who provides the tactics; the pharaoh, Theoclymenus, and his clairvoyant sister Theonoe much of the comedy. Theonoe gives her support to a plan pretending that Menelaus has died at sea. Helen will marry Theoclymenus as soon as she has been able to fulfil the necessary rites – offshore, with a boat and a crew who are waiting on the beach. Helen is at last able to take Menelaus off for a much-needed bath and a change of clothes.

All works well, at least for Helen and Menelaus. When far enough from land they attack the local rowers and, as a survivor reports, throw them overboard before heading for home. The pharaoh is aggrieved, especially with his sister: 'Outwitted! And by a woman! What a fool I've been. Bang goes my wedding!' (ll. 1621–2). The arrival *ex machina* of Helen's brother Castor, not dead, but now one of 'the Heavenly Twins', soon convinces him to forgive his sister and the Chorus conclude with the stock ending about the unexpected.

It is probably in this ability to juxtapose the comic and the serious that Euripides most advances his drama from that of Aeschylus or Sophocles. Such a mix will not tickle every palate: nor did it during his own lifetime. A sense of the ridiculous in the midst of horror, and savagery in the most absurd of situations, appear to have been a function of the satyr play. There, though, the scope was limited by the form. Euripides took it out into his mainstream tragedies. Such an approach was not a mark of flippancy and only in part, of cynicism. There is a Greek adjective, *spoudaios*, which means 'worth taking seriously'. It could be applied equally to tragedy and to comedy: and to any play of Euripides.

II. POWERFUL FORCES: THE GRAND PASSIONS

5 WAR AND THE MILITARY

Rhesus, Trojan Women, Suppliants, Iphigeneia at Aulis

The story that Euripides was born on the day of the battle of Salamis in 480 BC and that Sophocles sang in a victory chorus is probably no more than a later historian's bogus attempt to link the three great tragedians. Aeschylus fought in that battle – there is no doubt about that – as he had at the battle of Marathon when the Athenians liberated themselves, if only temporarily, from the menace of the Persian invaders. Salamis, ten years later, was more comprehensive. The sea-battle was witnessed by much of the population of Athens who had been evacuated from their city. Aeschylus immortalised it in his play *Persians* which includes a graphic description from a Persian messenger back in Susa of how the Greeks outwitted and outmanoeuvred the Persian fleet.

Whether or not the three dramatists were linked by Salamis, the story serves as a timely reminder that to the Greeks of the fifth century BC, and hence for all surviving Greek Tragedy and Old Comedy, peace was an interlude between wars rather than the natural condition of life. Perhaps for many countries in Europe, Asia, Africa and South America it has always been so. A large proportion of the countries of the world require a period of military service for all young men and, in some, for young women too. In classical Athens all male citizens were liable for military service up to the age of sixty. Aeschylus saw action in two memorable battles and probably a lot of minor ones. Later in the century Sophocles was twice elected as an army general. Euripides, who wrote some of the most explicitly anti-war plays in the world repertoire, must have done his share of fighting, and, it would seem, understood war as an inevitable part of the human condition.

Of the nineteen surviving plays of Euripides the great majority have some sort of framework of war. Usually it is the Trojan War or the civil war in Thebes, even if the background is as tenuous as the belated return home of some of the Greeks after the sack of Troy or the exile of Amphitryon from Thebes. *Iphigeneia at Aulis* takes place before the war against Troy begins; *Hecuba* and *Trojan Women* soon after the Greek victory; *Phoenician Women* at the climax of the Theban civil war. *Children of Heracles* largely revolves around an engagement between Athens and Argos; *Suppliants* around a request to bury the fallen dead. Perhaps surprisingly, the only

81

extant tragedy set within the action covered by Homer's *Iliad* is *Rhesus*. Whether early or late Euripides, or before or after Euripides' working life, the dialogue and dynamics of *Rhesus* offer a unique picture of the military under arms that has no dramatic parallel in classical times. None of the tragedies, from Aeschylus' *Persians* onwards, makes any secret of the hardships suffered in war. The Herald's speech in Aeschylus' *Agamemnon* has the authentic sound of a dispatch from the trenches and Euripides' *Children of Heracles* contains an especially graphic description of battle in action. Only *Rhesus* shows troops in the centre of a combat situation, from both sides, involving different ranks and commitment, the competent and the incompetent, the brave and the foolhardy.

Military display had a civic function within the Great Dionysia in Athens. The personal and the national issues, the moral and philosophical standpoints on war in general, and its conduct, do receive attention in *Rhesus* but are better addressed in other war plays, as we shall see later. *Rhesus* does offer some broad comments on warfare – questions to do with alliances, leadership, respect for the gods and so on – but is basically an adventure story, set among soldiers, soldiers, at that, whose motivation and dedication are often less than they might be. There is no mention of Hecuba or Andromache and only an oblique reference to Helen, and then not by name. There are two female characters but both are goddesses.

The play takes place at night, not in Troy, but in a Trojan forward camp outside the walls. The distractions of Trojan society are reduced to a minimum: effectively neither side is 'playing at home'. It is the shortest surviving tragedy, under a thousand lines, though a prologue or opening scene may be missing. The first quarter involves a discussion of tactics, mainly between Hector and Aeneas, after news has arrived that there is major action in the Greek camp and that it looks as though the Greeks are planning a withdrawal under the cover of darkness. A decision is taken to send a spy to find out what is happening and Dolon volunteers. He will not get far.

Information is then brought of the belated arrival of the eponymous hero Rhesus, a Thracian ally, whose reception from Hector is grudging. Rhesus and his troops are taken off to a campsite. The Chorus of Trojan soldiers exit, to be replaced by two Greeks, Odysseus and Diomedes, who have arrived on an assassination mission. Athena makes an appearance to divert their attention away from Hector or Paris as a target in the direction of the new arrival, Rhesus. A bizarre scene follows in which Athena fools the suspicious Paris by pretending to be Aphrodite. The Greeks arrive back having killed Rhesus, hotly pursued by the Chorus whom they elude, partly thanks to confusion in the darkness. The penultimate scene has Rhesus' wounded charioteer accusing Hector of treachery before the arrival of Rhesus' mother, the Muse Terpsichore, to lament the death of her son.

The contrast here between the various characters and character groupings is very marked and dramatically subtle. All but the goddesses, and a shepherd/messenger, are soldiers, but they are soldiers who are differentiated by rank. Hector may be commander-in-chief of the Trojans. He is certainly not deferred to by Aeneas who treats his impetuosity with concern but also with disdain. Hector's response to the news of a possible retreat by the Greeks is to suggest they rush down and attack them. Aeneas suspects a trick and advocates sending a scout while leaving the army to their rest. Hector isn't shown in much better a light when he responds to the news of Rhesus' arrival.

HECTOR.   Where was he
   when the hunt was up and we needed his spear? [...]
   I never could abide a latecomer. (ll. 324–33).

His greeting to Rhesus 'Son of a musical Muse' (l. 393) seems to have a built-in sneer, especially when he continues 'I speak straight, I'm no diplomat. Late, you're late. You should have been here . . .' (ll. 393–6). Rhesus turns out to be capable of giving as good as he gets:

RHESUS. Late I may be. Apparently, not too late.
   Ten years you've been at war, achieving nothing. [...]
   A single sunlit morning's all I'll need
   to storm their towers, catch the fleet at anchor,
   and kill off the Greeks. Troy saved in a day.
   Then I can go home after sorting out your little problem. (ll. 443–50)

Rhesus never gets as far as the battlefield. Hector's reaction to the news of his murder by Diomedes (Odysseus manages to opt for the less dangerous horse-stealing) is again hardly that of an inspirational leader in the field:

HECTOR.   They've got away scot-free
   to jeer at Trojan cowardice,
   and at me, your general. I'm a laughing-stock. (ll. 814–15)

If those in command do not always inspire confidence, the other ranks are more realistically represented than in any other play before the two parts of Shakespeare's *Henry IV*. The Chorus of *Rhesus* are Trojan sentries on night duty. Though they function as a choral unit, and speak mostly in lyric metre rather than iambics, they have a physical involvement with the actors and appear to be sentries first and Chorus second. Not only do they account for their presence (awakening Hector to alert him to the activity down on the shore), but also find plausible reasons for leaving half way through the play. They do not appear any more competent than the rest of the Trojans, nor especially dedicated to the cause.

> CHORUS. Whose watch is next?
> Who's my relief?
> The evening stars are down,
> The seven Plciades rising.
> The Eagle at its height.
> Come on, what's keeping you?
> Wake up. Sentry time.
> Can't you see the moonlight waning?
> It's dawn, almost dawn.
> Look east, the dawn-star.
>
> Whose watch was first, did you say?
> Coroibus, Mugdon's son.
> Then who?
> The Paionians woke the Cilicians,
> The Mysians woke us.
> Then fifth watch is the Lycians.
> That's what they drew.
> They need waking, don't they?
>
> Listen.
> Do you hear that?
> Over Simois, a nightingale,
> Singing her murderous lament,
> The child-killer.
> Such a lovely song.
> There go the flocks,
> Off to graze on Mount Ida.
> Listen, shepherd pipes.
> I can't keep my eyes open.
> Nearly dawn. Sleep. Wonderful.
>
> Where's that spy got to,
> The one Hector sent to the ships?
> Don't like to think. He's been a while.
> Ambushed, do you reckon, killed?
> We'll find out soon enough.
> I vote we go and wake the Lycians.
> They're fifth watch.
> We've done our stint.
>
> *Exit* CHORUS. (ll. 527–64)

Here is a group of believable, disgruntled soldiers who have been allotted the fourth watch of the night, and who have not been relieved on time by the fifth watch. They are fed up and feeling mutinous. Suddenly one of their number calls out 'Listen'. Everything stops for the song of a nightingale, as years later will the troops defending Gallipoli, and the gentle sound of a shepherd's pipe when the flocks head for their daytime grazing pasture. Peace in the midst of war: drowsiness after a disturbed night. Then they get fed up with waiting and desert their posts to look for their replacements. Practically, of course, the stage needs to be cleared for the entrance of Odysseus and Diomedes, but what a wonderfully competent way for the playwright to do it, whoever he may have been.

All these soldiers, from Hector and Aeneas through the two Greek heroes, to Rhesus and his Charioteer, constantly use the argot of war and warriors. It ties into an ethos of military procedure and a strictly military use of language. Part of the plot depends on the Greek password, 'Phoebus'. The Trojans, meanwhile, as is appropriate for forward troops, are sleeping under arms, 'beneath their shields'. The reasons people give for military action, or lack of it, involve the practicalities: the difficulties of driving chariots over the no-man's-land between armies and of getting over trenches; ramparts and stockades; the practice of ambush. Alongside the regular terminology of warfare, familiar from other literary contexts – spears and spear-heads, swords, javelins, shields, armour and so on – there are words, often familiar in other contexts, but with a specialist meaning – *skolopai*, 'pointed stakes placed in a ditch', *gephurai* for the 'embankments between armies', *hippêlatai*, 'charioteers', and *teichê* for 'earthworks round the ships', all found in Homer's *Iliad*. This is a world of night-raids, sentries, various kinds of weaponry, the sound of a war-trumpet and a range of technical terms that only cavalry could be expected to know. To place such emphasis on a play whose provenance is confused may seem strange, but Euripides or not, and 'proper tragedy' or not, this is a play that has been oddly neglected.[1] It is an adventure story where neither of the only two to die, Dolon and Rhesus, reveals himself in sufficiently heroic a light to elicit much concern. The revelation at the end of the grief-stricken Terpsichore, Muse of the dance and Rhesus' mother, together with her son's body, is a timely reminder that every casualty of war is a cause of mourning for someone.

Trojan Women needs no such reminder. It is an angry play. Whether or not it was inspired by a particular atrocity makes little difference to its

---

[1] I will return to the play when considering theatrical illusion in Chapter 9.

impact in whatever mould it is cast.[1] Only one of the characters is a fighting man, and that is Menelaus whose exploits off the battlefield were rather more distinguished than on it. Nor is the war any more in progress: it is the aftermath which Euripides chooses to stage. The most remarkable feature of *Trojan Women* is that it breaks one of the major rules of play-construction. It opens on a scene of devastation and despair: and gets worse. There is precious little relief or prospect of hope for any of the defeated Trojans. The prospects for the victorious Greeks are hardly better.

Poseidon, god of the sea and of horses, appears to open the play. He has taken the side of the Trojans during the war: indeed he and Apollo helped to build the city which the Greeks have just burnt to the ground. Now he gives an account of its downfall. He is visited by Athena, one of those who sided with the Greeks. In no other Euripides play is there a similar encounter between gods. The opening scene of *Alcestis* has Apollo clashing with the shadowy figure of Death and in *Heracles* Lussa (Madness) tries to argue with Iris. In *Trojan Women* the gods are both members of the Olympian family. Athena's appeal for a truce is a surprise:

POSEIDON. Have you brought some communiqué
   from Zeus, or from another of the gods?
ATHENA. No. I am here on behalf of Troy. I appreciate your influence
   and think we may have interests in common.
POSEIDON. Are you telling me your hostility has been set aside
   and you feel pity now that the city's in ashes?
ATHENA. As I said, a common interest. Would you be prepared
   to discuss our joining forces? I have a plan.
POSEIDON. Very well. But whose side are you really on?
   Greeks or Trojans? Which?
ATHENA. I wish to raise the spirits of my former enemies
   and ensure for the Greeks a disagreeable return home.
POSEIDON. Why this capricious change of heart?
   There's no middle road for you. It's love or hate.
ATHENA. My temples have been desecrated. Had you not heard? (ll. 55–69)

Couched in a kind of diplomatic language, this opening scene appears to

---

[1] The devastation of Melos at the time Euripides would probably have been writing the play (416 BC) is attested to by the historian Thucydides, who seems to have been as shocked as was Euripides by the slaughter of the entire male population and the selling into slavery of all the women and children. Aristophanes makes a direct reference to it too in his hard-edged comedy *Birds* (414 BC). The 'crime' of the Melians was that they claimed the right to remain neutral in the war between Athens and Sparta, a war which they thought was nothing to do with them.

have less to do with any of Euripides' theological opinions than to serve as a confirmation that wars, any wars, of whatever magnitude, have at their root vested interests that go far beyond the apparent political manoeuvrings. Whether or not Euripides would have agreed with such a reading, it is in keeping with what follows. The far from holy alliance of the two gods will ensure that few of the Greeks will be allowed to reach home at all. As most of even a modern audience will know, some of the Greek 'heroes' face up to ten years of wandering: few will have a happy homecoming. Once they have made their pact, Poseidon and Athena depart. Neither is seen again, Poseidon not even mentioned, Athena barely. But the rest of the play is not about gods: it is not about voyages home. It is about the immediate fate of those whose city has been sacked, the women of Troy.

I suggested earlier that Poseidon 'appears' to open the play. After the gods depart, Hecuba's first lines show that she has been present throughout, sufficiently clearly for most translators to include a stage direction to this effect. She has not heard the gods. Poseidon has made only the briefest of references to her. The playwright's opening image is of the two who hold power debating coolly above, the victim of events lying prostrate below.[1] Hecuba and the Chorus, who soon join her from a tent behind, are waiting to find out to whom they have been allotted as slaves. The Greeks are in the process of breaking camp and these women are the detritus of war. Hecuba's daughter, Cassandra, the prophetess whom no one can understand, is still inside. Talthybius, the Greek herald, arrives with his list. Agamemnon has picked Cassandra, not as a servant for Clytemnestra, but 'to share his bed in secret' (l. 252). Hecuba protests that Cassandra is dedicated to Apollo: to no avail. She asks about another daughter, Polyxena. Talthybius equivocates: 'She has been assigned to serve at the tomb of Achilles' (l. 264). There is one last daughter, or rather, daughter-in-law, Andromache, the wife of her dead son Hector. She goes to Neoptolemus. As for Hecuba herself, queen of Troy, wife of Priam, mother in addition of Hector and Paris, she will be a slave to the hated Odysseus.

The next stage of this selection process follows. Cassandra arrives from

---

[1] There is no direct evidence to suggest how a play began in the Greek theatre. The stage was open and a front curtain was not used until Roman times. However early in the day proceeding began, in the absence of artificial light apart from torches, characters had to make an entrance somehow. The sense that Euripides is consciously making use of contrast in space between 'heaven' and 'earth' is enhanced by his greater use of effects created by the two most familiar pieces of stage machinery, the *mêchanê* (stage crane) and the *ekkuklêma* (wheeled platform). Similar uses of such a physical juxtaposition can be found, notably in *Medea, Heracles, Electra, Orestes* and *Bacchae,* as well as in Aristophanes.

the tent brandishing flaming torches in a sickening parody of a wedding procession. In two extended outbursts, she forecasts, before being dragged away, that what has happened to the Trojans is nothing compared to what the Greeks will face. Andromache is then wheeled on, carrying her young son, Astyanax, on top of a pile of looted Trojan effects, princess and child reduced to chattels, people reduced to objects. There is worse. Andromache reveals what Talthybius meant when he said that Polyxena had been 'assigned to serve at the tomb of Achilles'. She has been sacrificed to appease the dead hero. As atrocity piles on atrocity, the returning Talthybius hesitantly informs Andromache of a decision from the Greek higher command that Astyanax is to be thrown from the walls, in case he should grow up seeking revenge for his father, Hector. The herald recommends she does not make too much fuss, so that she will at least get the child back for burial. As Astyanax is carried off in one direction, Andromache is removed to the ships in the other. The scene with Helen and Menelaus comes at this point (see Chapter 1, pp. 24–5). They arrive separately, but leave together. Talthybius' final entry is accompanied by attendants carrying Hector's battle-shield, on which the tiny corpse of his son has been laid. Here is the final graphic image of the desolation of war, a dead child presented to its grandmother on its dead father's shield.

Andromache has already been shipped out. Talthybius seems deeply shocked. There is no dissembling here. The herald has been a reluctant participant throughout, as he carries out the orders of others. This may be the thinnest of defences in a court of law or at a military tribunal, but does at least show that one of the Greeks can feel pity for what he is powerless to prevent. Andromache has asked that the women dress the child's body as best they may. Talthybius leaves them to private grief as they search among their last remaining belongings for any suitable adornment. The city, or what remains of it, is set alight. Hecuba is barely prevented from throwing herself into the flames. The play ends in a lament as she and the Chorus are driven to the ships to face their new life.

Amid such a relentless accumulation of suffering, the opening can easily be forgotten.[1] It must have been a shocking play in its time, with many of those who served at Melos in the audience perhaps. Euripides knew well enough the effect of war on both victor and victim. That *Trojan Women* continues to pack such a punch is, in part, the manner in which, in Euripides' own time, the Trojan War was more metaphor than history: and so it remains. Beyond this is the sequence of those moments

---

[1] The scene is sometimes cut altogether in performance.

when words fail and Euripides, the war artist, takes over, sending back his series of pictures from the front line: Cassandra and her torches, Andromache and Astyanax on the cart, the child's corpse on his father's shield, the tiny body dressed in whatever rags these women have been trying to preserve for the life they face. These are immediate; these are the emotive moments so powerful they carry the play remorselessly forward through despair. But when the tears are spent and the immediacy of this shocking tragedy has become dulled by life outside a theatre, what should remain, to haunt our dreams and all our futures, is two secure and comfortable untouchables debating policy above, an old and broken woman prostrate on the floor below.

Hecuba seems so similar in outline that it has been sometimes described as a companion piece to *Trojan Women* or even as a dummy-run for it. Though the immediate background is the same, the aftermath of the war with Hecuba and the women of Troy, their sons and husbands dead, waiting to be ferried out to new lives, there are significant differences which makes it a more suitable subject for discussion under a different heading (see Chapter 6, pp. 101–4). Instead, a different group of mothers take the stage, unhappy survivors of another war, the Theban civil war initiated by Eteocles and Polyneices, the sons of Oedipus and Jocasta. *Phoenician Women* gives Euripides' individual slant on the rival brothers, but in *Suppliants* the war is well and truly over. Whereas, in Sophocles' *Antigone* the collision between state decree and private principle leads to the fatal clash of wills between the daughter of Oedipus and her uncle Creon, the issue here is beyond a personal wrangle.

Suppliants is set at Eleusis, some twenty miles outside Athens, in front of the temple of Demeter and Persephone.[1] The connection with Thebes is not immediately obvious, especially as the first character to speak is the unfamiliar Aethra, mother of Theseus. Already present, however, are the Chorus and, it would seem, their grandsons, as well as Adrastus, king of Argos. All of them have taken refuge before the temple as suppliants. It is Aethra who identifies them and the reason for their presence. These are the mothers of the seven heroes who died unsuccessfully trying to take Thebes, a military engagement which ended with the deaths of the two brothers, Eteocles and Polyneices. Their grievance is specific. They want back the bodies of their dead children. They want to bury them. There is

---

[1] As with the settings of many surviving Greek plays, the declared location can still be visited. The archaeological site at Eleusis is one of these, as are others at Mycenae, Colonus or Delphi. Like all surviving Greek plays and, indeed, a majority of the world's repertoire, the action takes place on a stage whose similarity to any given locale is driven by theatrical, not geographical, priority.

an unresolved problem about these mothers to which I will return below.

The Thebans have flouted the accepted conventions of war and refused to return the remains of those who died in battle. The Argives are now appealing for Athenian help, not because Athens has much direct involvement, but because Athens is seen as the only real dispenser of earthly justice. In Euripides too jingoism must have its place and flag-waving still resonates wherever outside interference in the actions of other nations becomes the subject of debate. Already the suppliants have the support of Aethra and when Theseus arrives he closely questions Adrastus about what on earth he thought he was up to in getting involved in the first place. Adrastus admits failure of judgement which led to the loss of his finest men. 'It's what happens: war is a nasty business' (l. 119), retorts Theseus. Adrastus responds that the causes of the war are no longer the issue: this is about morality in its conduct. A reluctant Theseus sees no reason why he should pick up the pieces after someone else's blatant mistake but his mother argues for a duty of intervention, to respect the gods and to uphold moral law on which civilisation itself is based. 'Your country thrives through action' (l. 323) proves to be her clinching argument. The king of Athens finally agrees:

> THESEUS. Here's what I'll do. I'll go and get the bodies released.
> I'll convince the Thebans by argument: and if that fails,
> by force. The gods will support us in this.
> I need the whole city to agree, of course,
> and so they will if this is what I want. Once I've explained,
> they'll understand it's in their own interest.
> This is a democracy, after all. Everyone has a vote. (ll. 346–53)

This is a tricky speech because it is ambiguous: and it is ambiguous both in the decision that Theseus has made and in his justification for making it. It is also a specific example of Arrowsmith's 'anachronization', a democratic system being at odds with Theseus' status as a king. To those believing in his right to interfere in someone else's fight his actions are modest and appropriate: and will continue to be so. To those who deem it unacceptable that he should threaten force against another city because he dislikes their king's behaviour, his action is that of an aggressive dictator whose claim to consultation of the people is the rankest cynicism. The 'just war' is hardly a novel idea, with or without the inverted commas. Not only is the speech tricky: it is dynamite.

Theseus just has time to give instructions when they are interrupted by a Theban Herald. The debate switches from one about intrusion to a question of government and the play changes direction. Theseus backs democracy, the Theban Herald monarchy, the Theban hardly helping his cause by forbidding Theseus to allow Adrastus to stay in Athens. Nobody tells a king of Athens to whom he can grant asylum. The argument is now between two superpowers over which can lean more heavily on the other and, when Adrastus is so incensed as to swear at the Theban, it is Theseus who tells him to hold his tongue and not to put his oar in ahead of the king. This may be in part a declaration of support: it is also a strong put-down to the king of Argos who is now little more than a bone for the top dogs to fight over.

When Theseus lays out what is to happen – hand over the bodies or we come and get them – they return to the original argument in the following exchange:

> THEBAN HERALD. Were you born to take on all comers?
> THESEUS. Only the disrespectful: not decent people.
> THEBAN HERALD. That's your trouble, you Athenians: everyone else's business.
> THESEUS. Great effort brings great reward. (ll. 574–7)

There is a revealing word in Greek, *polupragmosunê*, best translated as 'officiousness' or 'busyness', in the sense that it is used in the medieval Corpus Christi cycles to note the quality of excessive energy which leads to minding everyone else's business. The issue of taking up the causes of others was a subject of considerable debate in Athens, seen by many as a mark of assuming your own society so superior that you have a duty to try to make everyone else conform to your philosophy and template of government. Why does that sound so familiar?

No sooner has the Theban Herald retreated than Theseus gives the order for invasion: whether this is more from a sense of pique than of justice is a moot point. In no time a Messenger has returned with news of a glorious victory, but there is no shirking the action of battle:

> MESSENGER. I was close by the chariots and the cavalry,
> and saw the horror of it all. What to describe first?
> Dust-clouds rising heaven-high: so much dust.
> Groups of horsemen swaying to and fro, falling,
> caught up in harnesses or stirrups and dragged across the rocks.
> Mangled. Blood, rivers of blood. Some men cut
> to pieces, others hurled from their cars, skulls smashed,
> or crushed beneath the shattered chariots. (ll. 686–93)

Hand-to-hand fighting is less a feature of modern soldiering, but the destruction as brutal as the aftermath of a suicide bombing.

The Athenian mission is successful. The bodies are brought back.

Theseus returns with tales of heroism and has exercised restraint in declining to attack Thebes itself. Adrastus praises the fallen. But just as everyone is celebrating a famous triumph, a new character appears on the roof. It is Evadne, wife of one of the seven, Capaneus, and sister of another, Eteoclus. As her father, Iphis, and the rest look on in dismay she hurls herself into her husband's funeral pyre. The shock of her suicide, never mind the sheer staging in a theatre where such action must have been rare, casts a different light on the official jubilation. Euripides has another surprise up his sleeve, if not so dramatic. The sons of the seven sing a dirge over their fathers' remains, but vow revenge. Athena, patron goddess of Athens, arrives *ex machina* and tells Theseus in no uncertain terms to require an oath from Adrastus, on behalf of all the Argives, never to attack Athens. Then she addresses the sons and sanctions their future revenge on Thebes, as soon as they are grown up. Even peace terms endorse the possibility of their fracture.

This is a complex and uncomfortable play about the processes of war, which does not shirk its conduct and its repercussions for those who are affected, women and children in particular. They, in turn, bring us back to the question of the 'seven' mothers, who serve as Chorus and give the play its title. Seven is not the expected number for a Chorus in Greek tragedy. At this time, it is generally agreed, there should have been fifteen, though in the following century there is a record of a chorus of seven for comedy at Delphi. Some nineteenth-century critics suggested adding in the seven sons, or seven attendants, their arithmetic being more approximate than their sense of symmetry. A more simple solution is to suggest that 'seven' is a figurative number, standing for grieving mothers as a collective, the play demanding more than a literal interpretation.[1] Assuming we can put any trust in the play's authenticity, Euripides is clearly aiming at free allegory throughout. This does not mean that the comments, both on authority and on warfare, are not serious or that there is not a reliable thematic truth beyond literal detail. It is simply a fresh sense of what a chorus may stand for beyond immediate identity.

Children of Heracles has another king of Athens, Theseus' son Demophon, again getting involved in what is really someone else's concern. This time it is against Argos in favour of some Thebans, at least

---

[1] During Argentina's 'Dirty War' in the nineteen seventies, some thirty thousand activists disappeared. The mothers of the Plaza de Mayo in Argentina, in their white scarves, dwindled eventually to a token five, but they served as representatives for all whose children had vanished without trace. An opera featuring the story of four such mothers by Luis Bacalov, under the title of *The Mother Was There*, was performed in La Plata in 2007. Amnesty International can point to any number of other parallels.

by ancestry, though the children of the dead Heracles are Argives and subject to Eurystheus' jurisdiction in life, as was their father. Eurystheus has had the children condemned to death *en bloc* and, accompanied by the elderly Iolaus, they have been trying to escape ever since. Athens is again advertised as a safe haven for refugees. Copreus, the Argive herald, argues that the Argives have every right to carry out their country's laws outside their own boundaries. Athens is having nothing to do with that sort of argument, but the alternative may be war. Athens, again a democracy under the rule of a king, is threatened with civil war, so divided is opinion on the street, especially when the local prophets demand a human sacrifice. Macaria, one of Heracles' daughters, volunteers to die for the cause. Battle commences, with the miraculous outcome already described for the rejuvenated Iolaus (see Chapter 4, pp. 73–4).

The interesting moral issue crops up when Eurystheus is brought in in chains in the presence of a Chorus who are, significantly, old men of Marathon, the scene of one of the Athenians' greatest military triumphs and constantly recalled with awe. The code of war requires, as far as these old men are concerned, that you cannot kill a prisoner-of-war. For Alcmena 'a dead enemy's a good friend'; and it is she who finds a solution that suits her vindictiveness.

For another view of the army, this time as an entity, in contrast to the group of individuals in *Rhesus*, it is necessary to return to *Iphigeneia at Aulis*. Agamemnon tells Clytemnestra to bring their daughter to the camp at Aulis to marry Achilles, intimating that Achilles has refused to go to Troy unless Agamemnon gives him one of his daughters as a bride. Clytemnestra is delighted. Achilles is a catch. The plot proceeds through the discovery of the subterfuge and Achilles' attempt to set things right, especially as, by this time, none of the central characters appears in favour of the sacrifice Agamemnon has planned, neither he, nor Menelaus, nor Achilles, never mind the shocked mother and the putative victim. But beneath all the determination to rectify a situation that no individual any longer wants, there is the army, a constant undercurrent: Greece 'is mad', as Agamemnon says (l. 411), and the army wants blood.

Though subtly understated, their feelings, and the importance of their feelings, are made clear from soon after the beginning of the play. Agamemnon in the delayed prologue tells the story of Helen's being allowed to make her own choice of a husband, something unusual, perhaps unique, in the societies where these plays are set. The remainder of her many suitors swore an oath that they would unite in supporting her husband should there be any future occasion when the marriage was threatened. Helen chose Menelaus – 'I wish she hadn't,' says Agamemnon – but later fell in love with Paris and ran away with him. Menelaus called in his favour, 'upon which the Greeks raced to arms, arriving in this narrow strip of land at Aulis with a huge flotilla, shields, horses and chariots' (ll. 80–4). Agamemnon was picked as commander-in-chief and, while they were becalmed, Calchas told Agamemnon and his brother that there had to be a sacrifice. Menelaus refused to countenance withdrawal and so the fatal letter was sent. The enthusiasm of the army for war at this point is noted, but of no great consequence.

When Menelaus intercepts Agamemnon's second letter to Clytemnestra, retracting his earlier one, Menelaus reminds his brother of how he canvassed for the job of general:

> MENELAUS. You were so humble, do you remember? Shaking hands
>   with all and sundry: 'My door's always open: to anyone,
>   at any time'. Striking up conversations with people,
>   even when they weren't interested. Sucking up to everyone.
>   Till you got the job. Then it was a different story. (ll. 339–44)

Going to Troy, Menelaus, suggests, was simply for Agamemnon an ego-trip. Agamemnon replies, giving as good as he gets, but a messenger interrupts. Clytemnestra and Iphigeneia have arrived and there is a rumour running through the army. They know Iphigeneia is in camp and they want to know why. For a wedding? Or what? Has Agamemnon simply been missing his daughter? Unexpectedly it is Menelaus who now has a change of heart and declares they must disband the troops. But Agamemnon recognises that things have already gone too far and that there is no way he can get out of sacrificing his daughter:

> MENELAUS. But why? Who's going to make you kill her?
> AGAMEMNON. The army, the whole Greek army.
> MENELAUS. Not if you send her back home again.
> AGAMEMNON. That I could conceal, but not the rest of it.
> MENELAUS. Rest of what? You're not scared by the rabble, are you?
> AGAMEMNON. Calchas will tell the army. Reveal the oracle.
> MENELAUS. Not if we kill him. Simple. (ll. 513–19)

But Odysseus knows, and Odysseus will reveal the truth if Agamemnon goes back on his word. The vengeful troops will pursue them back to Argos. All Agamemnon can hope for is to keep Clytemnestra in the dark as long as possible.

Whether or not Agamemnon's prediction is an accurate one, his fear of the army is palpable. As he grows more afraid of them, so they seem to grow more frightening, all the more so for having no onstage representative, either through character or Chorus. Momentum begins to build. After the uncomfortable meeting of Agamemnon with his wife and daughter Achilles arrives as though he were the army's spokesman and claiming that he has the Myrmidons, his personal company of troops, under control:

> ACHILLES. But they keep pressing me: 'Achilles, what are we
>   waiting for? How long do we have to hang about here?
>   before heading for Troy? If you are going to do something,
>   then do it, or take your men home. We've had enough
>   hanging about, waiting for Agamemnon and his brother'. (ll. 814–18)

Once Achilles and Clytemnestra have found out from the Old Man what is going on, Achilles, though grossly insulted himself, is aware of how Clytemnestra has been treated. He does not wish to meet Iphigeneia: 'The soldiers will talk. You know what they're like when they're away from home, foul-mouthed and filthy-minded' (ll. 1000–1), but is determined to save her. Clytemnestra warns that Agamemnon is too frightened of the army. Achilles is confident they will listen to him and leaves to sort it all out. Meanwhile Clytemnestra confronts Agamemnon in a speech (see Chapter 10, pp. 180–2). Agamemnon's response is abject and addressed not to his wife, but to his daughter:

> AGAMEMNON. Look at the size of the fleet we have here,
>   how many Greek chieftains under arms.
>   They cannot go to Troy with its fine high towers
>   unless I do as the prophet says I must,
>   and sacrifice you. There is a lust rampaging
>   through these troops, a compulsion to set sail for Troy
>   and teach the barbarians they cannot go round
>   raping Greek wives and get away with it.
>   And they'll slaughter the lot of us, the girls too,
>   back in Argos, if I try to ignore this oracle. (ll.1259–68)

The return of Achilles confirms that Agamemnon's fears amount to more than spinelessness:

> ACHILLES. Poor woman . . . Daughter of Leda . . .
> CLYTEMNESTRA.   Yes, that is me.
> ACHILLES. Terrible things. They're screaming . . .
> CLYTEMNESTRA.   What things? Who?
> ACHILLES. About your daughter. The Greeks . . .
> CLYTEMNESTRA.   Oh no. Please no!
> ACHILLES. They want her sacrificed . . .
> CLYTEMNESTRA.   No one disagreed?

ACHILLES. I tried. I was shouted down.
CLYTEMNESTRA.   Shouted down?
ACHILLES. They threatened . . . to stone me.
CLYTEMNESTRA.   For trying to save my girl?
ACHILLES. For that.
CLYTEMNESTRA.   Who would dare lay a hand on you?
ACHILLES. Every single Greek, that's who.
CLYTEMNESTRA.   What about your Myrmidons?
ACHILLES. Starting with my Myrmidons. (ll. 1345–54)

The account of the death of Iphigeneia is in all probability the product of a later hand, the play having been either uncompleted, or unrevised, at Euripides' death. The details in the Messenger's account still confirm the role played by the army in the whole affair. They are all present for this human sacrifice. Instead they witness a miracle and are apparently satisfied. Whatever occurred, it is enough to get them to the war, which is where they want to be.

The range of approaches employed by Euripides within this set of plays covers both aspects of military behaviour and attitudes, and the effects that war has on everyone involved, combatant or non-combatant. Aeschylus set his *Persians*, the only surviving tragedy on a historical rather than mythical theme, back in the home of the defeated aggressors, Susa, the Persian capital. In so doing the playwright was able to demonstrate the folly of the action of King Xerxes in initiating the war, and in his conduct of it. There is also some room for sympathy. Sophocles too is inclined in *Ajax* and *Antigone* to spend more time on the losers than the winners. Euripides is certainly not alone in the compassion he extends to victims, a civilising dimension of all three tragedians. What is exceptional is his pinning down the attitudes of those directly involved at the front line, the way in which being at war changes them, and is for many both exciting and the occasion to exercise their one and only talent. As soon as the front line involves civilians, then the pain overwhelms everything else and reduces women and children to being the real casualties, whether queen, Muse, wife or daughter of the commanding officer. Whatever it is in human nature that triggers the instinct to swarm and destroy, Euripides knows no remedy. He makes no attempt to provide answers beyond giving examples to serve as reminders of what we all risk when leaders are allowed, for whatever reason, authentic or manufactured, to commit to action whose prime purpose is destruction.

6 REVENGE

Electra, Hecuba, Children of Heracles, Andromache, Medea

> CHORUS. What gift of the gods could be finer for man
> Than to raise up his hand o'er the head of his foe,
> Triumphant. (*Bacchae*, ll. 878–80)

The Greeks thought of the future coming up behind them where they could not see it. The past was in front, visible, impossible to wipe away. For a culture that invented drama before history, the amalgamation of past within present embodied in tragedy offered lessons from the past as well as examples for the future. No tragedies should be easier to appreciate today than those which relate to revenge, stretching one long arm backward into the future even as the other points grimly to the affronts and transgressions of the past. Our mythologies, perceived or actual, are buried in histories that refuse to lie down, wrongs rooted in previous centuries sometimes, but still serving as an excuse for refusing to forgive and move on. The vocabulary of warfare, politics, religion, even entertainment, is dominated by words like 'retribution', 'retaliation', 'reprisal', 'compensation', 'vendetta', 'vengeance': words that can be found every day of the week in the press, applied to anything from military incursion to playground bullying. St Paul's advice in his Epistle to the Romans ('Vengeance is mine, saith the Lord') was not to forget about revenge, but to leave it to the Lord. But who can deny a sneaking itch to side with the cinema's vigilantes in westerns (and easterns), when justice seems denied by law or lawlessness?

There is hardly an action in a Greek tragedy that cannot be traced to an incident of revenge. Indeed precious few dramatic situations, serious or comic or both, are not founded on retribution, one way or another. Revenge, or desire for revenge, seems to be our birthright. The Athenian playwrights never denied the power of the curse to leap across generations. The past unmasked in the present is as much a major theme in Ibsen as in Wilde, Miller or Dürrenmatt. The first great dramatic exploration of revenge and justice inevitably is to be found in Aeschylus. His *Persians* concerns the invasion of Greece by Persia, in response to their defeat ten years earlier at Marathon. *Seven Against Thebes* deals with the internecine strife between brothers when one reneges on an agreement to share power. *Suppliants* is an appeal for protection by the fifty daughters of Danaus who will react to forced marriage by forty-nine of them murdering their husbands on their wedding-night. *Prometheus* shows the Titan pegged out on a rock in the Caucasus as punishment for his opposition to Zeus. In the *Oresteia*, Aeschylus offers something more detailed and more complex, a situation created from two contrasting imperatives when to avenge the murder of a father, a son must become murderer of his mother.

Aeschylus is inconclusive about whether Clytemnestra kills her husband Agamemnon as the result of blood-curse passed down from several generations back through the house of Atreus; her love-affair with her cousin Aegisthus; Agamemnon's sacrifice of Iphigeneia before going to Troy; or his return with Cassandra as a concubine. The last can hardly have much to do with preparations made before Agamemnon and Cassandra arrive. In *Libation-Bearers* motives are clearer, though they involve a moral paradox. Apollo has instructed Orestes to avenge the murder of his father or face numerous torments, including those instigated by the Furies. Vengeance means the murder of his mother, an act which will also incite the Furies.

In the final play of the trilogy, *Eumenides*, Orestes flees to Athens, the Chorus of Furies in pursuit, and is put on trial at a new, specially created Court of the Areopagus, a citizen court over which Athena will preside. Old justice or new? An eye for an eye or a means of breaking the cycle? That the verdict has to make a decision on this specific occasion about whether killing your husband or your mother is the more heinous crime is almost a side-issue. Who administers justice is the real concern. Orestes is acquitted, if only by the casting vote of the goddess. The new court becomes the conduit for dealing with vendetta. Revenge is devolved from the individual to the body politic. A new concept of justice is born, one that is more fitting for a democratic society. Fifty years later Euripides in *Orestes* will set the same issue in a socially developed Argos that has an established legal system. The outcome is a capital verdict against Orestes and Electra, that only the timely arrival of Apollo can annul.

When Sophocles considered the same question in his *Electra*, justice has become dominated by the directive from Apollo. Matricide is summarily sidelined as an occupational hazard for the avenger and, if this sounds an outcome which returns to a primitive notion of morality, it is in effect a declaration of Sophocles' dramatic priority. His *Electra* is a revenge play no doubt, but more of a character-study than a moral or legal piece. The spirit of natural law encounters a more serious debate in *Antigone* where

Creon's decree that the body of Polyneices must remain unburied is purely pragmatic, Antigone's opposition a reaction of instinct, appealing to natural law. In *Ajax* the impulse to revenge from the hero after a personal slight is thwarted by the intervention of Athena. Deianira, Heracles' wife, turns unwittingly into an avenger of her husband's infidelity in *Women of Trachis*, when seeking naively only to rekindle her husband's love. In the two Oedipus plays and *Philoctetes*, revenge is not a central motive, though Philoctetes' hatred of Odysseus is a result of the treatment he has received in being abandoned on a desert island.

Euripides has his own agenda when it comes to revenge. There are numbers of aggrieved individuals in his plays, but what interests him as a playwright seems to be the progression from grievance to action. It is all too easy for revenge to masquerade as justice when it is at most a reprehensible, if human, element within it. Euripides, philosopher as he was and probably an acquaintance of Socrates and Plato, seems to have been well aware how Electra will make claims for justice through actions that spring wholly from a spirit of revenge. In his *Electra* the title character seems so fixated in her desire to punish her mother and step-father that everything and everybody is subordinated to it. Vengeance, though, does not come cheap. As for many with an obsessive goal, achieving that goal results in something that more resembles emotional collapse than release. No apologies are offered here for making the murder of Aegisthus an impious act, the murder of their mother explicit and abominable:

ORESTES. Did you see how the poor woman bared her breast
    as we were killing her?
    Sprawled on the ground the limbs that gave me birth.
    I nearly fainted. [...]
    As she cried out, she put her hand on my chin:
    'My child, I beg you . . .'
    She touched my cheek,
    and the weapon slipped from my hand.
CHORUS. The poor woman! How could you bear to look
    at your dying mother,
    as she breathed away her life?
ORESTES. I covered my eyes with my cloak,
    thrust the sword through her neck
    and put my mother to death.
ELECTRA. I urged you on.
    My hand was on the sword with yours.
    Most terrible of all, I drove it home. (ll. 1206–25)

If the fanatical impulse in *Electra* suggests that at the far end of vengeance lies mental disintegration, there are three major tragedies of Euripides where genuine suffering leads to breaking-point. In *Trojan Women* (see Chapter 5, pp. 85–9), Hecuba begins the play prostrate before a pair of conniving gods. She loses in swift succession surviving members of her family, down to the youngest. At the end, physically prevented from release through suicide, she is hauled off to live out her life as a slave. There is no comeback, no consolation, no hope. In *Hecuba*, the situation is similar, so is the character of Hecuba – or so at first it appears.

There are no gods in *Hecuba*. The play opens instead with a ghost, the ghost of Hecuba's son, Polydorus. He announces himself in a prologue and tells the audience what has happened. At the beginning of the war, his father Priam had sent him away to the protection of Polymestor, a 'guest-friend', and so, under an obligation to the Trojan king. With Polydorus Priam sent a store of gold so that, in the event of the Trojans losing the war, Polydorus and whichever of his brothers survived, would have means to carry on and perhaps restore the fortunes of the house. As soon as Troy fell, Priam and Hector with it, Polymestor put Polydorus to death and stole the gold. Then he threw the body into the sea.

The ghost of her son gives way to Hecuba, as desperate as her counterpart in *Trojan Women*, perhaps more so: she cannot walk without assistance. The Chorus are again women from Troy, but several of the events which occupy the early scenes of *Trojan Women* have already happened. The allocation of the Trojan captives has taken place. Troy has already been left behind. The Chorus are aware of what is to happen to Polyxena, sacrificed at the tomb of Achilles. Cassandra is already with Agamemnon. Odysseus comes to fetch Polyxena and Hecuba reminds him of an incident from earlier in the war. Odysseus had sneaked into Troy as a spy, dressed in rags and having bloodied his face as though from a wound.[1] He was recognised by Helen who informed Hecuba. Abject and on his knees, Odysseus begged for his life and Hecuba allowed him to leave. Now she asks for a favour in return: she wants Odysseus to save Polyxena. Odysseus is unrepentant: 'I said whatever was necessary to save my life' (l. 250). He offers Hecuba her life, which is not under threat, and puts forward a hollow defence for the killing of Polyxena which amounts to little more than a shrug. Polyxena responds with the submissive dignity that Euripides reserves for the young, condemned and accepting their fate.[2] Odysseus has the grace to avoid looking her in the eye, but hides his face

[1] The incident can be found in Book IV of the *Odyssey*.
[2] Macaria (*Children of Heracles*), Menoeceus (*Phoenician Women*), Iphigeneia (*Iphigeneia at Aulis*) all submit uncomplainingly to their fate.

in his cloak. Hecuba offers herself instead. Polyxena will have none of it:

POLYXENA. Take note of what I say, Mother. You, Odysseus,
  Be patient with my mother. She has reason to be angry.
  And you, poor Mother, don't try to fight authority.
  Do you want to be thrown in the gutter,
  an old woman, beaten and bloodied,
  your daughter violently torn from your arms?
  Is that what you want? You deserve better.
  Take my hand, dear Mother, give me a hug,
  cheek against cheek. One last time. And let me go. (ll. 406–11)

As Polyxena leaves with Odysseus, Hecuba falls to the ground, all strength, all resistance spent: and lies there throughout the next choral ode till Talthybius makes his first appearance. So far, there are variations from *Trojan Women*, but the outcome seems the same.[1] Talthybius gives an account of how Polyxena died, shockingly, but with sufficient dignity to have impressed the watching Greeks who have joined in preparing her for burial. Hecuba asks only that the Greeks leave her alone for her mother, and Talthybius departs. A covered corpse is carried in, found by a woman on the beach. Hecuba assumes it is that of her daughter. No one dares tell her otherwise. When she uncovers the face she discovers Polydorus, the son she had believed safe in Thrace. Stabbed to death and thrown into the sea, he has now washed up on the coast where the Greeks and their prisoners are currently becalmed.

In *Trojan Women* calamity after calamity is piled on Hecuba till she is capable only of attempted suicide: even that is refused her. In *Hecuba* something different happens. In this treachery by a former friend she finds, not something to crown the terrible outcome of defeat in war, but a well of resolve. The snuffing-out of decencies, typified by Odysseus rejecting the obligation to someone to whom he owes his life, was inflated by his arguments in favour of the sacrifice of Polyxena: the public interest; soldiers need incentives; heroes need recognition. Now Hecuba grieves for her last son, but in doing so, she passes beyond grief and discovers revenge. The bringing-on of the dead body of Polydorus happens barely half way through the play. The extent and depth of Hecuba's transformation occupies the rest.

Agamemnon, the Greek commander, arrives to find out why Hecuba has been so slow in going to deal with her daughter's body. He sees the

---

[1] Which play was performed first and what might have been the relationship between the two is open to speculation. Whichever was the 'alternative' version, they both show the cruellest aspects of war, without apology and without relief.

corpse and asks who it is. Instead of replying, Hecuba turns aside and delivers several short speeches addressed to herself, almost in soliloquy, wondering out loud how to respond, while Agamemnon tries to converse with her. It is a strange and unfamiliar device for a Greek tragedy, consciously planted to emphasise Hecuba's altered state of mind, from defeat to cold calculation. Her last such lines, 'Vengeance for my children needs this man. Why hesitate? Necessity demands risk, win or lose' (ll. 749–51), turn into a direct appeal to Agamemnon. Agamemnon seems aware that something has changed, his immediate reaction being for him too, like Odysseus, to offer Hecuba her freedom. She turns him down, then tells him about Polydorus. Her full address to Agamemnon is included in Chapter 10, pp. 182–4. It is possessed of a cunning unlike any of her previous remarks. She 'handles' Agamemnon, in a similar manner to Medea dealing with Creon, Aegeus and Jason.

Agamemnon is canny enough not to confuse pity, which he claims to feel, with responsibility for what may happen:

> AGAMEMNON. For the gods' sake I want that perjured friend of yours
>   to get what's coming to him. As long as the army,
>   that is, doesn't think I'm doing this, plotting
>   against a king of Thrace, just because of Cassandra.
>   That really is a matter of some concern to me.
>   The army likes the man. Your boy was an enemy. (ll. 852–9)

Hecuba is perfectly happy to manage on her own, as long as Agamemnon is complicit. He does have doubts about how she will succeed:

> AGAMEMNON.   Where will you turn for help?
> HECUBA. There are women in the tent, Trojan women.
> AGAMEMNON. What? The prisoners, do you mean?
> HECUBA. We'll do it together, the women and I.
> AGAMEMNON. Women against men?
> HECUBA. There's strength in numbers: and in guile. (ll. 879–84)

This steeliness is so different from the Hecuba of the first half of the play, it almost resembles the makeover of the aged Iolaus in *Children of Heracles*, from dodderer to hero of the battlefield. Agamemnon agrees to play his part, on his conditions, and a servant is dispatched telling Polymestor that Hecuba has a message for him: and, she adds, he should bring his two young sons with him. This echo from *Medea* (almost certainly an earlier play) gives an added frisson to what is to come.

Polymestor arrives, with his sons, and receives assurances about his health and well-being: he is full of commiseration for Hecuba's situation. She quizzes him about Polydorus and about the gold. Both, he assures her, are perfectly safe. She then informs him that the family treasure is hidden near the temple of Athena in Troy, but that she managed to smuggle other valuables from the city and that they are now concealed inside the tent. Polymestor is a little wary by this time, but she persuades him that there are only women inside and that he should bring the boys in with him. While the Chorus sing of justice, screams from indoors make it clear that Polymestor has been blinded and his sons killed. A triumphant Hecuba emerges, followed closely by a distraught Polymestor. Now it is he who is on his knees. His cries bring Agamemnon back. The commander-in-chief plays the innocent neatly and invites Polymestor to give an account of what happened. Polymestor justifies his murder of Hecuba's son and then becomes the messenger of his own disaster, describing exactly how the women set on his boys and himself inside the tent: and very brutal it was, without hesitation and without mercy. Hecuba answers Polymestor clinically, point by point, but forcefully. Agamemnon's summing-up is brief but cogent. When Polymestor had so gravely flaunted the laws of hospitality Hecuba's response was justified:

> POLYMESTOR. Beaten and by a woman. That's justice.
>   For an inferior. For a slave woman.
> HECUBA. You don't think that's justice? After what you did?
> POLYMESTOR. My children! And my eyes!
> HECUBA. Hurt, does it? So? Do you think I do not hurt?
> POLYMESTOR. You bitch! You're enjoying this: what you did to me.
> HECUBA. You think I shouldn't enjoy my revenge? (ll. 1252–8)

Polymestor, after acting as his own messenger, now turns into his own *deus*, forecasting Hecuba's end, Agamemnon's and Cassandra's too. The shocked Agamemnon orders him to be removed and abandoned on some desert island. The play comes to an abrupt conclusion.

The extent to which Hecuba's jubilation is shared by an audience may depend on the extent to which we can applaud such violence. As in *Medea*, that is surely Euripides' purpose. What he is doing, this clever and dangerous playwright, is make everyone complicit, Chorus and the hypocritical Agamemnon, but especially the audience. Do we condone the blinding of a man and the murder of two children? Yes, his crime was great. But this has nothing at all to do with the war, with the fall of Troy, with Helen or Menelaus, or even with Odysseus. That is what really distinguishes this play from *Trojan Women* and makes Hecuba less a tragic queen deprived of home and family than a victim of terrible events, who finds relief and joy in exacting the most vicious revenge for all of it on someone who was responsible for only a part of it. And because Euripides is so good at manipulating moral paradox, our own humanity and compassion are put to the test and, in all probability, submerged beneath the gratification of retribution.

The issue is clearer in *Children of Heracles* where the act of vengeance only lightly disturbs the eminently satisfying spectacle of an oppressor getting his comeuppance. The children of the great hero, harried from pillar to post after their father's demise, are trying to escape being stoned to death, the fate to which they have been condemned back in Argos. This was what Eurystheus has decreed, though the exact reason is never properly spelled out. That Eurystheus was scared of Heracles was common enough knowledge, but Heracles' descendants appear to offer little threat. Apart from Hyllus, who has managed to rustle up some support but is represented in the play by a servant, only Macaria of Heracles' children seems to have a name, though that is not in the Greek text where she is identified as no more than *parthenos*, 'an unmarried girl', the name supplied by translators from other sources because they feel she needs one. Iolaus, the children's protector, is old and feeble, at least initially. Their only other companion is their grandmother Alcmena, who is game enough though hardly a danger to the city of Argos and its king. Eurystheus, when he enters after being captured in the battle, justifies himself as being well aware that a feud will pass from one generation to the next. He not only expects Heracles' sons will some time seek revenge for the way he treated their father, but also assumes it to be their right. This naturally justifies his attempts to get rid of them, though they have done nothing except run away from him.

There seems to be a contemporary subtext to *Children of Heracles*, not all of it any longer accessible after such a gap in time. When it comes to exacting revenge, there certainly is something discernible, though nobody appears to be seeking it: or not quite anybody. The children of Heracles are guilty of no act against Eurystheus: nor are Iolaus and Alcmena. They do not have the means. Demophon initially has no quarrel with Argos, but takes what he sees as the moral course in defending the oppressed. Eurystheus has nothing against anybody for what they have done, only for what he thinks they might do: perfect excuse for the pre-emptive strike. The action proceeds. Athens sides with the refugees. Macaria sacrifices her own life. The battle gives occasion for the decrepit Iolaus to regain his youth and capture the villain. The conditions of melodrama are apparently satisfied.

The play, however, is not yet complete. There is an avenging Fury here in the person of Heracles' mother, Alcmena, who on her first appearance had seemed little more than part of a comic double-act with Iolaus. It is Alcmena to whom a Messenger brings news of what happened in the battle between Athens and her allies against Eurystheus, including the wonderful contribution of Iolaus.[1] Her response: 'Zeus, thank you for your concern over my affairs. Better late than never' (ll. 869–70), seems a bit grudging, but maybe she is entitled to be.[2] She concludes a relieved and fairly light-hearted speech by wondering 'What was Iolaus' bright idea in having captured Eurystheus not to have killed him?' (ll. 881–2). The Messenger surmises that Iolaus did not want to deprive Alcmena of the chance to confront her enemy and reminds her, in what still seems light-hearted mode, that she had suggested giving the Messenger his freedom for the news he has brought. The Chorus are elated and Eurystheus is at last led in, in chains. Alcmena unleashes a justified harangue for his causing her family so much suffering which she concludes as follows:

> ALCMENA. A coward's death is more than you deserve.
> One death is not enough for such a villain.

After which comes the following exchange with a Servant:

> SERVANT. The man cannot be killed.
> ALCMENA. Then what's the point of taking him prisoner?
> SERVANT. No point at all. We must release him to the Argives.
> ALCMENA. What law is this that says he can't be killed?
> SERVANT. Our law, the law of the rulers of this land.
> ALCMENA. What? You don't believe in killing your enemies?
> SERVANT. In battle, but not when they're prisoners of war. (ll. 958–66)

The argument continues, with Eurystheus joining in, offering reasons for behaving as he has. Alcmena is implacable. This sometime comic figure is adamant. She wants blood:

> ALCMENA. I tell you how we get round this. I'll kill him myself,
> I'll hand over his corpse to whoever comes to fetch him.
> Then his death will be nothing to do with this city.
> Just for me, his death. Justice for me. (ll. 1022–5)

Eurystheus has a further speech, a very odd one, whose meaning is

---

[1] The demonstration of abnormal strength is a feature of Dionysiac power as exhibited in *Bacchae* by Agave and her sisters. The transformation of Iolaus, whether real or illusory, is a Dionysiac attribute.

[2] Alcmena was the wife of Amphitryon to whom Zeus took a fancy. While Amphitryon was away on manoeuvres, Zeus made himself appear identical to Amphitryon and got up to some manoeuvres of his own. The result was Heracles. The situation has been treated for its comic potential in numbers of stage versions from Plautus onwards. Giraudoux called his play *Amphitryon 38* (1929) having discovered thirty-seven earlier adaptations. See also *Heracles*.

anybody's guess, before Alcmena instructs the attendants to take him off indoors where she will finish the job. The city of Athens emerges with its hands clean, or clean enough. Alcmena, on behalf of her whole family, gets the vengeance she wants, and perhaps deserves. The burst of savagery is a little perturbing, but not so as unduly to affect a sense that this is a suitable outcome.

Hecuba and *Children of Heracles* show old women gaining revenge for the crimes committed against their children. Family wrongs are frequently the cause of acts of vengeance in Euripides. *Ion*, a play which is more potential tragedy than tragedy tragic, has Creusa plotting the death of Ion who she thinks is being foisted on her as a son by her husband, Xuthus, when in actual fact she is his real mother and Xuthus is not his father. For all the comedy already identified in *Ion* (see Chapter 4, p. 66), Creusa has certainly had a life fraught with problems, and her decision to try and poison Ion is encouraged by one of Euripides' homicidal old men. A lucky chance averts the disaster and a frantic Creusa is on the point of being murdered herself by a resentful Ion when the Priestess emerges to sort everything out in a manner which raises as many questions as it resolves. Though Ion's reaction is pure instinct in the face of an attempt on his life, the play defines the moment where revenge overlaps with jealousy. It is this equally strong motivation for violence which lies behind the actions of the central characters in *Andromache* and *Medea*.

The situation in *Andromache* offers a new dimension to the sense of personal injury. It is set in Thessaly, a few years after the Trojan defeat by the Greeks. The parcelling-out of the captive women saw Andromache, Hector's widow, allocated to Neoptolemus, son of Achilles. Andromache has learnt, as a captive of war had to if she were to survive, how to live as a slave. She witnessed the killing of her husband by Achilles but has now had a son by Neoptolemus who has subsequently married Hermione. It is primarily around the conflict between these two women that the drama revolves, fuelled by Hermione's childlessness, for which she blames Andromache. Here she is, the legitimate wife, daughter of Menelaus and Helen, with money and influence, faced by a former queen, now a slave, who has the son she cannot conceive. Hermione is jealous and wants Andromache dead. She also wants the child dead. Andromache for her part is frightened for their lives, but still has some spirit despite a precarious sanctuary. Neoptolemus, probably wisely, is out of the country.

Though the play has a driving, if sometimes convoluted, narrative line, it is the sparring between the two women that sticks in the mind. Hermione arrives accusing Andromache of using drugs to make her barren and reminding Andromache of how their circumstances have changed. The central encounter between the two is ferocious and steeped in accusations, not all of which can possibly be true. There are a few catfights in surviving Greek tragedy (*Trojan Women* and the *Electra*s offer examples), but none other over a man. Hermione means to have the former queen scrubbing floors in the palace and will furnish her with a 'golden pail' to remind her of her new station. She taunts Andromache with the death of her former husband, Hector, and the child she has had since:

> HERMIONE. You have no Hector here, no Priam, no wealth.
>   You're in Greece now. You, you are so dimwitted,
>   you pathetic creature, you were happy to go to bed
>   with the son of your husband's murderer. And bear his child.
>   Foreigners, they're all alike, father in bed with daughter,
>   mother with son, sister and brother at it.
>   Nearest and dearest kill each other. And no law to stop them.
>   We don't want your practices round here. (ll. 168–76)

Andromache proves not so easy to intimidate. She has no desire to have more children. And as for Hermione:

> ANDROMACHE. It needed no drugs from me to turn your husband off.
>   Your being unfit to live with was enough for that.
>   Being a pleasant person, not beauty, makes someone
>   welcome in bed. Now that does work like a charm [...]
>   If your husband can't stand you, it's your stuck-up attitude. (ll. 205–14)

There's no denying that this free-for-all is a lot of fun. The motivation of the two women is intriguing. Hermione is driven by a desire to get her own back on Andromache for proving everything that she is not. Andromache may be on the defensive, but has no intention of giving in without a struggle. She proves capable of wiping the floor with Hermione's father, Menelaus, with or without a golden pail, but lets herself be tricked into surrendering the safety of her sanctuary. At Hermione's instigation, she is facing death, and her son too, when Peleus rides to the rescue and dispatches Menelaus back to Sparta with his tail between his legs, leaving his daughter to her fate.

The boot is now on the other foot for Hermione. Convinced that Andromache will in turn take revenge on her, she rushes about tearing her hair and threatening self-harm. She too finds an unexpected crusader in the improbable person of Orestes who turns up out of the blue with an offer of help. Hermione indulges in an extended speech of self-recrimination at the end of which she knows where to lay the blame:

HERMIONE. Why so jealous when I had everything I wanted?
    I was rich. I ran the household. Any children of mine
    would be legitimate; any others mere slave-bastards.
    But never – let me repeat that – never
    should a man of sense let his wife entertain gossips.
    Women who go visiting are up to no good.
    One will undermine another's marriage for profit;
    another who's corrupted wants someone else to corrupt.
    Many are simply wanton and infect homes.
    So take care. Lock and bolt your doors.
    These intruders are a disease. They cause nothing but trouble. (ll. 938–53)

What an extraordinary outpouring, with little relevance to the immediate situation, as it happens. Orestes, who has contrived to have her husband Neoptolemus lynched at Delphi, whisks Hermione off to Sparta. It is tempting to believe that she and Orestes deserve one another. This is a swift-moving and complicated plot, but one in which motives for revenge revolve around the possession of women by men, almost as an ironic complement to the conduct of the war against Troy and its initial cause.

Medea has nothing to do with any war, but is simply about a man leaving his wife for another woman, and what it means for her. True to the pattern found in the other plays, Euripides is more concerned with the circumstances that create avengers than the working through of a prolonged vendetta. The wife is a foreigner, not a Greek. She helped him in his early career, but is now something of a liability. In the final scene, when the appalled Jason confronts Medea, or tries to – she is by this time in her dragon chariot with the dead bodies of their sons and he is below, fruitlessly beating at the doors of the house – he unleashes the most scathing verbal attack on her:

JASON. You plague. You hateful thing. You woman
    detested by god, by me, by every mortal man.
    You dared to draw a sword and plunge it
    into children, your children, my children.
    You do this and can still look at the sun
    and at the earth. No crime's more monstrous.
    My curse, till death! Now at last I see you as you are.
    I never realised when I brought you to Greece
    from your home, that primitive country,
    that you were a traitor, to your father and your land.
    A degenerate. Now the gods heap retribution
    on me for your slaughtering your own brother
    before you ever embarked on the fair ship *Argo*.
    Only a start, that was. We married.

You had my children. Now you've killed them.
Why? Sex, just for the sake of sex.
No Greek woman would have done that.
Yet instead of one of them, I'd deigned to marry you.
What a wife you turned out to be.
An animal, not a woman,
a savage, some prehistoric monster.
Nothing I can say would touch your sort.
Your skin's too thick by far.
Vile. Leave, then, drenched in your children's blood.
Leave me to grieve my fate.
No new marriage to enjoy,
Never again to speak to the boys I fathered
and brought up. A beaten man. (ll. 1323–50)

Infanticide, fratricide, degenerate, un-Greek, an animal, a savage.
Medea's response appears cool to the extent of being disinterested:

> MEDEA. We could debate at some length about this,
> I think, but there's no real point.
> Zeus knows how you've been treated and what I did.
> I deserved better than contempt for my bed,
> rejection for something tastier. Oh, no.
> You mocked me, Jason. While that brand-new bride
> and her father Creon wanted me out of here.
> 'Animal', am I? 'Not a woman'?
> 'Savage. Prehistoric monster'?
> That's what it took to crush your heart. (ll. 1351–60)

This explanation for her doing what she has, for killing his sons as the
only way to touch her husband, shows how wrong he is to believe she has
no feelings. The cost to her is beyond his comprehension. This is no
impulsive act, nor one that most could contemplate, but a resolution,
nonetheless, that does lie at the far end of all too many broken relationships. Medea's final speech to her children is among the most searing
Euripides ever wrote (see Chapter 10, pp. 169–71). It reveals her not as
some demented witch, but as a mother.[1]

If it seems out of sequence to consider this final speech before the rest
of the play, the reason is to suggest a link through to Medea from Hecuba,

---

[1] In the celebrated production by Japanese director Yukio Ninagawa (1978), performed in
a style incorporating elements of both noh and kabuki, Medea was played by a male actor
in full kabuki costume. At the moment of her decision to kill the children, she threw off her
elaborate headdress and costume to stand revealed in a red shift, made male with every
veneer of borrowed 'civilisation' sloughed off.

both women who pass through despair to reach the point where they can without compunction murder two young children. In both cases it is an act of revenge, but the cause may seem unequal. The loss of her children and her world creates a new and destructive Hecuba who will blind a man and murder his sons: Medea is simply jilted by her husband before killing their two sons. The Chorus in *Medea* are initially phlegmatic about what has happened:

> CHORUS. Your husband's deserted you
> For someone else's bed.
> That's not the end of the world.
> God will work it out.
> You mustn't take so hard the loss of a husband. (ll. 155–9)

The Tutor later echoes them:

> TUTOR. You're not the only one to be parted from your children.
> You have to grin and bear it. People do. (ll. 1017–19)

That leads back to the beginning of the play and the identification of Medea as someone very 'different', very 'un-Greek', but in a way that the other characters in the play are incapable of understanding. Her journey can be traced from here, from loving mother to killer: she is both. There is some inkling too of why the playwright allows her to escape earthly justice and get away with what she does: the rarest of dramatic avengers in any drama since Euripides, one who kills but is not killed. What Jason turns her into and what he cannot understand in her makes Medea the avenger who, to destroy her husband, destroys her own motherhood.

In the prologue to *Medea* the Nurse speaks of the circumstances that have brought Jason and Medea to Corinth where the play is set. This is not Jason's native city and, for all he later disparages her as a foreigner, he is a foreigner himself. But he is a Greek and anyone who was not a Greek was a 'barbarian', an 'un-Greek'. Jason has announced that he intends dropping her to marry the Princess and she has reacted with a passion that worries the Nurse:

> NURSE. I know her but she frightens me,
> in case she sharpens a knife for her own heart,
> creeping silently through the house to her bed,
> or tries to kill the king, or the new bridegroom,
> provoking some irreparable disaster.
> She's an odd one.
> You'd be a fool to cross her lightly. (ll. 39–45)

Immediately Euripides has the Tutor bring in the children who will prove the means to her revenge. Both these two servants take Medea's side over Jason's desertion of her so that he can marry again, and the Nurse warns the Tutor to keep the children out of her way. He removes them. Four hysterical outbursts off stage from Medea seem to confirm her concerns to the newly arrived Chorus, but when Medea appears in person, her control is already similar to that of Hecuba, a control fuelled by hate. What is different from Hecuba is that Medea is in a position of comparative strength. She has the latitude both to make plans and to execute them. This she exploits first by gaining the breathing space she needs from Creon. In her first encounter with Jason he tries to establish himself as the reasonable one, the one who does not over-react, who thinks things through and makes balanced decisions: 'So hate me, if you like, but I bear no grudge towards you' (l. 463). She is, after all, far better off now than before:

> JASON. You're good with words, Medea. Perhaps it seems
> unchivalrous to suggest that it was simply Love
> whose arrows forced you to save my life.
> I don't want to make an issue of it.
> The assistance you gave was quite valuable.
> But you did get better than you gave,
> I think it's fair to say.
> To begin with, instead of that uncivilised place,
> you now live in Greece, a seat of justice
> and the rule of law instead of mindless violence.
> Everyone in Greece knows how clever you are.
> You're famous. If you'd still been living
> at the back of beyond, no one would have heard of you.
> For my part, a house crammed full with gold,
> or the skill to sing and play like Orpheus,
> would have no meaning without the fame.
> I've spoken so far of my own achievements
> but you did initiate this debate.
> As for my marriage, my royal marriage,
> that was a clever decision, you must agree,
> as well as a sensible one, the best thing really
> for you and the boys. No, just wait a moment.
> When I arrived here from Iolcos,
> weighed down by a series of disasters,
> what greater ambition could I have had,
> as an immigrant, than to marry the king's daughter?
> It was not – and I know this is what upsets you –
> that I'd stopped loving you and fancied some
> new woman or wanted a bigger family.

The boys. They're fine. No complaints there.
But so we could live a respectable life –
that's what it all comes down to. (ll. 529–59)

This speech, perhaps, is what convinces Medea, possibly puts the idea into her head, that the only way to touch Jason is through the boys. Previously she had managed to get the Chorus to go along with plans to kill the Princess and Creon. Faced with a Jason who claims to have a monopoly on being rational and forward-thinking, she needs something more extreme. What use in killing the Princess if he has so little interest in her that she is only a means to advancement? If he can maintain that he has introduced Medea to civilisation, what weapon does she still have to thwart his ambition?

The next Chorus sequence shows that they may have agreed to go along with Medea, but they recognise an intensity in her that is beyond their experience:

CHORUS. Passion. Too much passion.
  No merit in that,
  No reputation there.
  Love, gentle love,
  Is a gift of the gods.
  I'll settle for that,
  With no searing, no poison,
  No obsession, no pain.

  Control. Moderation.
  I'll pray for them,
  I'll be comfortable with them.
  God preserve me
  From that madness,
  The affliction that is sex,
  Without rhyme, without reason.
  Affection, but not passion. (ll. 629–43)

It as almost as though this 'civilisation' of Corinth is incapable of something so primitive as revenge which they cannot recognise until overtaken by it. They pray for protection from passion, but at the same time sign up for Medea's. A few scenes later and after Medea's farewell to her children their perspective has changed:

CHORUS. A woman shouldn't probe
  The fine subtleties of myth,
  Or the struggle for survival.
  But I have. Often.

We have a voice, we women,
To help us share in meaning.
An instinct. Some of us.
Only a few, perhaps, but some,
Not incapable of reflection.

And I say this. Those who miss out
On experience,
Who never have children,
They're the lucky ones.
They never know, the childless,
They never have the chance –
What a child may bring,
Joy or grief, grief or joy.
The childless never see
That first sweet enchantment
Shrivel, with time, into despair.

How to bring them up.
How to have something to leave them.
Will they turn out frivolous?
Will they turn out decent?
There's no predicting; and no end to it.
But worst, the worst
Of any human experience:
You become prosperous: they grow –
Good children, fine young people –
And then some accident . . .
Death steals them away,
Spirits them underground.
How does anyone survive that?
Why make yourself vulnerable,
Mortals to be toyed with by gods? (ll. 1081–116)

This is revenge too, the revenge of the gods, on any who seem too successful, too happy or too complacent. It is also the most pessimistic sentiment to be found, I believe, in any Greek tragedy. The Chorus have come to understand, a little at least, the cost to Medea of her actions.

The final line, 'Mortals to be toyed with by gods', introduces one more revenge tragedy, Euripides' final play *Bacchae*. But *Bacchae* is about many other things as well as revenge. It differs from other revenge tragedies by being an unfair match between mortal and immortal. There can only ever be one winner. Numbers of Greek tragedies depict gods as spiteful, malevolent even, Apollo (*Ion*), Hera (*Heracles*) and Aphrodite (*Hippolytus*) among the more culpable, but they operate at a distance or through intermediaries. The Dionysus of *Bacchae* makes no bones about what he plans and how, as an immortal, he will defeat his mortal cousin. No other god in Euripides appears in the leading role. The prominence of Dionysus in *Bacchae* has to be the starting point for any enquiry into the supernatural world within Euripides.

7 IMMORTALS AND MORTALS

Alcestis, Iphigeneia Among the Taurians, Electra, Rhesus, Ion, Hippolytus, Bacchae

Only four of Euripides' nineteen plays (*Children of Heracles*, *Iphigeneia at Aulis*, *Medea* and *Phoenician Women*) do not include an immortal or supernatural character with a prominent part to play. Such non-mortals are mostly gods from the Olympian pantheon, Apollo (twice), Athena (four times), Aphrodite, Artemis, Poseidon, Hermes and Dionysus. Castor and Pollux (the Heavenly Twins) arrive at the end of two plays – Castor does all the talking.[1] There are also numbers of demi- or semi-divine immortals and appearances from other fringe deities, Thetis (mother of Achilles), the Muse Terpsichore (mother of Rhesus), Iris (the messenger of the gods) and a couple of more sinister figures, Madness and Death. There is a monster, in *Cyclops*, the one-eyed Polyphemus, and, as this is a satyr play, its standard Chorus of rustic animalistic creatures, the satyrs, and their leader Silenus. Euripides introduces only one ghost, that of Polydorus in *Hecuba*, but in the same play another, that of Achilles, has a say in what happens without appearing.[2]

If these seem a somewhat freakish *dramatis personae* for a playwright who is acclaimed for his realism, it is worth drawing attention to Shakespeare's castlists which include fairies, apparitions, visions, soothsayers, witches, spirits, ghosts galore, Time, Rumour, fiends and even Goths.

In most of the Euripides plays in which they appear gods, or demigods, are figures of authority, though no more moral leaders than they are depicted by Homer. They may have particular concerns or represent some vested interest: usually they begin the action or conclude it in a prologue or epilogue, either setting the scene or resolving the plot. Whether they appear at the beginning or the end does, of course, make a considerable difference to their effect and dramatic purpose. Apart from Castor and

---

[1] Castor and Pollux were brothers of Helen and Clytemnestra, but the exact contents of Leda's famous egg, after she had been raped by Zeus in the guise of a swan, are variously reported (and credited).

[2] In Aeschylus' *Oresteia* Clytemnestra is the only 'running' character. She appears in all three plays, but in the last as a vengeful ghost reproaching the Furies for falling asleep (literally) on the job while meant to be pursuing Orestes.

Pollux who, being twins, tend to be inseparable, gods seldom hunt in pairs, though they may frame a play, one at the beginning, one at the end (as in *Hippolytus*) or provide an epilogue where a mortal has delivered the prologue (as in *Electra* or *Iphigeneia Among the Taurians*). Euripides rings the changes and, whatever the hostile critics of previous generations may have thought, does not decide to end a play with a divine intervention because he has painted himself into a corner and cannot think of any alternative means of extricating his characters. Underpinning Euripides' dramaturgy is a precocious ability, for almost two thousand years before Shakespeare, to manufacture and make the most of a dramatic situation. This is one of the qualities that does travel across time.

Euripides' own theological stance is not of great consequence here. The purpose is to identify why Euripides merits study after all these centuries and, more importantly, deserves a place on the contemporary stage. Whether or not he believed in the Olympians in any fundamentalist sense is not really any more significant than whether anyone still does. The gods in his plays are a dramatic device. In that, his position is probably similar to Shakespeare's over ghosts, or both of them over dreams and omens. They are as significant as the situations in which they crop up and the manner that the characters react to them. Their function differs according to the point in the action at which they appear.

The encounter between Poseidon and Athena, on different sides in the Trojan War but colluding over its consequences, has already been noted (see Chapter 5, pp. 85–9). That scene alone would give licence to treat the gods as having a figurative reality beyond their literal identity: all those for whom war is a means to personal gratification or profit. Such dispensation is almost unnecessary when the mortal characters are treated in the same sort of way, identified by their labels – Agamemnon, Helen, Electra – but enjoying, beyond their mythical status, a certain elasticity. For the rest of *Trojan Women* and throughout *Hecuba*, human beings inflict the pain and fellow human beings do the suffering. There is, incidentally, only a single example of a god being a recurring character within any play of Euripides. Dionysus opens *Bacchae* and Dionysus effectively closes it. In all sorts of ways every play of Euripides is heading towards *Bacchae*, as the following chapters will demonstrate.

Among the more conventional prologues, the opening of *Alcestis* is still something of a curiosity. Apollo enters, the god of prophecy, the god of music and harmony, the god associated with the oracle at Delphi, the god of healing. He was the brother of Artemis, goddess of hunting, of chastity and, slightly incongruously, of childbirth. He is the god also whose behaviour is more often called into question by Euripides than any other. At the beginning of *Alcestis* he tells of an incident in his past where Zeus (his father) had killed Apollo's son, Asclepius, with a thunderbolt.[1] Apollo in retaliation killed the Cyclopes who were the manufacturers of those thunderbolts – an interesting refinement on the politics of government and intervention. Apollo's sentence from an infuriated Zeus was a year's community service which he duly completed as a cowman to Admetus, king of Pherae. So grateful was he for his kind treatment during his sentence that he fooled the Fates into promising that, when it was Admetus' time to die, the king could find a substitute to take his place. The only relation Admetus could find to agree was his wife Alcestis. She is now on the point of death. Apollo, who one might think – and Euripides possibly did – should have learned his lesson over cheating death, is about to depart to 'avoid pollution' when Death arrives in person. Death resents Apollo's interference with the gods of the underworld and refuses to make special allowance for Alcestis. Apollo forecasts that 'a man' (Heracles) is already on his way to Pherae and will save Alcestis. He then departs. Death too leaves to complete his work and claim Admetus' wife.

This unusual encounter between an Olympian god and one of the powers from below sets up the fable. There are hints too of other questions that the playwright poses. Is there a way of cheating Death? And, if there were, what right has anyone to ask another to take their place? Here it seems to have backfired on everyone, Apollo included, whose good turn fractures the natural order of things, something ventured upon only in exceptional circumstances. Fortunately for Alcestis and Admetus, and, as it happens, Apollo, Heracles counts as 'exceptional circumstances' because he too was fathered by Zeus (which makes him Apollo's half-brother). Heracles will be – though he has not yet reached his twelfth labour for Eurystheus – one of those few who does manage to descend to Hades and to return to earth. On this occasion he will encounter Death at the tomb of Alcestis and successfully wrestle for her life.[2]

Apollo seems at first sight to be the only god to appear in *Orestes*, arriving in the nick of time to legislate on a situation that really has got

[1] Apollo makes no reference to it here, but the usual reason for Zeus' action is given that Apollo's son Asclepius restored Hippolytus to life for Artemis, but to include that here would be a complication too far.

[2] Heracles is usually treated in Greek tragedy and comedy as more mortal than demigod, though he gets promotion into the company of the immortals after death. One of Sophocles' plays is about the circumstances leading up to his death (*Women of Trachis*), but in another (*Philoctetes*) he appears *ex machina*, to resolve the problem of getting the marooned Philoctetes, with Heracles' bow, to the battlefield at Troy.

out of control. This Argos is not a place for gods at all, having a perfectly adequate legal system for dealing with crimes of homicide, though not too competent at handling the sort of people who perpetrate it. Cleverly, Apollo arrives in the company of Helen. Not only is she not dead, though Orestes and Pylades were pretty sure they had slit her throat three hundred lines ago – the audience too, after hearing her death-cries reverberate round the palace – but he has promoted her, courtesy of Zeus, to a position in the heavens. She is, therefore, now an immortal, as happens to many, though by no means all, of those fathered by a god but who have to live their life on earth as mere humans. Sorting out the rest is chickenfeed by comparison (see Chapter 4, pp. 69–70).

Several plays conclude with an immortal when they have opened without. The reasons for their appearance are never quite the same but serve a similar dramatic function. *Iphigeneia Among the Taurians* is one of these. This too is a neglected play because it seems to cover similar ground to *Helen*, but is neither as funny nor as pleasing. It does involve, as does *Helen*, a post-Trojan War scenario. At the end of *Iphigeneia at Aulis*, a Messenger reports that Iphigeneia was laid out for sacrifice, but at the last minute was substituted by a deer sent by Artemis. Nobody seems entirely convinced by this Messenger, but in the text that we have, however unrevised, there is no sign of an Artemis turning up to explain why she performed this miracle, if indeed she did. In *Iphigeneia Among the Taurians*, which has no production date but must have preceded the posthumous *Iphigeneia at Aulis*, Iphigeneia has for many years been a priestess of Artemis in the Crimea. Like Helen, ensconced in Egypt, she has only a hazy idea of what has been going on recently. She rehearses, without obvious rancour, the situation which led her to the point of death and her nick-of-time rescue by Artemis. The goddess transferred her to a temple where her duty, prescribed by King Thoas, has been to prepare for death any foreigners, especially Greeks, who happen to turn up, 'though the actual slaying is somebody else's job' (l. 40), she fastidiously explains.

Now she has had a dream of home and interprets a destructive earth-quake which it included as an indication that her brother Orestes must be dead. Fortunately she is not much of a soothsayer and moments after she exits to prepare suitable libations, Orestes and Pylades enter: warily, because they have heard what happens to Greeks. They are here because the Furies, or a breakaway faction unhappy with the result of the trial on the Areopagus, are still hounding Orestes for killing his mother. Apollo has told him he must go to the land of the Taurians and fetch back to Athens a statue of Artemis. Orestes and Pylades case the temple, looking for a way in, and depart to wait for nightfall. In no time they have been spotted on the beach, one of them suffering a seizure.

A herdsman brings news to Iphigeneia about how the pair of them have been captured. They are brought in and an interrogation fails to reveal the fact that one of the two is Iphigeneia's brother, even when she agrees to let one of them go if he will take a message home to Argos. Eventually it becomes clear, even to these two, that they are brother and sister. Most of the remainder of the play involves finding a way to escape and to take the missing statue with them. Thoas is tricked into allowing the idol to be ferried out to sea for cleansing. The report of the Messenger, who returns to tell the king of their escape, suggests that the Greeks had more to fear from the elements than from Thoas' men. Thoas is on the point of setting off in pursuit himself, while uttering dire threats against the Chorus (who are Greek slaves), when a god interferes, not Artemis who might have been expected to show some exasperation at the hijacking of her bust, but her half-sister Athena to whose city it is to be taken. Athena has plenty to say about what is to be done with the appropriated statue. She also has some advice for Orestes, who 'can hear the voice of a goddess, however far away you are' (l. 1447). Thoas capitulates immediately, so impressed that he volunteers to provide a free passage home to the entire Chorus. The ease with which all obstacles are overcome defines the play as one of Euripides' romances which hardly needs a god to unscramble.

The same could be said for *Helen* where, for the sake of consistency, it should be pointed out that Helen, before or after *Orestes*, is technically a demigod already and hence half-sister to Athena, Artemis, Aphrodite, Hermes, Apollo, never mind Heracles and Clytemnestra; it is also her full brothers, Castor and Pollux, who make an entrance at the end on the machine to stop the enraged Theoclymenus from slaughtering everyone in sight. Helen has concerns about her birth and about being a 'freak', in addition to her resentment at being blamed for the Trojan War (see also Chapters 1, pp. 22–5 and 3, pp. 75–8). Some of this is comic, some far from it. During the scene with Teucer early in the play, without confessing who she is, Helen asks for any information he has about Helen's family and he tells her about the death of Thestia's daughter, Leda:

TEUCER. Leda, do you mean? Dead and buried.

HELEN. Did she die of shame at Helen's disgrace?

TEUCER. Something like that, they reckon. Noose. Round the neck.

HELEN. What about the sons of Tyndareus [Castor and Pollux]?

TEUCER. Dead? Or alive? Depends which version you believe.

HELEN. Which is the nicer version? All this makes me so unhappy.

TEUCER. The nicer version says they are gods now. Like stars. Up in heaven.

HELEN. That sounds all right. What's the alternative?

TEUCER. Suicide. Because of their sister, of course. (ll. 133–42)

Happily, the first account proves the more reliable, as they verify by convincing Theoclymenus that Helen has to go back to Greece with her husband. Castor then suggests, slightly mystifyingly, that:

> CASTOR. We could have saved our sister earlier than we did,
>   any time after Zeus made us gods, in fact,
>   but we had to give way to what was destined
>   and to the other gods who wanted it like this. (ll. 1658–61)

And they conclude with what almost amounts to an aphorism, but may rather be one of Euripides' running themes:

> CASTOR. The gods are not ill-disposed to those of noble birth,
>   but they make them face more than their share of hardship. (ll. 1678–9)

The Heavenly Twins, also known as the Dioscuri, complete *Electra* too, though in more detached, or perhaps more critical, mood. This is a play so severely realistic that it inevitably encompasses greater variations of tone, from domestic detail to the horror of the murder of Clytemnestra. There is certainly no greater social contrast between prologue and divine intervention. *Electra* for the most part turns its back on god-sanctioned morality along with any approach to the story with which the audience might have been more familiar. Orestes' killing of Aegisthus is at best reprehensible, at worst a flouting of most of the unwritten laws of common decency. Orestes and Electra proceed jointly to stab their mother to death and are suddenly confronted by her two brothers. Castor wastes little time in giving his verdict on what has just occurred, addressing, apparently, only Orestes:

> CASTOR. We have seen the murder of our sister,
>   your mother. She got what she deserved.
>   But it should have never have been at your hands.
>   As for Apollo, Apollo . . . Well, he is my lord.
>   I have nothing to say. He's wise, of course,
>   but there was no wisdom in this oracle.
>   What's done is done, and now you must live
>   with the consequences, as Fate and Zeus require. (ll. 1242–8)

Such a reluctant assessment of what has just taken place has less to do with this involving the death of their sister, or indeed of the murderers' mother, than serving as a broad condemnation of everything that has happened; and of Apollo for whatever part he may have played in recommending it. From here Castor simply picks up the pieces like a collector of body parts

after a nasty car crash. Electra to marry Pylades; Orestes to head for
Athens and a trial at the Court of the Areopagus; Orestes to found a city
in Arcadia; funeral arrangements for Aegisthus and Clytemnestra; Helen
already heading for home from Egypt with Menelaus; a reward for the
poor Farmer. It comes out like a shopping list, a restocking of the mythic
pantry after the reality of a hideous and bloody episode.

Just when the end seems at hand, the Chorus ask if they may have a
word. The text is uncertain and the speakers are confused but, when
Castor agrees, seems to read as follows:

CHORUS. Since you are gods and brothers of the dead woman,
    why didn't you keep the Furies away from this house?
CASTOR. What must be must be, because of Fate,
    Necessity, and Apollo's unwise words.
ELECTRA. May I say something too, divine twins?
CASTOR. You may. I blame Apollo for this bloody business.
ELECTRA. What Apollo, what oracles ordained
    that I should be my mother's murderer?
CASTOR. You shared the deed and a common fate,
    one and the same;
    the same curse from your ancestors crushed you both.
ORESTES. Sister, after years of separation, I finally see you,
    yet straight away I am severed from your love.
    I shall leave and be left in turn.
CASTOR. She has a husband and a home,
    and doesn't deserve to be pitied.
    All she has to do is leave Argos. (ll. 1298–1313)[1]

The dual condemnation, of Apollo for authorising the whole sorry affair
and of Electra for thinking only of herself, is in keeping with the broad
reading of the whole play as a fierce riposte to any playwright, Aeschylus
and Sophocles included, who could see this as remotely resembling a
heroic tale. It is a vicious but superb indictment of false heroics.

The arrival of Thetis for the last scene of *Andromache* is a surprise,
though there are a few ends to tie up. Andromache and her son have not
been seen since their earlier liberation by Peleus. Thetis was not an
Olympian goddess but an immortal sea nymph, who had been
condemned to marry a mortal, Peleus, when she was one of the few who
successfully rejected the advances of Zeus. After the birth of Achilles that
marriage fell apart apparently, in unspecified circumstances. She and
Peleus are the grandparents of Neoptolemus whose murdered body has

[1] Following Diggle's Oxford text (1994) with a re-ordering of lines.

just been brought back from Delphi. At first sight she seems to turn up to offer Peleus some consolation. Despite the admirable way he has conducted himself in supporting Andromache and putting Menelaus to flight, he now finds himself alone and without family, his marriage well behind him. Or is it? Suddenly here is Thetis and in a mood to reward the old man for his virtue. Hers is a bossy speech, bossier even than most *ex machina*. She confirms what is to happen to Orestes and Hermione and makes provision for Andromache who can now go off and marry her brother-in-law Helenus, not exactly Hector, but something of an improvement on being Neoptolemus' occasional bedmate. Then she turns to her ex-husband:

> THETIS. So that you will think with joy of our marriage,
>   I mean to free you from the cares of human life
>   and make you immortal. Then you can live with me
>   in Nereus' house for the rest of time, a god with his goddess.
>   And as you walk dry-footed from the sea,
>   you will be able to watch our beloved Achilles,
>   your son and mine, in his island home by the Euxine.
>   Go first to Delphi, the city built by god,
>   with this body [Neoptolemus], and bury him. Then to the sunken cave
>   by the Sepian rock. Sit there and wait, and I will come
>   from the sea, with fifty sea nymphs to bring you home.
>   Whatever is fated, that you must do. Zeus has ordained it. (ll. 1253–69)

Whether this seems an atypical sentimental ending or a deeply ironic one, is far from clear, but it cannot be both in the same production. What Euripides does seem to do is offer a range of incidents and reactions to them that move rapidly, but easily, from the tragic to comic, from pathetic to romantic. Within that framework the full circle of love-affair between mortal and immortal fits surprisingly elegantly.

Athena has a role in three other Euripidean tragedies apart from *Iphigeneia Among the Taurians* and *Trojan Women*.[1] Hers are more often guest appearances, suitable for the patron goddess of the city where the plays were first produced and which is a byword for the institution and administering of justice. In *Suppliants*, with its local setting, she has little more to say than a word or two of advice to Theseus about how to conduct negotiations, and to warn Adrastus and the Argives to keep their noses clean in future. She does urge some of the sons to seek revenge as

---

[1] She has been a major character in Aeschylus' *Eumenides* where she founds and presides over the Court of the Areopagus which acquits Orestes of the murder of his mother. She is the only god to appear in person in any of the surviving plays of Sophocles, that being *Ajax*, where her gloating over the afflicted Greek hero dismays even her champion, Odysseus.

soon as they are grown up, but her attitude suggests more contemporary polemic than dramatic imperative.

In *Rhesus*, which is anyway a curiosity for other reasons, she reveals an unexpected talent. Odysseus and Diomedes have entered the Trojan camp, determined to assassinate Hector. Fortunately, or unfortunately, Hector is not in his tent having gone to show Rhesus where he and his newly arrived troops can set up camp. The Chorus have left too, fed up with waiting for their replacements as sentries. Their target not being at home is a problem for the two Greeks, so they decide to leave and go back to their camp. They are prevented by the sudden and rare appearance of a *deus* in mid-play, taking a part in the action and seriously affecting its outcome. It is Athena who has come to tell them that it is more important that they go and kill Rhesus. Odysseus quickly agrees and then Athena says:

> ATHENA. Paris is coming. I can see him heading this way.
>   Some sentry must have alerted him,
>   an unconfirmed rumour of your mission.
> DIOMEDES. Accompanied or alone?
> ATHENA. Alone. On his way to where Hector sleeps.
>   to warn him about spies.
> DIOMEDES. He should be the first to die, surely.
> ATHENA. You may not transcend what is fated.
>   Paris is not yours to kill.
>   Quick, now. After the man who is destined to die
>   at your hands. I'll pretend to be Paris' ally,
>   Aphrodite. I'll lie to him because I hate him. (ll. 627–39)

Odysseus and Diomedes leave and an absurd scene takes place with Athena masquerading as Aphrodite. Do all goddesses sound alike in the dark, or is she doing her Aphrodite voice? She manages to disarm Paris and off he goes. Neither of them appears again.

Late in the play the arrival of the Muse to mourn Rhesus, her lost son, shows the response of a mother, amid all these military matters, to the realities of war. She reveals to Hector that the death of Rhesus was the work of Athena, Odysseus and Diomedes, and in her turn condemns Helen, 'widow-maker by arrangement to Troy' (l. 913). In a sympathetic moment she suggests that she will bear her loss better than will Thetis whose son, Achilles, is also destined to die. Her last lines reiterate the feelings of all bereaved mothers, mortal or immortal:

> MUSE. Such pain to have mortal children who may die.
>   To bury a child. If you had any idea,
>   you'd choose to live life barren. (ll. 980–2)

In *Ion*, another of Euripides' romances, though only by a short head, the prologue comes from Hermes, yet another son of Zeus and the messenger of the gods. He is the god of good luck and in Athens it was customary to have a small statue of him with an erect phallus outside your front door. On the day he was born Hermes killed a tortoise and, using its shell, invented the lyre before lunch. By mid-afternoon he had rustled fifty cattle from his half-brother Apollo, for which feat he also became, somewhat bizarrely, the god of thieves. His exploits in *Ion* are not half so unruly. He opens by introducing himself as the *latris* of the gods, a humble term meaning at best 'servant' or even 'dogsbody'. He then describes how, many years ago, Apollo had raped Creusa, daughter of the king of Athens. She managed to keep her subsequent pregnancy secret and gave birth to a child which she abandoned in the same cave where she was assaulted, leaving it in a crib along with some recognisable ornament of her own, nature unspecified. Apollo asked Hermes, his half-brother, to go and recover the baby, cradle and all, and deposit it on the doorstep of his temple at Delphi. Apollo's reluctance to acknowledge paternity turns out to be a major topic of concern later in the play. Hermes did as he was asked and the baby was discovered the following morning by the Priestess. She 'took it up for pity' (l. 47) and raised him, both unaware of his parentage.[1] The boy grew up and became a temple attendant while, back in Athens, his mother Creusa had an arranged marriage with Xuthus: but the couple are childless. They have now come to consult the oracle about their problem. Apollo has decided to tell them that the foundling is Xuthus' child and that he should be given the name of Ion. This way he can be recognised by Creusa and taken back to Athens and none will be the wiser about Apollo's involvement.

The reason for Hermes being mixed up with this devious plan is no more than that it is he who has been the go-between in the whole affair. None of the main characters at this stage has anything but a partial understanding of what is going on. Hermes is aware too that even for the god of prophecy the best-laid plans have a habit of ending up off-piste. Only after a string of misunderstandings, some comical, others less so, plus the presentation of Ion's various objects found with the baby, are son and mother reunited and stepfather suitably gulled. Ion, however, is not satisfied:

---

[1] This is another reference which suggests that Shakespeare may have known his Euripides rather better than is usually assumed when he was writing *The Winter's Tale*. 'I'll take it up for pity' is what the Old Shepherd says when he discovers the baby exposed on the shore of Bohemia by Antigonus. The return and unveiling of Alcestis offers a more extended parallel to the statue scene in *The Winter's Tale* when Hermione 'comes back to life'.

CREUSA. Apollo really is your father.
ION. Then why did he hand me over to a different father
and say that this Xuthus is my father?
CREUSA. Not father, exactly. He didn't say that.
He was simply making a present of you: in the same way
as someone might get a friend to make a son his heir.
ION. Does Apollo tell the truth or not? Is his prophecy lies?
I have to say, Mother, I'm very uncomfortable with all this.
CREUSA. No, listen, my dear. The way I see it, Apollo has done this
all for you: settled you in a noble household.
You wouldn't have had that as Apollo's son. No inheritance.
No father's name either. I covered up what happened,
and secretly tried to kill you, remember. So handing you over
to a different father is his way of helping you out.
ION. That's not good enough, thank you very much.
I want some answers. I'm going in there now
to ask Apollo straight, is he my father or isn't he. (ll. 1531–45)

At this moment a god appears *ex machina*, Apollo, one might expect, the only person to convince Ion of his mother's version of what happened: or, second best, Hermes, the other one who has been in on the whole conspiracy from Ion's birth. Instead, in flies Athena (yet another half-sibling of Apollo):

ATHENA. It is I, Athena, who gave my name to your city,
arriving posthaste, at Apollo's request.
He thought it best not to come in person,
in case what has passed between you should prove
a cause of recrimination. (ll. 1555–9)

She quickly confirms Creusa's account, has a few forecasts of her own about Ion's future and commends Apollo for all his kindness to Creusa: easy labour, healthy child, unsuspicious family, rescue by Hermes. And not a word to Xuthus, right? Ion is happy, Creusa is happy, Xuthus is happy: though it is difficult not to believe there will be a bit of gossip below stairs when the Chorus get back to base. Concluding the play with a different god from the one who opens it serves, it would seem, to throw the apparent solutions into doubt rather than confirm them, or, at least, suggest there are unresolved ethical issues here for an audience.

The other play where this happens asks a bigger question. *Hippolytus* is a classic example of a frame plot – almost. The prologue is delivered by Aphrodite, goddess of physical love, *erôs*. Her opening remarks make no bones about what she stands for:

APHRODITE. Amongst those who live and see the sun,
   between the Black Sea and the western boundaries,
   I privilege those who most look up to me.
   Those who treat me with disdain, I crush.
   We gods are really no different.
   We bask in men's respect.
   I'll show you shortly how true this is.
   The son of Theseus, Hippolytus,
   spawn of that Amazon woman,
   and raised by the pure and godly Pittheus,
   is the only person in the whole of Trozen
   to rate me most contemptible of all the gods.
   Goes to bed with no one. An anti-womaniser.
   Artemis is whom he reveres, daughter of Zeus,
   brother of Apollo, and his pattern of perfection.
   He cavorts around the greenwood in her company,
   he, his goddess and his hunting hounds,
   denuding the country of its entire wildlife.
   I feel no animosity towards them, of course.
   Why would I? But, for all this contempt of his,
   I am going to have to chastise Hippolytus. Today.
   My plans are made. They have been for a while.
   They just need a little fine-tuning. (ll. 3–23)

Not much scene-setting here. Aphrodite plunges straight in and, unlike some more neutral deliverers of prologues, gives the clearest of pictures of where she is coming from and of her target. She is out to get Hippolytus and she has contrived to afflict his stepmother, Phaedra, with a passionate sexual longing for her stepson. This, she forecasts, will lead to disaster. Theseus will find out. He will then curse his son and, as Poseidon awarded Theseus three curses as a gift, this will be enough to finish Hippolytus. As for Phaedra:

APHRODITE. [...] her reputation will remain intact
   but she will die nevertheless. I do not reckon
   what happens to her as of any great significance,
   compared with the satisfaction I shall derive
   from seeing my enemy get what's coming to him. (ll. 47–52)

None of the gods encountered so far, in any of the Greek playwrights, reveals such a personal level of vindictiveness, but Greek myth is well stocked with similar examples. It is more alarming to find it in a god, not because we expect anything morally superior from a Greek god, but because the power they have to exercise is so much greater: and the lack of a conscience unassailable.

At the other end of the play, a messenger brings news of how spectacularly effective Theseus' curse has proved, and concludes with a fervent declaration of his belief in Hippolytus' innocence 'even if the whole female sex had hanged themselves, and filled a forest with messages' (ll. 1252–3). Artemis makes her entrance at this point to convince the still sceptical Theseus. The king has no option but to believe a god, and one of the functions of epiphanies is to convince doubters. Artemis spares Theseus nothing. Hippolytus was guiltless: she describes Phaedra too as possessing a certain nobility, despite the false accusation against him. She seems to get almost as much pleasure at kicking Theseus when he is down as Aphrodite does in setting it all up in the first place. What she will not do is utter any words of condemnation against Aphrodite:

ARTEMIS. The rule amongst us gods is that none of us
   will interfere with any other. We remain detached.
   Were it not for my fear of Zeus' ruling,
   you should know, I would never have permitted
   my favourite mortal dying in such disgrace. (ll. 1328–34)

Favourite he may have been, but when the shattered body of Hippolytus is stretchered in, she is broadly sympathetic, but 'tears would be unacceptable' (l. 1396). Any revenge she may have in mind will need another occasion, though she is already on to the case. It is an uncomfortable encounter though 'you are very dear to me' (l. 1398), and becomes quite heated when Hippolytus pronounces a regret that a human may not curse a god. Artemis suggests a proper reconciliation between father and son, but cannot stay any longer as she would be defiled by having to watch a mortal breathe his last. She leaves at this point and the final scene does revert to the earth-bound characters. Hippolytus dies in his father's arms.

What are we to make of these antagonistic goddesses and of the ways of life they advocate? Two people have died here. Do they simply represent temperamental opposites, the lesson to be learnt that no one should assume that their way of life is the only one tolerable? Do we feel pity for poor non-combatants caught in the crossfire when a couple of gods are indulging in a private spat? Or dismiss the whole episode as fate, chance, bad luck, destiny, necessity, with or without initial capital letters? This last, 'Necessity', seems to be what everyone has recourse to, mortal or immortal, when they try to probe too closely what the gods have been up to. There is a school of thought that Euripides was as atheist as he was misogynist, and introduced gods on to the stage in order to show they could not exist. Just as many are convinced that, for Euripides, the value of introducing gods as characters, in *Hippolytus* or any other play, has more to do with what they represent than any tangible existence or non-existence. A tragedy such as *Trojan Women* makes the latter seem so, but it does not work that way in *Electra*, *Suppliants* or *Andromache* where immortals make their entrance expressly in order to address mortals. There are various reasons for their intercessions. Who but Artemis wields enough authority to convince Theseus he was wrong? Who but Apollo could tidy up the muddle at the end of *Orestes*; or other than Athena, tidy up Apollo's muddle at the end of *Ion*? Who but Castor and Pollux or Athena could reconcile Theoclymenus or Thoas to losing their long-time Greek guests: except, perhaps, Athena or Castor and Pollux? Whether or not Euripides would have agreed – and why a writer should maintain an unwavering theological standpoint throughout his life, God alone knows – all these dramatic gods need to be viewed within their immediate dramatic context.

Bacchae is more important in this than any other single play, Dionysus' contribution being unlike any other divine intrusion in tragedy.[1] He delivers prologue and effectively epilogue, has two major scenes in between, and has by some way the longest role. The play is about him and what he stands for in a way that does not apply to any other god figure in Euripides. Dionysus may be part-human, part-divine, but the combination has emerged with a different balance to that found in Heracles and Helen, or Castor and Pollux. His birth and origins 'sewn in the thigh of Zeus' form part of the background to the play, disputed by everyone one way or another: his grandfather, Cadmus, founder of Thebes; aunts Agave, Ino and Autonoe; and cousin, Pentheus, the present king of Thebes. Teiresias, the blind prophet, usually a reliable purveyor of the truth, has a pedantic explanation of the mythical version and Cadmus a cynical take on it (see also Chapter 2, p. 34). Neither god nor prophet, nor anyone else, is wholly convincing in their interpretation of what may really have happened. Such confusion is a part of the dramatic method. Euripides offers in the play a confrontation between a god from a human mother, who has the power of a god and the feelings of a human; and a king who believes in the gods, but not in this god.

The stage situation is confused by Dionysus' decision to disguise

---

[1] The only other Greek play in which Dionysus is a character is Aristophanes' *Frogs*, first performed at the winter festival of the Lenaea in 405 BC. So successful was it that an immediate revival was sanctioned, this taking place probably at the same Great Dionysia as *Bacchae* received its first production – maybe even on the same day.

himself as a man, while deploying his godlike power. The nature of that power and its relation to theatre will be considered later (see Chapter 9, pp. 164–7), but it does mean he can perform miracles, or appear to do so. Apart from Athena's charade in *Rhesus*, other stage gods are satisfied declaring themselves and showing their superiority in terms of what they know about past and future. Their ability to dictate human conduct, as far as is compatible with their fellow gods, is enough for them. The Aphrodite of *Hippolytus* is a spiteful creature who causes the downfall of Hippolytus, Phaedra and Theseus, but none of them gets the chance to plead their cause. At the end of *Bacchae*, when Dionysus returns, no longer in disguise, he confronts Cadmus and Agave, above and aloof from the remains of Pentheus before them. There is a break in the manuscript covering the actual entrance of Dionysus whose speech picks up in the middle of one of those familiar, but unfathomable *ex machina* expositions where some god forecasts the weird and wonderful futures of the affected and afflicted characters.[1] Cadmus has no time for this and interrupts:

> CADMUS. Dionysus, we implore you. We admit that we were wrong.
> DIONYSUS. Too late. You acknowledge me far too late.
> CADMUS. We know that, but you are too severe.
> DIONYSUS. You offended me, me a god.
> CADMUS. A god should not show passion like a man.
> DIONYSUS. Zeus agreed to all this long ago. (ll. 1344–9)

Cadmus' anguished protest is far more telling than Dionysus' feeble response and it gives some indication of how, at least in this play, the material presence of a god offers a key, not to what the play is about, but to the debate with which the playwright is engaging: between civic and religious authority, the world of the conscious and the subconscious, the rational and the irrational. The role of Dionysus in this is a central one. Familiar as our dramatic culture has been with allegorical figures, from the morality play onwards, slotting in the Greek pantheon should be as easy as accepting on stage any of the characters from classical, or indeed biblical, mythology. In an Athenian audience with a whole range of belief about the actual existence of the Olympian hierarchy, there was probably a frisson of excitement every time a god put in an appearance, especially when, as in Euripides, they are so often subject to awkward questions over their behaviour. Today they may be a means of creating a pattern of

---

[1] He tells Cadmus that he will be transformed into a snake, as will be his wife Harmonia, before leading an army to sack Delphi, being punished for that and ending up, thanks to Ares, in the land of the Blessed.

existence in which human attitudes and responsibilities can be raised and argued over: they also invite interrogation of the whole nature of power and how it is used.

This is not the whole debate. It moves into a different dimension when the gods are used as an excuse for human behaviour and it is to the idea of divine madness that we must now turn.

8 SANITY, MADNESS AND RESPONSIBILITY

Orestes, Heracles, Bacchae, Electra

When Helen enters to talk to Electra at the end of the prologue in *Orestes*, in transition, as it will turn out, between mortal and immortal status, she seems to be more dizzy than divine:

> HELEN. Electra, daughter of Clytemnestra and Agamemnon,
>   and, after all this time, still a virgin, how are you,
>   you poor dear, you and that brother of yours,
>   the pitiful Orestes who slew his mother?
>   There is no likelihood of my suffering pollution
>   from talking to you. I blame Apollo myself.
>   I am sorry about what happened to my sister, though,
>   Clytemnestra. After I sailed off to Troy,
>   though why I did that – madness, sent by some god –
>   I never saw her again. Yes, I'm sad about what happened to her. (ll. 71–80)

The off-hand manner in which Helen absolves herself of responsibility for her 'bolting' with Paris, may have had some comic intent and is drastically at odds with what others think of her actions. A more familiar defence might have been that, if Aphrodite promised Paris the most beautiful woman in the world to pick her as the winner in the celestial beauty competition, and she, Helen, was the most beautiful woman in the world, she could hardly be blamed for fulfilling divine will. The extent to which individuals could be held accountable for their actions is a major issue in the tragedies of Aeschylus and Sophocles, principally because of the intervention of gods in human activities.[1] In Euripides, this intervention takes a number of forms from being little more than an excuse for bad behaviour to the result of temporary insanity. The nature of the dividing line between the two becomes more cogent, rather than less so,

---

[1] Apollo's directive to Orestes to avenge his father's death is explicit. The god himself successfully undertakes the case for the defence in *Eumenides*. The Greeks accept without contention that Athena is the cause of the hero's brainstorm in *Ajax*. The play's argument revolves around whether, after committing suicide, he should be given due honour for his past achievements or abandoned without burial for the attempted massacre of his fellow soldiers.

in our world, with greater understanding of mental health but a more highly cultivated blame culture where the simply feckless will find anyone else answerable rather than themselves.

The eagerness of so many in *Hippolytus* to absolve Phaedra from her part in her stepson's death may be the result of Aphrodite's unashamed use of her as an agent when it is Hippolytus she really means to destroy. When Phaedra is first brought out on her sickbed, she reveals a mix of symptoms. She has no strength in her muscles (l. 199); she cannot tolerate the weight of a headdress (l. 201); she longs to drink spring water and lie in a meadow (ll. 209–11). In moments she wants to behave as a huntress inspired by Artemis (ll. 215–20 and 228–31), while sounding more like a bacchant, under the influence of Dionysus. The Nurse describes her as *paraphrôn* (l. 232), 'out of one's right mind'. Phaedra picks it up almost as a cue: 'I was mad, brought to my knees by the decree of a *daimôn*' (l. 241).[1] This difference between the will of some hostile god and the vaguer involvement of some dispassionate entity reads almost like the difference an accused might make between genetic tendency and mere bad luck. Phaedra's cool, almost detached statement about the nature of love is included in full elsewhere (see Chapter 10, pp. 178–9). The Nurse's advice to Phaedra is to give in. The Chorus sings an ode about *Erôs*, sexual desire personified, and the need to respect him, however destructive.[2] But if Phaedra's love is an obsession, a madness, sanctioned by a vengeful goddess, there are different questions to be asked about the madness that makes her not only commit suicide, but leave a message accusing of rape the man who has rejected the Nurse's advances on her behalf: or the madness that makes a father curse his son because of such an accusation, knowing such a curse will prove fatal.

A different kind of insanity haunts *Heracles*. At first sight the playwright seems to return to a Sophoclean model, but there is a strongly Euripidean structure and a wholly Euripidean resolution. The play opens with Heracles' wife, Megara, three of his young sons, and Amphitryon, the hero's earthly father, 'the one who shared his wife with Zeus', as he disarmingly introduces himself in the prologue. They are in Thebes, the city founded by Cadmus and where the protracted saga of Jocasta,

---

[1] *Daimôn* is a difficult word for which to find any English equivalent. 'Fortune', 'Fate', 'Destiny', 'the Deity', all seem loaded terms which introduce some different concept. 'Demon' is misleading, and leaving it as a transliteration seems the best solution (see Walton, 2006, pp. 99–101). Orestes uses it when justifying himself to Menelaus in *Orestes*.

[2] *Erôs*, Eros or the Roman, Cupid, is usually portrayed in art as some sort of chubby child with a mini bow and arrows which he aims at the hapless. This is an image fostered by the notion of romantic love from the Hellenistic period. For ideas at the time of Euripides on love as a kind of madness there is still no better place to look than Plato's *Symposium*.

Oedipus and his children/siblings will later be played out to its bitter end. For now it is where Heracles married Megara, daughter of the king of Thebes, and volunteered to undertake twelve labours to help his father win back the throne of Argos from Eurystheus. Hera, for the usual reasons of antipathy towards the results of her husband's amours, augmented here, it is tempting to suggest, by the tactless pun on her name for this particular bastard, has helped in devising the missions impossible, eleven of which Heracles, with death-defying exploits, has overcome. The twelfth and last seems to have been one too many, a visit to Hades to bring back to earth Cerberus, the three-headed dog which guards the gates of Hell. In his absence, Lycus has killed Megara's father and usurped the throne. He now intends to secure his position by slaying the entire family of Heracles who have taken precarious refuge at an altar, with only the clothes they stand up in and no food.

This is not a detached prologue and, as Amphitryon finishes his summary, Megara joins in, blaming unspecified gods for their current distress: 'We're not exactly insignificant' (l. 63), she protests peevishly. The children keep asking where their father has got to – Amphitryon's a man: why does he not do something about it? Amphitryon tries to reassure her, but Megara is not much use in a crisis. Nor are the most decrepit Chorus in any Greek play who totter in, propping one another up with difficulty while recalling their glorious pasts.

If this seems, and not for the first time, to border on pastiche, the arrival of the evil Lycus to debunk Heracles' exploits reinforces such speculation. Amphitryon can only retort with a spirited, if hardly compelling, justification of bows and arrows as weapons of war and a few toothless insults. Lycus responds with instructions to his servants to go and fetch a cartload of oak logs from Parnassus, so he can burn all the suppliants to death. He then directs a few threats at the Chorus to which they do not take kindly and fiercely respond – the man is an immigrant! How dare he go calling them 'slaves'? Megara begins to assess the situation more realistically, believing the best they can hope for is a dignified death. Amphitryon, chastened too, asks Lycus to kill Megara and himself first so that they do not have to witness what happens to the children. Lycus grants Megara permission to take the children indoors and dress them for their execution before departing himself. Amphitryon follows up with an outburst against Zeus:

> AMPHITRYON. Oh, you are quick enough to sneak into men's beds
> and secretly have their wives against their will.
> But you have no notion of saving flesh and blood.
> God, are you? You have the morals of an imbecile. (ll. 344–7)

A long choral ode follows, one of the longest in any Euripides play, before Megara and the children return, dressed for burial. Suddenly the melodramatic opening scenes do not seem so funny. Megara's farewell to her children is moving and Amphitryon's address to the Chorus impressive.

Then melodrama promptly appears to reassert itself. At the critical moment, unannounced, though perhaps not unanticipated, in marches Heracles. Before you can say Eleusinian Mysteries, he has found out what Lycus has been up to, given a quick résumé of his own recent adventures and dispatched everyone off stage, the little boys trailing behind him, clinging so tight 'I'll just have to be the boat and tow my dinghies in behind me' (ll. 631–2). It is such a charming image that it seems all must turn out well. Finishing off Lycus takes little time and the Chorus sing a song of delight, praising the gods for sorting the good from the bad and rewarding them accordingly. As in all proper melodrama the interests of justice have been duly served.

But this is not melodrama: this is Euripidean tragedy, and at its most tragic. To the surprise of the Chorus two figures suddenly appear above: gods from the machine, perhaps, to tie up ends. Iris introduces them:

> IRIS. You are looking at Madness, daughter of Night,
>   old men, and I am Iris, messenger of the gods.
>   We mean no harm to your city. We have one target only:
>   the man they call son of Zeus and Alcmena.
>   He was protected, until his labours were complete.
>   Hera and I could not touch him. Now they're over,
>   and Hera wants blood, children's blood. So do I.
>   So, Madness, daughter of darkest Night,
>   show hard heart and inflict on his mind the nightmare
>   of infanticide. Home in, under full sail.
>   Make him dance, skimming his boys across the Acheron
>   to Hell. Then he'll appreciate the wrath of Hera.
>   And mine. Without his punishment what are we gods?
>   Men would rule and we would be nothing. (ll. 822–42)

Madness (*Lussa*) is reluctant to obey: 'I take no pleasure in afflicting mortals' (l. 846). An extraordinary dispute ensues between god and personification, paralleled only elsewhere by the confrontation between Apollo and Death in *Alcestis*. In *Alcestis* Apollo argues for life. Iris argues for death. Despite all the protests of Madness, Iris overrides her in the name of Hera and requires her to perform her function. All Madness can do is protest: 'Let the Sun bear witness, I act against my will' (l. 858), and alleviate the worst so that Heracles is unaware of what he is doing until his attack has passed. But she is still Madness and goes about her business:

MADNESS. There! He's in the traps, shaking his head,
eyes rolling, Not a word, but the eyes,
gorgon-like, revolving in their sockets.
Panting now, like a bull at the charge,
he roars his summons to the spirits of Hell.
Soon I'll have you dancing to my tune of terror.
Back now, Iris, to Olympus, on your dainty feet,
while, all invisible, into Heracles' house I seep. (ll. 867–73)

Such an abstract scene, a theatrical evocation of a psychotic episode, does have echoes of Sophocles' *Ajax*, but is in every way made more horrible by how it is framed and the manner in which it is incited.

Amphitryon, inside, can do nothing. Nor, outside, can the Chorus, beyond accompanying the mayhem, dancing their own dance, 'A dance, without the thyrsus or joyous drum of Dionysus [...] scarlet, not of the trampled grape, but spilled blood' (ll. 889–92). Eventually, a Messenger emerges with all the ghastly details of what he has seen, almost too dreadful to describe. Heracles' insanity was initially outlandish – 'We servants didn't know whether to shake with laughter or terror' (l. 950) – rapidly turning to pure horror as he mistakes his own children for those of Eurystheus, and slaughters them, one by one, in vile reversal to the promise made by Lycus. Then he turns on their mother, Megara. Only the intervention of Athena, who strikes him senseless, saves Amphitryon from a similar fate.

Euripides spares the audience little. The bodies are wheeled out, Heracles lying among them, tied down and still unconscious. As the shattered Amphitryon grieves, Heracles starts to come round, disorientated, unaware of where he is and with no recollection of what has happened or why he is tied up:

HERACLES. Father, why are you in tears? Covering your eyes?
I'm your loving son. Why are you so distant?
AMPHITRYON. My son. Yes, you're still my son, whatever you've done.
HERACLES. What have I done? That could make you cry?
AMPHITRYON. Enough to make the gods weep.
HERACLES. That sounds ominous. What are you talking about?
AMPHITRYON. If your wits have returned, see for yourself.
HERACLES. What's happened? Has my life changed somehow?
AMPHITRYON. If you've stopped raving like a Bacchant, I will tell you.
HERACLES. I haven't the faintest idea what you mean.
AMPHITRYON. Let me look at you. Closely.

HERACLES. Like a Bacchant? I don't remember. Anything. (ll. 1111–22)

Amphitryon gently confronts his son with the evidence of what he has done, as, later, Cadmus in *Bacchae* will coax back his daughter Agave from the crazed state in which she tore her son to pieces, believing him to be a lion. Heracles has only moments to take in the enormity of it all before Theseus enters, the friend who shared his escapade to Hades and owes to Heracles his return home. Though the rest of the play is taken up with the aftermath, all serves to accentuate the play's unusual rhythm.

Theseus, after hearing of the treachery of Lycus, has arrived to assist Amphitryon, only to find the place littered with dead bodies. At first he fails to see Heracles, collapsed on the ground, head covered by his cloak, but Theseus immediately suspects the hand of Hera in what has happened. He tries in some way to restore Heracles' sense of dignity. No blame is implied for what Heracles has done: nor is Madness as an entity mentioned, not even by the Chorus who witnessed her appearance and took part in the devastating dance of insanity which overtook the whole dramatic action. For the last three hundred lines of the play, from the entrance of Theseus, the Chorus say nothing beyond a concluding couplet after the bloody tableau is withdrawn and the main characters exit. Most of the dialogue is between Theseus and Heracles, with Heracles having two major speeches, Theseus one.

Heracles' first speech is included later in its entirety (see Chapter 10, pp. 176–7), primarily as a piece of unusual self-analysis, especially from a character whose central purpose in life so far has been as a man of action. Putting a new perspective on a familiar character is a Euripidean trademark, but seldom in such an extreme fashion. Theseus uses Heracles' insights to dissuade him from taking his own life. His catalogue of the misdemeanours of the gods, for none of which do they see fit to resign from Olympus, almost returns the play to comedy. It is a calculated speech which ends with the offer of a visit to Athens for purification and some reinstatement of Heracles' status as a saviour of mankind. Heracles, in another lighter moment, suggests that he had never personally set much store by these tales of the gods and put them down to malicious insinuations by playwrights. He agrees to Theseus' proposal, asking, in addition, only that his friend comes and gives him a hand to get the damned dog (Cerberus) back to Argos. He bids a tender farewell to his father, with the promise that he will return to conduct his burial when the time comes.

The shifts in mood in *Heracles* are startling as the action of the play veers from predictable to unpredictable, from comic to tragic, from sanity to lunacy. If we are looking for a pattern – and where would critics be were it not for pattern – this is a walking example of Aristotle's *peripeteia*, reversal of expectation. Directors and actors need them too: it is moodshifts that give a play a performance shape. In another way it is a complex theatrical evocation of the onset of mental illness and a demand in the most acute of circumstances for sympathy for the sufferer. *Lussa*, the reluctant agent of Heracles' temporary insanity, is a personification of a condition recognised elsewhere as typical of anyone out of control, from the berserker in battle to various forms of the frenzied, from fanatic to rabid to erotomaniac.

The word 'madness', as opposed to the allegorical figure in *Heracles*, is used in a number of Euripides plays, among them *Bacchae*, where a principal character, or rather several of them, lose their 'sanity' at the direct intervention of a god. A chameleon of a play which could claim discussion in any chapter in this book, *Bacchae* offers parallels between what Heracles and Agave suffer, but in *Bacchae* the state of mind of the afflicted is far more widespread and manipulated than the sudden psychosis that is *Lussa*. *Lussa* is invoked, but not until late in the play.

When Pentheus has retired into the palace in *Bacchae* to dress himself as a woman, Dionysus, still in his human guise, addresses the Chorus, devotees of his religion though unaware of his identity:

> DIONYSUS. Straight into the trap. Where he will find,
> oh my women, his Bacchants and a death sentence.
> Dionysus, close at hand, now it is up to you.
> We will pay him out, but first befuddle his wits,
> make him mad. Never in his right mind
> would he put on a dress. Possessed, he will. (ll. 847–53)

The phrase 'make him mad' has the literal meaning of 'instil into him a light-headed *lussa*'. So *lussa* here is a sensation that Dionysus controls, not an agent of Hera, as in *Heracles*. After Pentheus returns, in drag, to be mocked by Dionysus, the two of them leave to confront the cruel end the god has planned for the king. The Chorus then sing a short ode in which they urge the 'swift hounds of *Lussa*', as though an entity, to stir up the women against the '*lussôdê* [afflicted by madness] spy' (ll. 977–81). The strongest emotions, passions and instincts take on a personality in Greek tragedy, those in particular that are the cause of disaster or that trigger human failing. What is particular to the *Bacchae* is the nature of this 'madness' which Dionysus both controls and exemplifies. Dionysus' weapon is delusion. His revenge on the women of Thebes is an aspect of his own nature:

DIONYSUS. I have driven them mad.
  Homes abandoned they roam the mountains,
  out of their senses, deranged. (ll. 32–4)

The ecstatic Chorus who have accompanied him are nothing to do with
the women of Thebes who are up in the mountains. They are Asian
followers whose open hostility to anything Theban is to a surprising
extent tolerated, apart from a passing threat from Pentheus after con-
signing Dionysus to the dungeons:

PENTHEUS. Take him down. Put him in the stables.
  He can dance in the dark in there.
  As for this pack of followers he brought with him,
  I'll sell them or set them to work sewing
  instead of making all this din. (ll. 510–14)

The Chorus of Bacchants are a great deal more than a glorified fan club.
As Lussa in Heracles is a personification of Madness, so this Chorus are a
corporate personification of the Dionysiac experience. Their various
choral odes demonstrate the peaceful and pleasurable aspects of the
religion, its enormous appeal to the house-bound and restricted women of
Greece, while showing an aspect of freedom that threatens all Pentheus'
notions of control. Any emphasis on Dionysus as a god of drink or as an
advocate of promiscuity seems to be largely a figment of Pentheus' own
imagination. Teiresias and the Messenger may not be the most convincing
of converts, but much of their description of the religion draws attention
from two perspectives to what is wrong with Pentheus' opposition:

TEIRESIAS. There are two main principles in human experience,
  just two. The first is Demeter,
  Mother Earth, whatever you care to call her.
  She nurtures us humans by the gift of solid food.
  Then there's Semele's son who discovered wine,
  a liquid to match her mortal gift with his,
  a gift to soothe the troubled mind
  and bring us restful sleep, the best of all remedies. (ll. 275–84)

  As for the women, Dionysus does not require chastity,
  but a temperate mind controls any circumstance.
  Take note of that. The Bacchic rites alone
  never lead to corruption. (ll. 313–8)

MESSENGER. They were all fast asleep, stretched out,
  some reclining on pine branches,
  others amongst the oak leaves.
  They were lying anywhere, but decently.

No sign of the drink and music you had led us to expect.
No debauchery in the bushes. (ll. 683–8)

This god, my lord, whoever he is,
accept him in the city.
His power is phenomenal, greater even than I have told you.
He is the one, as they say, who gives us wine
to ease our ills. And without wine, there's no love either,
and precious little else for a man to enjoy. (ll. 769–74)

Teiresias may come over as a figure of ridicule in his Bacchic get-up and
with his pedantic explanation of the birth-myth, but he is closer than
anyone else to understanding the true nature of Dionysus when he talks
of the strange gift of prophecy: 'Bacchants like madmen have method' (l.
299); or identifies as Dionysiac 'soldiers, stricken with panic' (l. 302). The
Messenger tells too of miraculous events among the women on the
mountain: milk, wine and honey conjured from the earth; fawns nursed
at the breast; an attack from which the herdsmen barely escaped; cows
and calves torn to shreds; children kidnapped; fire in the women's hair;
iron weapons bouncing off and doing no harm. Real or imagined, to
witnesses these things *seem* real.

All the characters who encounter these strange events contribute to the
picture of the god's true nature while hinting at the impending outcome
for Pentheus, who is brought down by the very Dionysiac qualities in
himself he tries to deny, the 'madness' which Dionysus unleashes in him.
The encounters between the two revolve around a debate over who is in
his right mind and who is out of it. When Pentheus confronts his
grandfather, Cadmus, intent on going to worship Dionysus in the
mountains, his anger is directed almost entirely at the prophet:

PENTHEUS. Leave me alone. Go on. Dance about, if you must.
   I want none of this foolishness.
   But the man who taught you this folly,
   he shall get what he deserves.
   Go immediately to his seat of prophecy,
   and uproot it. Use crowbars if you have to.
   Leave nothing standing.
   Throw all his trumpery to the winds.
   Perhaps then he'll take me seriously.
   The rest of you, search the city.
   I want him found, this freak who infects our women,
   corrupting our beds. And when you catch him,
   tie him up and bring him here.
   We'll see how he dances when it's raining stones. (ll. 343–57)

Teiresias' response is immediate:

139

TEIRESIAS. Oh, you fool, you do not realise what you are saying.
    Witless before, you're now stark mad. (ll. 359–60)

'Folly', 'freak', 'fool', 'stark mad': such is the language of this struggle for the high ground of reason. The Chorus sing an exultant ode of longing for freedom from restraint and the risk of repression; at the same time, paradoxically, they seem to applaud 'judgement':

CHORUS. What is the result of an unbridled tongue,
    What is the end of lawless misjudgement?
    The outcome disaster, only disaster.
    A life lived in quiet, a life tranquil and sane,
    Preserves the house and keeps it from harm.
    The gods, far-off, still gaze upon mortals.
    Overstepping the mark is simply fool's wisdom,
    Gaining him nothing who chases too far.
    This way lies madness, attempting the summit,
    Ill-judged and ill-starred, crashing to earth. (ll. 386–401)

Such contradictions are part and parcel of the picture being built up of this bipolar religion, soothing but intemperate, gentle but turbulent, controlled but ecstatic:

CHORUS. Our lord, son of Zeus, delights in the feast.
    One goddess I name who pleases him more.
    Giver of comfort, giver of joy,
    Allowing young men to relish their youth.
    The goddess he loves is the goddess of Peace.
    To rich and to poor he brings gifts of enchantment,
    Gifts he bestows through the virtue of wine.
    But the man who declines, by day or by night,
    To live life as pleasure, he loathes.
    Wisdom is keeping apart from the rational.
    Grant me instead what the simple believe. (ll. 417–31)

Most of the quoted passages throughout this book are not from choral odes. Choruses tend to be outside the dramatic line and what they say does not necessarily subscribe to coherent argument. *Bacchae*, as has often been noted, has a Chorus that is unlike any other in Euripides. This is not, as was once suggested, because of any reversion to a more primitive dramatic structure in this late, perhaps last, play. Rather it is an advance, already explored in part in a play like *Heracles*, that allows the Chorus a new flexibility, to have both a reality and a prejudice which the audience may share or reject. The Chorus in *Bacchae* have a central role to play as supporters of the religion and as the religion itself, especially when

Dionysus is present, their leader, though not recognised as their god.

A Servant arrives, after being sent to arrest the 'stranger', an easier job than he had anticipated, but one that has made him decidedly uneasy. This 'stranger' has an aura about him. Pentheus is aware of it too, his interest almost sexual:

> PENTHEUS. So, my friend. You're not so bad-looking, I see,
> not as far as women are concerned,
> which is why you came to Thebes, no doubt.
> Such long hair. Not a wrestler, I think. All down your cheeks.
> Very luscious. How pale you are. Not much in the sun,
> are you? Under cover mostly, hunting Aphrodite? (ll. 453–60)

Pentheus tries to interrogate this intruder, but the disguised god gets the better of him, at least in argument, reducing the king to threatening to cut his hair and confiscate his thyrsus.[1] At the same time Pentheus is clearly intrigued, though he orders him to be taken off to prison. Dionysus escapes, in circumstances that properly belong in the next chapter (see Chapter 9, pp. 164–7), rather than here. Pentheus is mortified, but before he can do anything about it, a second Messenger has arrived to relay the mystifying incidents involving the 'maddened' women of Thebes up in the mountains. Far from changing his mind about how to deal with this outbreak, Pentheus' reaction is to call out the army. The more infuriated Pentheus becomes, the calmer Dionysus' reaction. The turning point in the play comes soon after when Dionysus offers assistance in bringing back the women. So significant is this scene that it is worth including almost all of it:

> DIONYSUS. My friend, listen to me.
> This still could be turned to your advantage.
> PENTHEUS. What can I do? I cannot let my subjects
> overrule me, women at that.
> DIONYSUS. Why should I be plotting anything
> beyond using my skill to assist you?
> PENTHEUS. You're in this together, plotting
> to install this religion here.
> DIONYSUS. Why yes, I am. I am in this together with a god.
> PENTHEUS. That's enough from you. Fetch me my armour.
> DIONYSUS. One thing more! [A!] You would like to watch them
> up there in the mountains, wouldn't you?
> PENTHEUS. Watch them? Why, yes. I'd pay

---

[1] A thyrsus was a staff, decorated with ivy and vine-leaves, with a pine-cone on top, carried as the marker, or emblem, of a devotee of Dionysus.

good money to see what they are up to.

DIONYSUS. Why this great desire to see them?

PENTHEUS. There's no great pleasure in watching women drunk.

DIONYSUS. But you would like to take a look, pleasant sight or not.

PENTHEUS. Yes I would. As long as I was sitting quietly
out of the way among the trees.

DIONYSUS. They'd sniff you out if you tried to watch them furtively.

PENTHEUS. That's very true. Out in the open then.

DIONYSUS. Do you want me to show you a way? Is that what you want?

PENTHEUS. Yes. You show me the way. Now, I want to go now.

DIONYSUS. You'll have to wear a costume. A linen dress, perhaps.

PENTHEUS. Dress? What do you mean? Dress like a woman?

DIONYSUS. They'd murder a man if they saw him, now wouldn't they?

PENTHEUS. Yes, of course. You're right. You've thought it all out.

DIONYSUS. Call it inspiration. From Dionysus.

PENTHEUS. A clever idea. Now what?

DIONYSUS. Come indoors. I'll serve as your dresser.

PENTHEUS. I don't think I've the nerve. Not dressed, like a woman.

DIONYSUS. Do you want a peep at the Maenads, or do you not?

PENTHEUS. A dress, you say? What sort of a dress?

DIONYSUS. A full-length dress. And a wig, a long one.

PENTHEUS. Any other kind of decoration?

DIONYSUS. You ought to have a headband.

PENTHEUS. Is that everything?

DIONYSUS. Yes, except for a thyrsus and fawnskin.

PENTHEUS. Dress up as a woman? I couldn't do it.

DIONYSUS. The alternative is bloodshed and a battle against the Bacchae.

PENTHEUS. All right. I'll do it. I have to see them before anything else.

DIONYSUS. Far more sensible than countering one evil with another.

PENTHEUS. How will I cross the city without being recognised?

DIONYSUS. We'll use quiet roads. I'll take you.

PENTHEUS. Rather than have those Bacchants
laugh at me. I'll go inside. I want to think about it.

DIONYSUS. As you wish. I'm ready, whatever you decide.

PENTHEUS. I'll go then. I'll go and prepare my weapons.
Either that, or do what you suggest.

Exit PENTHEUS (ll.802–46)

This seduction – there is really no other word for it – is the crucial
crossover between sanity and madness for Pentheus, god-inflicted as is the
madness of Phaedra or of Heracles, but taking place before our eyes. The
moment of truth comes after Pentheus' line 'That's enough from you.
Fetch me my armour' (l. 809), and Dionysus responds 'One thing more.
You would like to watch . . .' (l. 810). 'One thing more' is, with apologies,

translator's licence. In the Greek there is the single-letter exclamation '*A!*', then 'You would like to watch them up there on the mountains, wouldn't you?' Something specific happens at this point. One possibility is that Pentheus has turned away to address an attendant, or even begun to make his exit. At any rate, Dionysus stops him in his tracks and begins the process of control, of reeling him in. It is a director's problem, but one that Euripides signals and the reader must not miss. From here on Dionysus applies more pressure, his influence sometimes described as resembling hypnosis or the effect of a drug, transforming the king from puritan to voyeur. Pentheus goes indoors, apparently still unsure of what to do, but Dionysus has no doubts:

> DIONYSUS. We will pay him out, but first befuddle his wits,
> make him mad. Never in his right mind
> would he put on a dress. Possessed, he will. (ll. 850–2)

When Pentheus and Dionysus return, the full extent of Pentheus' delusional behaviour has become clear:

> PENTHEUS. I can see two suns, I think,
> and the seven-gated city of Thebes, double.
> A bull. I think you look like a bull,
> horns on your head? A wild animal.
> Did you used to be an animal? You've become a bull. (ll. 918–22)

This is, in fact, a repetition of the delirium Pentheus reportedly suffered during Dionysus' earlier escape from prison, when he sees Dionysus in his true form, the form in which he will later come back *ex machina*, no longer 'disguised as a man'.

So far the only real harm wrought by Dionysus is to have made Pentheus an object of mockery. Much worse is to follow when he engineers the discovery of the king in his hiding-place, a scene that is described in the vivid messenger speech (see Chapter 10, pp. 188–90). There is a further example of Dionysus' power to delude with the arrival of Agave brandishing her son's head on her thyrsus, the rest of his body being carried in by his grandfather Cadmus. When Cadmus restores her to her senses, it is almost an exorcism as he coaxes her back to sanity:

> CADMUS. Oh my dear. When you realise what you've done,
> your pain will be unbearable. Madness
> is the best that you can hope for.
> AGAVE. What's wrong? Why so solemn?
> CADMUS. Look up. Look at the sky.
> AGAVE. What am I meant to be looking at?
> CADMUS. Is it the same as before, or do you see a change?

AGAVE. It's brighter, perhaps, a little clearer.

CADMUS. And the confusion in your mind. Is that still with you?

AGAVE. I don't understand. I was confused.

   But that seems to be passing.

CADMUS. Can you hear what I'm saying? Tell me if you can.

AGAVE. What were we talking about, Father? I can't remember.

CADMUS. What family was it you married into?

AGAVE. You gave me to Echion, the one they call the dragon-spawn.

CADMUS. Yes, and the son you bore your husband?

AGAVE. Pentheus. Our son is Pentheus.

CADMUS. And whose . . . whose head is that you're cradling in your arms?

AGAVE. A lion's. That's what the hunters told me.

CADMUS. Look at it. No, fully. Look.

AGAVE. What is it? What am I holding?

CADMUS. Look again. Carefully. Now do you realise? (ll. 1259–83)

Madness is not the same in *Bacchae* as it is in *Heracles*, though both are instigated by gods for their own ends. These gods may have an axe to grind and they grind it. But Aphrodite (in *Hippolytus*), Hera (in *Heracles*) or Dionysus (in *Bacchae*) call into question individual responsibility for one's actions. This proves to be one of the most critical debates in Euripides. If Hera instructs Madness to afflict Heracles, does that absolve Heracles from the consequences of criminal action? If a psychotic behaves in a similar way and kills his wife and children, how should society react to protect itself? This was not a new question for the Greeks, nor for their dramatists. Sophocles tackles the same issue in both Oedipus plays: and in *Ajax*. There is a double question. Is Ajax to blame when it was the goddess Athena who sent him mad in the first place, to prevent him attacking his allies? Beyond that, is it as reprehensible to kill a load of sheep as to kill enemies, if he was mad enough to believe it was his enemies that he was killing? In all the examples above, the gods appear simply to isolate and inflate a single aspect of someone's character and drive them into overweening obsession.

Elsewhere, as in the example of Helen in *Orestes* above, the playwright plays on the fact that in certain cases, pleading some god-inflicted state of mind is simply a useful way of ducking the consequences of one's actions. What of Orestes himself in the same play? For the Greeks madness was not a simple affliction: nor was it necessarily a debilitating, or a permanent one. The big question is where personal responsibility can be disowned and personal weakness passed off as god-sent. That means looking at another two plays where derangement appears to have a major part in the plot. Though Helen uses the excuse casually in *Orestes*, the state of mind of Orestes himself, in the first part of that play, is more complicated.

In Electra's prologue she speaks of her brother's condition after the killing of Clytemnestra six days earlier:

ELECTRA. Since that incident, poor Orestes lies in his bed,
    wasting in body, his mind driven in circles
    by his mother's blood. I hesitate to mention
    the goddesses who create such terror, the Furies. (ll. 34–8)

Orestes wakes up, speaking himself, attributing his state initially not to persecution by the Furies, but to fever. Then a sudden vision of his mother and of the Furies hits him. This time it is Electra who tells him that there is really nothing there: it is all in his mind. He raves in delirium, mistaking Electra for one of the Furies while she tries forcibly to restrain him. Abruptly, he returns to sanity. It is an alarming sequence, the result of an act of violence, rather than heralding one. Orestes wonders why ever they decided to kill Clytemnestra, whatever Apollo might have said, when it was not going to bring Agamemnon back, with Electra claiming 'When people are not ill, but think they are, it can be every bit as debilitating' (ll. 314–15). This madness may be less driven by some primitive goddess, she seems to think, than by the mind preying on what has happened: conscience even? When Menelaus arrives he is shocked to see Orestes:

MENELAUS. God, what a sight you are. You look half dead.
ORESTES. You're right. More dead than alive, but alive . . . just.
MENELAUS. That matted hair. You look like a savage, you poor man.
ORESTES. It's what I've done, more than what I look like.
MENELAUS. Dry eyes. The look in those cold eyes.
ORESTES. Nothing is left me. Except a name.
MENELAUS. I wasn't expecting to find you so . . . changed.
ORESTES. It's me all right. Me, the mother-killer.
MENELAUS. I heard. But, please, spare me the details.
ORESTES. I'll spare you. Though the *daimôn* piled trouble upon me.
MENELAUS. What is the matter? What precisely are you suffering from?
ORESTES. Conscience. I know the terrible things I've done. (ll. 385–96)[1]

The mix of theology and psychology is confused in this celebrated passage, perhaps on purpose. There are few issues which so divide people to this day as the extent to which temporary insanity should be treated

---

[1] The Greek here is *sunesis*, a word with a variety of meanings including 'self-awareness', or, in the present context, 'conscience'. As M. L. West pointed out in his edition of the play, the Greeks were becoming aware of the concept before they had a regular word to define it. See also Snell (1964).

rather than punished. If Orestes is suffering from some kind of breakdown, is the source medical or is it religious? Apollo is cited, but only critically, for instructing Orestes to kill his mother. The Messenger who reports the Argive public trial is informative. Diomedes advocated banishment; someone else stoning to death; another man thought Orestes should be awarded a golden crown for killing an adulteress. In the end the Argives decide not to condemn Orestes, Pylades and Electra to death on condition that they commit suicide that very day. Conscience, or no conscience, Orestes makes a rapid recovery and, in no time at all, aided and abetted by the appalling Pylades, is back on the killing trail, prevented from further butchery only by the maligned Apollo.

This is a country mile from the feeble Orestes who havers about in *Electra* trying to avoid her finding out that he is her long-lost brother, if in rather less glamorous guise than she would have wished. There is a case to be made that in *Electra*, Electra is as deranged as any of them, Phaedra, Heracles or Agave: and nothing to do with any god either. She is certainly erratic and a systematic fantasist. She maintains she has only rags to wear when the Chorus have just offered her a dress (ll. 191–2), and then that she has to make her own clothes (ll. 304–8). She talks of her hair being 'soft with combing' (l. 259) when Orestes assumes she is a slave because of her confessedly shaven head (l. 241). She gives a report of Aegisthus' conduct which is at odds with the courteous welcome he gives to Orestes and Pylades (ll. 327–8). When she gets to confront his corpse, she accuses him of being under Clytemnestra's thumb and having married above his station:

> ELECTRA. Then there's your women – no topic for a virgin –
>   so I'll keep quiet, but give you a hint.
>   You pursued women simply because
>   you lived in a palace and were so good-looking.
>   I'd always prefer a husband with rugged looks:
>   no pretty boy for me.
>   A real man's children will be fit to fight,
>   not just to dance in a chorus line. (ll. 945–51. See Chapter 10, pp. 184–6,
>   for the whole speech.)

The play is veined through by Electra's egotism (how many times does she remind everyone in sight she is still a virgin?), fuelled by her loathing of her mother. After an edgy exchange between Orestes and the Old Man over how to deal with Aegisthus, the question arises of what to do about Clytemnestra. 'How can I kill both of them at once?' asks the apprehensive Orestes (having just been told that Clytemnestra had not accompanied her husband to the feast). And Electra, silent since the incongruous 'recognition' scene, has the answer: 'I'll take care of Mother' (ll. 646–7). Head-to-head with her daughter, Clytemnestra seems defensive, ashamed of her past and keen to assist after being told Electra has had a child. Electra cannot resist putting the boot in:

ELECTRA. As soon as your husband was away,
   even before he'd ordered your daughter killed,
   you were sitting in front of your mirror,
   combing your lovely golden hair.
   Any woman who dolls herself up
   once her husband's left home
   should be written off as a whore.
   Anyone who shows her pretty face outdoors
   is up to no good.
   You were the only woman in Greece
   to celebrate a Trojan victory.
   If Troy was losing, your expression clouded over,
   because you didn't want Agamemnon back. (ll. 1069–79)

Are we expected to believe this or is it a further example of her obsession? Electra's self-absorbed reaction to the murder of Clytemnestra eventually induces a reproof from Castor. Such behaviour may or may not be a form of personal madness, untouched by divine hand. Electra is at the very least as nasty a character as any in Greek tragedy, and nobody blames a god for that.

Euripides offers his lengthy catalogue of violent action, as do Aeschylus and Sophocles in plays like *Eumenides* or *Ajax*. He explores as they do, motive, action and justification. But the questions he asks are asked in a different way, and are ones for which we still seek answers. How acceptable is a defence of 'temporary insanity'? How can it be identified when agreement may be divided between the expert witnesses of prosecution and defence? What are the levels and boundaries of diminished responsibility, between lawful and unlawful killing? How do we judge or defend ourselves against a Heracles, an Agave or a Medea; or an Orestes or Electra, for that matter? How do we define forms of legal redress, and address all manner of antisocial behaviour from the thoughtless to the drug-induced?

Any message these plays had for their first audience is likely to have become muddied after such a length of time. That does not matter. What matters is that *Heracles*, *Hippolytus* or *Bacchae* are plays that have provided a whole series of different messages to different generations of scholars, critics and audiences. They are as protean as *Hamlet*, as *The Master Builder* or as *Waiting for Godot*. The great plays reach out to any and every age. The rest of this book is devoted to Euripides' modernity.

III. THEATRE THEATRICAL

9 PLAYING THE GAME: ILLUSION AND REALITY

Hecuba, Suppliants, Ion, Rhesus, Helen, Bacchae

In the previous eight chapters the plays of Euripides have been approached from a number of different perspectives, all of which have their origins within the preserved texts (in translation), but are linked by some dynamic present-day application. Such associations will not necessarily reflect the central concerns and interests of Euripides in his own time. They may not accurately reflect a political and social culture alien in many ways to our own. They do provide some bridges to the past: they do suggest that the greatest theatre from any period has survived through offering complex metaphors for the broad processes of living, the bones of a source culture on which is grafted the flesh of contemporary reception. Themes of family, marriage, children, women and class furnish parallels and ring bells. Human personality in all its savage, stubborn or merely selfish aspects is easily recognisable. Dramatic structure and rhythm point to the vicissitudes and relentless unfairness of life and lives, whether the cause be hostile gods, human frailty or simply being in the wrong place at the wrong time.

In the next three chapters, I want to turn to the theatrical qualities of Euripides' writing that argue for his central position in the world's dramatic diet. Two of these involve the dramatic material he supplied, albeit for male actors in masks, which transfers readily into the mouths of actors without masks, male and female; and the contribution Euripides may have made to the stage technique of a selection of major playwrights from the last hundred or so years. First, though, there is the question of identifying in more detail the manner in which Euripides revolutionised and defined the very marrow of the theatrical experience.

In 1938, Johan Huizinga, a Dutch professor of History, published a book entitled *Homo Ludens*.[1] The argument that 'play', with its special

---

[1] 'Man at Play' is a reasonable translation of the Latin title, but fails to do justice to the range of Huizinga's line of reasoning. The book was originally published in English as *Homo Ludens* in 1949, with a new edition from Paladin in 1970 which included an introduction from George Steiner that is both grudging and patronising.

rules and limits, was a fundamental animal instinct to be found in many aspects of human activity was familiar, as any major study of cultural history and its practice can show.[1] From Plato onwards, and the Ionian philosophers before him, the nature of play and pretence within human experience were both identified and, in Plato's case, shunned, as having far too dangerous implications for an orderly society. Shakespeare, Calderón, Molière, Strindberg, Pirandello, O'Neill, Brecht, Pinter, Friel, Stoppard, a hundred other playwrights, have investigated ways in which theatre can engage with its own medium. As the early part of this book has incidentally shown, in Euripides truth and untruth, reality and falsehood, reason and unreason battle it out in the 'game of life'. Huizinga's singular achievement was to trace the prevalence of 'play' as both a serious and a teasing aspect of behaviour: play as a central facet of all social association. The breadth of his reference is daunting, ranging through cultural phenomena of widely differing countries and periods, their origins, rules and applications, to see what is shared or what overlaps. He looks at law, warfare, philosophy and poetry, assessing the function of 'play' in establishing rules and procedures. The crossover from everyday life to culture as a reflection of that life dexterously moves to the world of social *mores* and fashion, including theatrical performance, from the Renaissance to modern times.[2]

Much of Huizinga's basic argument is rooted in the culture of ancient Greece where his own understanding of the nature of ritual is both a help and a hindrance. Only drama in Greece, he asserts, was truly linked to play, but he then suggests that 'The Greeks, the very people who created drama in its most perfect form, applied the word "play" neither to the drama itself nor to its performance' (p. 167).[3] This he attributes to Hellenic society being so 'profoundly imbued with the play spirit that they never saw it as anything worth commenting on' (p. 167). His understanding of that spirit, however, owes more to the world of the Cambridge anthropologists than to any sympathy with the nature of theatrical performance:

[1] The Russian director, Nikolas Evreinoff (his preferred spelling), wrote a series of short monographs in the years immediately before the Bolshevik Revolution which were eventually published together as *The Theatre in Life*, in which he proposed that there was no aspect of living (or dying) which was not 'theatre'. See also twentieth-century writers in anthropology, linguistics, philosophy and cultural theory, among whom Richard Schechner (1988) has perhaps been the most influential for Theatre Studies.

[2] Huizinga's previous *The Waning of the Middle Ages* (1924) had provided a platform for V. A. Kolve's matchless study of play and game in medieval drama (1966).

[3] The Greek verb *paizô* (from *pais*, 'child') does cover sport, mockery, dancing, playing an instrument and simply having fun.

> As to the mood in which the drama was performed it was one of Dionysian ecstasy and dithyrambic rapture. The player, withdrawn from the ordinary world by the mask he wore, felt himself transformed into another ego which he did not so much represent as incarnate and actualize. The audience was swept along with him into that state of mind. (p. 168)[1]

This perception of Greek tragedy as Dionysiac, or Dionysian, in performance, something ecstatic, in a manner similar to how the Indonesian dance drama of the Barong, Rangda and Rarong involves trance and possession, now seems at odds with our understanding. The plays that survive, tragedy and comedy, are dominated by a broad political content ('political' in the sense of 'to do with the *polis*', the city-state) that required attention and an awareness of the medium in which they were being presented. The acting was masked, which may give a nod in the direction of ritual, but the text was novel on every occasion suggesting something immediate rather than familiar (as is the nature of ritual). Greek tragedy and comedy, by the latter years of the fifth century BC were dramatically complex and theatrically sophisticated. Huizinga seems not to be able to make a connection between what he says here and his earlier point that:

> The very existence of play continually confirms the supra-logical nature of the human situation. Animals play, so they must be more than mechanical things. We play and know that we play, so that we must be more than rational beings, for play is irrational. (p. 22)

If it is in the irrational that the true Dionysus is to be found, then it is in the exposition of the nature of life itself revealed through the dramatic experience, implying a more comprehensive notion of theatre in ancient Athens than Huizinga was able to encompass. This is certainly the territory where the search can now focus on what makes Euripides a playwright for the modern age.

Polytheistic societies have deities with functions. The Greek system of gods developed over a period of time and involved a progress through myth from primordial chaos to a world that could be comprehended, contained and, in some part, controlled. Before tragedy was 'invented' tales of the gods, their relationships and concerns were relayed mainly through oral poetry and certain ritual patterns which had proved themselves efficacious. The Olympian hierarchy covered all areas of natural and creative life, often – because there were so few of them – multi-tasking, as the modern buzz word has it, with a variety of

---

[1] The Greek word for 'actor' is *hupokritês*, 'answerer'; *drama* is 'something done', *theatron* 'a seeing-place' or 'an audience'.

responsibilities. Poseidon was god of horses, god of the sea and god of earthquakes, not because horses, sea and earthquakes had anything much in common, but because they represented something powerful and something of which it was sensible to be wary. Aphrodite had her work sufficiently cut out with the lust portfolio for there to be little time left for anything else, but Athena oversaw domestic crafts, such as weaving, alongside a responsibility for being patron of the city of Athens, dressed in armour a bit like Britannia. For better or worse Zeus presided over all. Alongside the Olympians was a sub-world of spirits, of places and elements, satyrs, Muses, nymphs and dryads. The assumption was not that any of this pantheon would provide guidelines for how to live your life, but that they were aspects of that life which needed to be comprehended, accommodated or appeased if life were to have some recognisable purpose and shape.

Shape it may have gained, but under control it was not. Reality refused to be so regulated. There was still some force at large, something between chaos and caprice. Life stubbornly refused to be either predictable or rational. The answer was to incorporate a god of the irrational. Dionysus, an eastern deity and a peripheral figure in Homer, joined the Olympian twelve and Hestia, goddess of the hearth, had to make way for him. Dionysus' functions were multiple, if harder to pin down than those of the other Olympians. Anything that could not be attributed to any other cause, or any other god, was the broad brief, but it included the whole gamut of the supranatural and what was beyond normal explanation. Wine was a part of this, the subconscious was a part of it. Exercise of exceptional strength was another: the miraculous fitted here. The experience of theatre gave a structure and an embodiment to such experience and when tragedy and comedy were invented, it was in honour of Dionysus that the dramatic festivals were held, an extension of ecstasy ('standing outside oneself'), for the individual to inhabit a place where anything could happen, a dangerous place.[1]

Huizinga may have felt that the nature of tragic performance was at odds with the sense of game, but even if 'play' in Greek is not generally used to describe a 'drama' the language of playing is widespread in Greek writers. One reason for Plato's rejection of drama and theatre was its association with 'fiction' and 'lying'.[2] It involves a kind of cheating, potentially both immoral and dangerous, which manipulates the emotions and creates spurious ones on behalf of people who do not exist.

[1] See also Nietzsche, *The Birth of Tragedy* (1872, trans. 1967).
[2] See in particular Plato, *The Republic*, 3 and 4, and *The Politics*, 8.

But there can be a different sense of cheat too. Hermes, as we saw earlier, was an inventive and precocious god. He was also, among other things, with his winged sandals, the god of dreams and the god of cheating. To cheat is common theatrical parlance in English-speaking theatre, with far less of a pejorative dimension than the word ordinarily implies in everyday discourse. Actors will cheat their way upstage, designers cheat a set or property to make it appear real rather than to be real. Musicians will cheat a passage of music to fit a tempo or a vocal line. Directors faced with some problem of the stage picture will cheat it. Part of the object is to tinker with space, or anything that fills space, in a manner that serves the performance: but without an audience being wholly aware of how they are being manipulated. This is the language of stage presence, of the illusionist, of the hairs on the back of the neck. It is part of theatrical craftiness, or just the craft of theatre.

Euripides has a fondness for toying with an audience, shifting between what they know and what the characters know, by playing on expectation, almost defying an audience to anticipate how a situation will be handled. The satyr play *Cyclops* dramatises one of the more fantastical adventure episodes from the *Odyssey* in which Odysseus and his crew land in Sicily seeking help and provisions. The Chorus of satyrs warn Odysseus that the Cyclops, the single-eyed giant Polyphemus, will be more inclined to eat them than feed them. Eventually several of Odysseus' men are killed and devoured, but Odysseus (the crafty Odysseus) gets the Cyclops drunk and blinds him before making his escape. This is a farce, more *Jack and the Beanstalk* than *Hecuba*, but the satyr play was an aspect of tragic submission, however comic; a distorted view which invited an anarchic look at how and why tragedies were staged. The audience are invited in *Cyclops* to accept that the Chorus open the play driving a flock of sheep into the cave (director's problem); that the ogre, who can hardly be much bigger than an ordinary actor, is capable of overpowering a group of war-hardened veterans; that Odysseus can sneak outside to tell everyone what has happened inside the cave, but that his men (those that are left) cannot use the same escape route.

But the game, as Huizinga points out, is more often serious than comic. Whenever Euripides begins a play with a god or gods, *Alcestis*, *Ion*, *Hippolytus*, *Bacchae* and *Trojan Women*, they always give away the outcome, sometimes with significant detail. Apollo in *Alcestis* forecasts the arrival of someone [Heracles] who will remove Alcestis from the clutches of Death. Hermes in *Ion* not only anticipates the plot but most of the turning points within it, admitting how much of it Apollo has asked him to stage-manage. Aphrodite claims responsibility for the upcoming deaths of Hippolytus and of Phaedra. Dionysus positively gloats over what he has already done and what he has in mind for Pentheus and Agave. Only in *Trojan Women* are the two gods more concerned with punishing the Greeks after the play is done than in giving away the plot. But then, *Trojan Women* does not really have a plot in the conventional sense, merely heaping atrocity upon atrocity, shock after shock, with little surprise. Suspense in all this group of plays depends less on catching the audience unawares than in the fine detail of the execution. It is a calculated method of work, one which Euripides signals, but one on which he relies only occasionally in the plays we have. His playmaking includes a variety of approaches.

One play involves a supernatural character with a wider vision than that to which the rest of the cast are confined. *Hecuba* opens with the appearance of a ghost, an *eidôlon*, Hecuba's son, Polydorus, lying dead on a beach but 'unmourned and unburied'. He has freed himself from his body and for three days has been flitting in the sky above his mother, but unable to reveal himself to her. Hecuba, as she will soon divulge, has had a dream. Dreams are one of the means whereby the dead communicate with the living in most mythologies, including the Old Testament, and have proved invaluable in the drama: like oracles, and like oracles, they are not always reliable and can be hard to interpret. Much of the dramatic action of *Iphigeneia Among the Taurians* is the result of a dream of Iphigeneia's which she construes as disclosing the death of her brother, Orestes. What the dream actually portends is, unusually, never revealed. Were it not for her misreading, the longest unbroken scene in Greek tragedy, more than six hundred lines while she fails to recognise her alive and present brother, could have been comfortably reduced: but then, how many great plays could have been polished off in Act One with a single action or a single sentence.

Polydorus does not appear responsible for Hecuba's dream, but his dramatic function is unusual. Euripides cannot take credit for first dramatising a ghost, a device which goes back to the earliest surviving Greek tragedy, Aeschylus' *Persians*. In *Hecuba* the ghost of Polydorus provides information about his death which could not have been forthcoming in the first part of the play from any other source. It is a play without a god because none is appropriate. The only living character who knows what happened to Polydorus is his murderer, Polymestor, who arrives too late to fill in all the necessary detail. As the opening of a play the scene is both startling and effective, while establishing, as prologues do, whether delivered by mortal or immortal, the point of entry into the story. This ghost has another function, though, a subtler one. Part of the horror for

Hecuba is the news that her daughter Polyxena is to be sacrificed. She is to be sacrificed, as Polydorus tells the audience, at the tomb of Achilles. She is to be sacrificed to a ghost, but this ghost, unlike Polydorus, does not appear, except in the report of a vision and a disembodied voice. Surprisingly too, it is the Chorus entering in disarray, who provide the information, functioning as a messenger might, or Talthybius who reluctantly reveals what is to happen in the similar situation in *Trojan Women*.[1] In *Hecuba* the turning upside down of the queen's world is reflected in a similar disruption of dramatic norm. The Chorus never for a moment question the report that Achilles himself, or rather his ghost, appeared standing on his tomb demanding a prize. There was debate among the troops about what should happen, but Odysseus won the day arguing in favour of the human sacrifice. So far there has been no direct mention of Achilles being a ghost. Eventually, when Odysseus confronts Hecuba and she volunteers to die in her daughter's place, Odysseus coldly replies:

> ODYSSEUS. It is not your death, old woman, that Achilles'
> ghost [*phantasma*] required of the Greeks, but hers. (ll. 389–90)

The use of a different word for the dead Polydorus (*eidôlon*) and the dead Achilles (*phantasma*) may have no special significance, but *phantasma* does have a secondary meaning of 'dream' or 'vision'. The theatrical crux comes when the wrapped body is brought in by a maidservant (another curious reversal) for Hecuba to uncover, believing it to be the sacrificed Polyxena. Instead, it is the drowned Polydorus, victim of betrayal by Polymestor. From this moment Hecuba's nature too is turned inside out, as we have seen, and the play heads for its bloody finale with Polymestor's blinding and the murder of his children by the women inside the tent.

There is a theatrical coup, but of a different kind, in *Suppliants*. The play is largely a dramatised debate between politics and humanity. The mothers of the fallen champions who tried to capture Thebes now want the chance to bury their dead sons. The logistics of exactly who these mothers must be and how there are enough of them to make up a proper Chorus has to be set aside as a conundrum or a casting issue.[2] When the arguments are over, Evadne, widow of Capaneus, one of the seven, and daughter of Iphis, who is also present, appears 'on a rock, like a bird,

---

[1] The speaker/s – there appear to be split single voices – describes herself/themselves as a *kêrux*, the word used for a formal messenger (*Hecuba*, ll. 98–152).

[2] The 'seven' appear to include the mother of one hero, Amphiaraus, who was swept alive into a chasm opened by the gods. They should also include the mother of both Polyneices and Eteocles, Jocasta, who is probably dead, and anyway, highly unlikely to be asking for help against her native Thebes (see also p. 92).

above my husband's funeral pyre' (l. 1046). She is apparently wearing her wedding dress. After some farewell remarks to her father, she hurls herself into the flames. As no one has so much as mentioned Evadne before she arrives, it is difficult not to treat this as a gratuitous piece of action to enliven a wordy play, but there's no denying it is unexpected.

The original setting for *Suppliants* that makes such a leap possible is not clear. Evadne's description of being 'on a rock' may mean little more than that she was standing on the roof of the *skênê*, the stage-building which, by the time of Sophocles and Euripides, seems to have been a fairly flexible construct, either a modification of some basic but movable stage units that allowed for an iconic representation of place, or a fixed building which made itself versatile by the use of an upper level, stage door or doors, and pieces of stage machinery. Of these latter the undisputed ones are the *mêchanê*, the stage crane, for entrances *ex machina*, and the *ekkuklêma*, a wheeled platform for the display of tableaux such as Heracles and his children (*Heracles*) or the murdered Clytemnestra (*Electra*). In several plays Euripides seems to draw particular attention to the details of the setting, or what the characters claim it to be. The delight displayed by members of the Chorus at the temple they find in Delphi has already been noted (see Chapter 4, pp. 66–7). In several other plays something similar seems to be happening. When Orestes and Pylades enter at the end of Iphigeneia's prologue in *Iphigeneia Among the Taurians* they know of the hostile reception accorded to foreigners and have come to make a recce prior to forcing an entry into the temple of Artemis to steal her statue:

> ORESTES. Pylades, have we arrived at the Goddess' shrine? [...]
>   Is this the altar where Greeks are slaughtered?
> PYLADES. The bloody hair left there should be proof enough.
> ORESTES. Are those trophies hanging up there on the walls heads? (ll. 69–74)

> You see these high walls
> surrounding the shrine. Should we use ladders?
> Won't we be seen? Or should we use crowbars
> and break into the shrine? (ll. 96–100)

Seeing that eventually they are not going to do anything of the sort, the detail is effectively window-dressing. So too in *Electra*, but there to a purpose. Electra has been married off to an independent Farmer who lives near the border. As far as Electra is concerned it is a 'peasant cottage' (l. 207). 'Suitable for a ditcher or a cowman' (l. 252), agrees Orestes. However humble, when the Farmer arrives and meets the two strangers who have brought news of Orestes he invites them in. Later, it is the scene of Clytemnestra's murder when Clytemnestra pays a visit in response to an appeal for help from Electra who claims to have given birth to a child. How far the setting would have reflected the state of this Farmer's home is a matter of conjecture. To Electra it is certainly not a palace. More importantly, it is not *the* palace.

A pattern is beginning to emerge here, something metatheatrical, in which the playwright loses no opportunity to draw attention to the practicalities of staging. *Ion* seems to confirm what the playwright is up to. The admiring survey of the stage décor when the Chorus make their first entrance is intriguingly matched by a later off-stage setting. Not knowing that Ion is her real son, Creusa has plotted to poison him. A Servant arrives as messenger to tell her everything has gone wrong. He describes the scene in some detail, as messengers often do:

> SERVANT. When Xuthus, Creusa's husband, had left the shrine
> he took this newly-discovered son of his to a feast
> and to a sacrifice he was organising in honour of the gods.
> Then he departed to where the Bacchic fire leaps up
> to sprinkle blood on the double peaks of Dionysus,
> and make belated offerings for the birth of a son.
> But first he left the following instructions:
> 'You stay here, my boy, and have the carpenters
> construct a tent, bounded on both sides. [...]
> The young man followed his instructions, building up
> the scaffold of a tent on pillars, though without walls as yet,
> and taking into account the position of the sun at midday
> and at sunset. He measured off a square, a hundred foot
> each side, ten thousand square feet in all,
> according to the mathematicians, to have room
> to invite the whole population of Delphi to dinner.
> Then he brought sacred coverings from the store
> and draped them over the frame. Everyone was amazed. (ll. 1122–41)

There follows an intricate description of the decoration on the curtains. What seems odd about this description is not so much the detail, irrelevant to the Servant's narrative and the play's plot, as the language in which it is couched.[1] It may be a description of the building of a temporary banqueting hall, but it uses the same terminology as for building a temporary theatre. The words translated here as 'tent' are *skênê* (in the plural) and *skênôma*, the terms used for the scenic background of

---

[1] This uninterrupted Messenger speech is over a hundred lines long, making it as long as any in Greek tragedy. A good half is simply scene-setting.

Euripides' theatre. The original settings in the Theatre of Dionysus were all 'temporary' in that they could accommodate a Farmer's cottage or a palace; the Cyclops' cave, a prisoners' tent or a temple: variations created by wooden pillars and drapes. Even theatres in some areas appear to have been constructed to take account of the position of the sun in relation to audience or players. The Servant's whole account reads like a witness view of a piece of set-construction, all the way up to the 'amazement' of the audience, a *thauma*, a word used on a number of occasions to describe extraordinary events in *Bacchae*.

Ion is riddled with theatrical association and even jargon. Some of the play's ambiguity, and Ion's scepticism, revolve around the props introduced to effect the recognition of Ion as Creusa's son. Their newness is suspicious and has to be accounted for. The Old Man has to 'palm' the poison to get it into the cup at the right time, only one of a whole series of deceptions – people pretending to be what they are not, or believing they are something they are not. Status and the acquiring of status have a sense of belonging to the world of casting rather than politics. The gods themselves appear to be taking roles and the Pythian Priestess gives the impression of being thrown into the action to avoid embarrassment to Apollo.

In a theatre of masks, as in any form of visual art, the level of belief is created through the link between a capacity to absorb convention and the human instinct to respond to it viscerally and emotionally. Brecht believed that this response should be one that dealt, not in sentimental acquiescence, but in an impulse to change. Euripides seems to show, I would suggest, that there is a different aesthetic at work here, one more complex than that of any manufactured a hundred years later to suit an Aristotelean formula. The theatre is exposed for what it is, a distorting mirror, an alternative universe, a second life: the game to show the reality that lies below the surface. Euripides' contribution to this was to be the first to create a realism of truthful response within artificial circumstance.

This is never more true than in the much-maligned *Rhesus*. Here is a play all of whose action is conducted during the hours of darkness, from the entry of the Chorus of sentries to alert Hector that something is amiss to Hector's misguided final lines to them:

> HECTOR. Guard dismissed. Wake the allies.
> Let them arm. Yoke up the chariots.
> Don't douse the torches till the trumpet.
> As soon as that sounds, I'll launch an assault
> on the Greek defences and set fire to their fleet.
> With this new day I mean to bring
> freedom to Troy. (ll. 986–92)

There are very few plays which take place completely in the dark. Peter Shaffer's *Black Comedy* (1965) opens with the curtain going up on a scene of complete darkness. Two characters start to talk, drawing attention to how the set looks and apparently moving freely about the stage: the audience get the uncomfortable feeling that some awful technical disaster has overtaken the production but that the actors are determined to carry on regardless. After four pages in the pitch black, all the lights snap up and we see, for the first time, the two characters, in a freeze for a couple of seconds before the man says 'God! We've blown a fuse!'[1] The audience realise that this was all intended and the play continues, having established the convention that, for the duration of this play, the characters cannot see when the audience can, and vice-versa. It is a fine comic conceit, but one that depends on artificial light.

One of the standards of the Beijing Opera is a play called *Where Three Roads Meet*. It is a slight piece: indeed it was originally no more than a curtain-raiser which proved so successful when Chinese acting troupes first toured to the West that it was rewritten and found a major place in the repertoire. Both versions revolve around travellers at an inn who become involved in a fight, the fight being conducted in what is for them the pitch dark, but is for the audience full light.

The possibilities are exemplified in the Jacobean theatre. In Thomas Heywood's *Iron Age II* (1613), whose plot concerns the sack of Troy, we find the stage direction '*Enter Agamemnon, Menelaus, Ulisses, with souldiers in a soft march, without noise*'. And, two pages later: '*Pyrhus, Diomed and the rest, leape from out the Horse, and, as if groping in the darke, meete with Agamemnon and the rest*'.[2] In other words, the players are required to *act* darkness.

That some action should begin before dawn is a commonplace of Greek tragedy and comedy, including Euripides' *Electra*, *Hecuba*, *Ion* and *Iphigeneia at Aulis*, though the opening scenes in all of these other Euripides plays indicate the time of day as a marker for the play's action rather than as a dramatic device. In *Rhesus* it is different. Darkness, in full light, dictates the play's action and, if the audience are not prepared to go along with that, then the playwright is sunk. There are expedients, of course. Lamps or torches can be carried, but all the characters constantly stumbling over one another would quickly pall even in a comedy. The multiplication of theatrical situations compensates for that. Odysseus recognising Athena by her voice and the goddess's subsequent pretending

[1] Peter Shaffer, *Black Comedy*, in *White Lies, Black Comedy*, New York: Stein and Day, 1967, p. 53.
[2] Thomas Heywood, *The Second Part of the Iron Age*, ll. 378–80.

to be Aphrodite to fool Paris contribute, but relying on darkness exaggerates the possibilities while serving constantly to remind an audience of the rule they have accepted.

More than any other tragedy *Rhesus* is a play of intrigue. It is set in a soldiers' world (see Chapter 5, pp. 82–5), but it is also, at least in classical experience, an experiment in theatre. The key issues are disguise, pretence and transformation. A god pretends to be another god; a Chorus pretend to be sentries; Dolon, the curious volunteer, agrees to act as a spy and, accordingly, puts on a wolfskin, to fool the enemy.[1] Not that it does: Odysseus and Diomedes not only 'unmask' him, but torture him into revealing the Trojan password, 'Phoebus', before killing him. Armed with their password the two Greeks sneak into the Trojan camp, intent on killing Hector too. When they cannot find him, Diomedes suggests they aim for Aeneas or Paris: 'How will we ever find them in the middle of the army in the pitch dark?' retorts the pragmatic Odysseus. 'It's suicide' (l. 587). The line is one of several planted reminders to an audience and presages the scenes that immediately follow.

Athena diverts the Greeks and they do away with the newly arrived Rhesus instead of Hector. They are almost caught and it is night-time that saves them. The scene speaks for itself, waiting only for a director who will balance the comic with the sense of adventure generated by the playwright:

> *Enter* ODYSSEUS *and* DIOMEDES, *and the* CHORUS. *It is still dark. Shouting and confusion.*

CHORUS. There they are.
 After them. After them,
 Get after them. Cut them down.
 Who's that? Who is it?

 Look. There they are.
 Over there. That's them, I tell you.
 Thieves in the night.

 They've woken the whole camp.
 Here they are. I've got them.
 Over here. Everyone, over here.
 They're caught.

 Now, you. What's your company?
 Where've you been? Where're you from?

[1] The disguise as a wolf is not quite as bizarre as some critics have found it. Wolves were, it would seem, not unfamiliar scavengers in and around the trenches of First World War battlefields.

ODYSSEUS. That's my business. You'll pay with your life for this.
CHORUS. Password. Or this sword in your gut.
ODYSSEUS. Was it you killed Rhesus?
CHORUS. You're the assassin, I think.
ODYSSEUS. Calm down, will you? Look, come over here.
CHORUS. Put a knife in him. Kill him. Kill the pair of them.
ODYSSEUS. Hold on a minute.
CHORUS. Not likely.
ODYSSEUS. I'm a friend. Don't kill me.
CHORUS. What's the password?
ODYSSEUS. 'Phoebus'.
CHORUS. Right. Hold your weapons.
   Those men. Do you know where they went?
ODYSSEUS. We saw them. Heading that way.
CHORUS. After them. Track them down.
   Shall we raise the alarm? (ll. 675–91)
    Exit ODYSSEUS *and* DIOMEDES.

The Chorus soon discover their mistake but by then it is too late. Pure theatre.

Two romance plays offer examples of an extension of the argument, if more briefly than they deserve: *Alcestis*, dealing with a resurrection and a restoration, and *Helen*, effectively doing the same. The final scene of *Alcestis* is one of pure theatre, with the audience fully aware of the revelation that is about to take place. After the funeral of Alcestis, and Admetus' realisation of what he has lost (see Chapter 3, pp. 46–57 and Walton, 2007 b), Heracles brings back a veiled figure, claiming to have won her in an athletic competition and asking for Admetus to take her into his own home:

HERACLES. I entrust her to your right hand and yours alone.
ADMETUS. My lord, you compel me against my will.
HERACLES. Do not shun her. Nay, present your hand.
ADMETUS (*without looking at her*). Like a man cutting off Medusa's head.
HERACLES. Are you holding her?
ADMETUS. I'm holding her.
HERACLES. Then take care of her and in future you can say
   What a generous guest the son of Zeus has proved.
   Take a look. Now, tell me if she resembles your wife a little.
   And change sorrow into happiness.
ADMETUS. What can I say? If this be magic,
  Let it be an art lawful as living.
  Strike all that look upon with marvel.[1]

---

[1] Some of these lines have been poached from *The Winter's Tale*, V, iii.

Is this truly my wife I look upon,
Or some god's illusion sent to mock me?
HERACLES. She's real. It is Alcestis.
ADMETUS. Some phantom, maybe, stolen from the dead.
HERACLES. I'm not some necromancer you welcomed here. (ll. 1115–28)

The game here is that the audience are well aware of who the concealed figure is, having already been primed by Apollo and by Heracles himself. The manner in which Euripides negotiates between what an audience know, what they may suspect and what comes as a complete surprise, is one of the features of Euripides' dramatic writing that feeds into Menander. In Euripides there are scenes when the audience are both better informed than the characters and less so.

Helen is another exercise in recognition and restoration, but one that probes more deeply into the nature of reality and of stage reality (see also Chapter 4, pp. 75–8). The play is positively marinated in theatre. Menelaus is constantly embarrassed by his costume. Helen is sceptical about her semi-divine origins, but cannot avoid the implications of having a doppelgänger supplied by the gods. Who or what is real? Every story seems to have two versions. Teucer passes on the news to Helen, who he thought looked like Helen, but now realises cannot be: though she is. 'But, enough of stories' (l. 143), he says, '*halis de muthôn*'.[1] 'I don't want to double my trouble' (l. 144). Theonoe, the king's sister, has second sight, but has an eccentric and partial way of employing her gift. People in *Helen* are constantly fooling other people: Teucer, Menelaus, Theoclymenus. At the end, when Theoclymenus has lost his bride-to-be and Menelaus with her, not one of Helen's brothers comes to sort him out but two, Castor and Pollux. *Helen* is not a confusing play, it is a play about confusion. Such a sentiment leads finally to a play that is both, *Bacchae*, the biggest mystery of all.

Critics have long appreciated that this last play has a theatrical frame of reference which, alongside its tale of the death of Pentheus for opposing the Bacchic religion, celebrates Dionysus as god of the theatre in its detail and structure.[2] The play is interlaced with references to disguise and cross-dressing, miraculous events, illusions and delusions, frantic music and dance, ironies and a sense of play, cruel play which leads to as shocking a scene as even Euripides ever wrote. Dionysus announces within half a dozen lines that he intends to spend most of the

[1] *Muthos* is the Greek word for 'plot'.
[2] See especially the Introduction to Dodds' edition (1944); Winnington-Ingram (1948); Kirk (1970); Castellani (1976); Seidensticker (1978); Foley (1980); Segal, C. P. (1982);

play in disguise. The first two characters to appear after the prologue are Teiresias and Cadmus, the blind prophet whose words so often presage disaster in the troubled history of Thebes, and the city's respected founder, both in costume as Bacchants. Agave and her sisters are dressed the same. Pentheus is almost as much in disguise as king of Thebes as when induced to masquerade as a woman, persuaded to turn into an actor and wondering whether he looks more like his aunt or his mother. He is overcome by the power of Dionysus. The Messenger who brings news of Pentheus' death begins his account of the journey to the mountains as involving just Pentheus and the Messenger, and that stranger [Dionysus] as the '*pompos theôrias*' (l. 1047), a difficult phrase that could be translated as anything from 'escort to the spectacle' to 'our guest director'.[1]

Throughout the play, what takes place is not quite what it seems, to such an extent that the audience is left in some doubt about what happens in front of their eyes, never mind whether or not the accounts of messengers are wholly reliable. Seeing what is not 'real' is a central part of the religion's fascination. The hold that Dionysus has over devotees and opponents alike is a simple counterpart to the appeal of theatre. There is one sequence which especially concentrates on this parallel. No scene in Greek tragedy, I suspect, has been more hotly argued over.

After the first confrontation between Dionysus and Pentheus, the king dispatches the 'stranger' to jail and himself escorts him indoors. The frenzied response of the Chorus is interrupted from off stage, the only occasion in Euripides when such an off-stage voice is not an indication of extreme distress:

DIONYSUS (*within*). Ahhh, Bacchae. Hear me, Bacchae. Hear my voice.
CHORUS. Who? Where? A shout. A cry.
  His. Whose? Calling. Who?
DIONYSUS (*within*). Hear me, Bacchae! I call again.
  It is I, Bacchae, son of Semele, son of Zeus.
CHORUS. Dionysus. Master. Dionysus. Join us.
  Lead us, Dionysus.
  Welcome! Bromius, Dionysus!
DIONYSUS (*within*). Come, earthquake, come.
  Shake the world to its roots.
CHORUS. Help us. Look. Look there. There.
  The palace of Pentheus. See how it shakes.

---

[1] There have been twenty-five translations of *Bacchae* alone published in the last hundred years as well as numerous adaptations and new versions. Unsurprisingly, the extent to which the play's theatrical overtones have been emphasised has varied widely.

Shaking to pieces. It falls. The palace is falling.
Dionysus within. Worship him. Worship.
We revere. We revere.
Look at the stones, the pillars, the beams.
Bromius cries and the whole house replies.
DIONYSUS (*within*). Lightning bolt! Flashing fire!
Engulf and consume all Pentheus' domain.
CHORUS. See how it blazes. Blazing fire
Licking over the holy tomb. Over Semele's tomb,
Semele, blasted by thunderbolt, thunderbolt of Zeus.
Fling yourself earthwards. Fling yourself fearfully.
Cast down your bodies. Fall down, you Maenads,
All-overturning, Zeus' child breaks the house down.
   Enter DIONYSUS.
DIONYSUS. Women, outsiders. Were you so terror-stricken
You fell to the ground? I do believe you may have noticed
How Dionysus wobbled the palace of Pentheus.
Up you get. Calm yourselves.
There, that's better. (ll. 576–603)

Precisely what happens here is one of the play's many mysteries. Is this an earthquake? Is the palace struck by lightning? Does it catch fire? Or collapse? Does the god manifest himself off stage, in his true form, only to re-enter in his disguise? And, if so, what aspect of his power is he exercising? The power to destroy, or the power to hoax, to beguile, to delude?

If this chapter is an accurate appraisal of Euripides' interest in the processes of theatre, then Dionysus is showing off. He is not the god of earthquakes; nor does he have at his disposal a bolt of lightning like the one with which Zeus reluctantly killed his mother. What he does have is the power of suggestion, the power to 'cheat'. He chides the Chorus for their concern about his welfare, outlining how he made Pentheus believe he had tied him up when it was a bull that he secured, set the palace and the tomb on fire (or did he?), and created a *phasma*, an 'apparition', before razing the palace to the ground (or did he?). The returning Pentheus has a lot to complain about, but the fact that his palace is in ruins is apparently worth not as much as a mention.

If this is intended as an example of the impact of theatre, like the introduction of Madness in *Heracles*, or the cheating of Death in *Alcestis*, then the Chorus have simply succumbed to suggestion. They appear not to detect an earthquake until Dionysus points it out to them, or to notice the fire until he informs them of it. What, then, is the nature of this theatre of Dionysus? To be carried away to a different level of belief is certainly an aspect of it. To create an imaginary version of life is another, through which to stare into the Gorgon's face, like Perseus and, via a mirrored reflection, find the strength to cut off her head and survive.[1]

Dionysus, it seems to me, creates his earthquake as Prospero creates his storm in *The Tempest*, as a demonstration of the playwright's imaginative power. Last plays bring out strange qualities in playwrights where the art they have practised is recognised as an aspect of the real life away from which they are beginning to move. But the whole of Euripides is a celebration of the art he has advanced beyond all reasonable expectations. The whole company are here, the whole theatrical set-up: Medea, the consummate actor; Ion, the competent stage-manager; Helen, the wardrobe mistress; Priestess of Delphi, props mistress; the Choruses as singers and dancers, and as audiences; Polydorus, the theatre ghost; Messengers who relay what is happening in the world outside; the celestial producers up there in the gods, counting their currency and demanding, as often as not, a happy end where none seems plausible; the mask-makers and the mask-wearers; the walk-ons and the stars; the leading men and leading ladies; the juveniles; the character actors; the understudies, the brazen and the superstitious (was there a taboo, I wonder, on quoting the 'Theban play'?); and a cast of dupes, deceivers, hypocrites, survivors, witnesses, martyrs, killers, victims, fantasists, prophets, clowns and lunatics. And presiding over all, Dionysus, the great and whimsical director, who has a taste for being worshipped but who carries in his hand the careers and reputations of everyone with whom he comes into contact.

---

[1] Perseus was the Greek hero who managed to cut off the head of Medusa whose gaze turned people to stone. He succeeded after borrowing winged sandals from Hermes, a helmet of invisibility from Pluto and a polished shield from Athena to serve as a mirror. See also Nietzsche (1967), p. 39.

10 GREAT ROLES

Medea, Alcestis, Heracles, Hippolytus, Iphigeneia at Aulis, Hecuba, Electra, Helen, Bacchae

Today's stage actors often complain that modern dramatists, whatever other virtues they might possess, have stopped writing great roles. Whether this is to be attributed to dramatic teeth being cut on scripts for television or the fact that, whatever the Oscar halls of fame appear to suggest, film performances are made or marred by directors and editors, the outcome is the same. There have been few stage playwrights of the last fifty years who have created characters as iconic as Peer Gynt, Lady Bracknell, Uncle Vanya, Mother Courage, Willy Loman, Blanche Dubois or Claire Zachanassian.

Greek tragedy does offer such parts: Prometheus, Clytemnestra, Oedipus, Antigone, Electra, Ajax, Heracles, Medea, Phaedra. If the list, however extended, favours female roles, though the actors were always male, then that reflects the preferences of the Greek tragedians for situations in which women were more prominent than ever they were in the public life of Athens. Greek actors were masked and the plays as we have them reveal a text for physical acting which depends heavily on the set speech and balanced dialogue: but there are entry points. Reconciling this apparent structural rigidity with the expectations of a modern audience is just one of the challenges facing today's translators and directors, as much as actors, but Euripides seems almost to anticipate the predicament through subtlety and nuance and by playing off an audience's complicity against their expectation. Sometimes he allows them to be ahead of the game, sometimes ensures that they are behind it. In any period that is the playwright's craft.

Actors approach a major role in different ways. Some will choose to leave everything to the rehearsal process where interaction with director and the rest of the cast offers the opportunity to try on, and try out, a range of approaches and possibilities. Others will prefer to do their major preparation in private, their homework, where they can address personal development within a role in their own time and fashion. In a speech of some length, whether narrative, introspective, declamatory or polemic, there are through-lines to be discovered, changes of direction, pauses for thought, points of emphasis, moments of quiet and moments of intensity.

In other words, and this applies equally to an entire role, they discover its pace. In Euripides this pacing is always there to be identified. Many of the major set-pieces that define character in Greek tragedy are sited in speeches of considerable length, sometimes balanced one against another in forensic style. This is a product, perhaps, of the original masked tradition, but such speeches, especially in Euripides, are crafted with an unerring sense of dramatic rhythm. Given a sympathetic translator, and that means one who can, by theatrical means, create links between past and present, the great roles of the classical stage ought to prove as amenable to the contemporary actor's scrutiny as are those created by Shakespeare, Ibsen, Chekhov or Miller. Simply, Euripides knew how to shape a speech as he knew how to construct a play. Great playwrights are a joy to work on because the search is always for what is there, not a means to cover up what is not.

Dissecting any single role would take longer than the present study warrants. Instead, the aim will be to pick out a number of speeches, briefly identify their context – a fuller version can be found in the Appendix – and invite the reader to consider what they offer to an actor. Choosing ten was not easy. Too much had to be jettisoned, too many plays ignored entirely. The fact that all nineteen of the Euripides canon have received some attention earlier tempered the concern. Inevitably the choice revolved round more familiar material. Male characters had to be represented as well as female. There needed to be a place too for Messengers, whose lengthy accounts of what they have seen elsewhere add such a surprising range of emotions and responses, from dismay to euphoria. All Euripidean characters listed as 'Messenger' are male (thirteen of the tragedies have at least one), but there are other 'messenger speeches' delivered by named characters, male and female, who report on off-stage events.

1. *Medea to her children*, Medea, *ll.* 1019–80

When Medea first declares to the Chorus that she means to kill King Creon and the daughter whom Jason plans to marry, she includes Jason in her plans: 'A day for me to transform the father and the daughter/ And my husband, three enemies into three corpses' (ll. 373–4). The Chorus have already sworn their compliance and take this with surprising equanimity. Not until after her first encounter with Jason and the timely appearance of Aegeus offering her an unconditional refuge, does she decide upon or, at least, reveal her full purpose: 'But what comes next, ah, there are the tears./ I have to kill the children. My children' (ll. 791–2).

This time the Chorus are appalled, but she claims there is no alternative. The children become irrevocably implicated in the murder of the Princess when Medea gives them the poisoned dress and coronet to take to the palace. The Tutor returns with the boys to say that the gifts have been accepted and the Princess has agreed that the children may stay in Corinth. She dispatches him indoors but keeps her sons with her:

MEDEA. Oh my boys, my boys. This is your city,
   your home where I must leave you motherless.
   Poor me.
   I leave for somewhere else, a refugee,
   without the joy of watching you grow up,
   of seeing your prosperity, wives, weddings,
   wedding-torches, wedding-beds.
   Selfishness, I suppose. It seems so pointless.
   Why did I ever cherish you?
   Why bear you at all?
   Difficult labours. Painful births.
   You have these hopes – I did, poor fool that I was –
   of growing old cossetted,
   with loving care to help you from this life.
   It's everyone's ambition. All gone.
   A lovely dream. Without you
   I'll live out my time fretting, embittered.
   You'll never set eyes on your mother,
   never again. You'll have moved on.
   No, don't. Don't look at me like that.
   Is that a smile? Will you ever smile again?
   What am I to do? They melt my heart.
   Dear friends, when I look at their faces,
   my willpower turns to water. I can't do it.
   Change of plan. I'll take them away.
   What point in wracking their father's heart
   if I break my own twice over?
   No! Never! Change of plan.
   And yet . . .What's the matter with me?
   They'd laugh at me, my enemies, for going soft.
   Coward! Coward! I must be strong.
   No weakening. No relent.
   Children! Indoors!
     Exeunt children.
   Now. Any of you who does not share my mind,
   go about your business. My hand will not weaken.
   No! No, you can't. Medea, you can't go through with this.

You poor fool, let your children go.
They'll live on with you. Be happy.
No! Never. By all the hounds of hell,
I'll not hand over children of mine
for my enemies to scorn and spit upon.
They have to die. And if that's going to happen,
I bore them so I have to do the killing.
All settled. There's no escape.
The coronet's on her head. The bride princess.
I know it. The dress is destroying her.
And I am starting on a terrible journey,
Terrible for my children too.
I have to speak to them.
Children, come here! Come here,
     Re-enter children.
Give me your hands.
Beautiful hands. Lovely faces.
I love you. Wish you well. But not here.
Your father appropriated 'here'.
A kiss. A hug.
Such sweet breath children have. Soft skin.
Off you go now. Go away!
     Exeunt children.
I can't look at you and do this.
No! Passion drowns my judgement,
passion, the force of destruction.

Medea does not leave at this point, but stays on stage to greet a messenger from the palace. Her speech is easy enough to follow. All that she reveals to the children is that she and they must be parted. After sending them indoors she calls them back for a last farewell, before transforming herself into their murderer; almost weakens, but steels herself in the knowledge that, whatever happens next, the children will be held in part responsible and put to death. People publicly changing their minds happens less often than might be expected in Greek tragedy. Medea's vacillation has no parallel even in Euripides, but is all the more powerful for showing her as much victim as murderess.

2. *Messenger to Medea and the Chorus*, Medea, ll. 1136–1230

Soon after Medea's farewell to her boys, the Messenger arrives from the palace with a description of the death of the Princess and her father,

Creon. What he has to say changes nothing. The decisions are made and all he does is provide a delay to confirm what has been anticipated. It is still, at nearly a hundred lines, one of the most prolonged and horrific such speeches in Euripides. The Chorus, despite their support of Medea, are almost as appalled as the man himself, who seems in deep shock from what he has witnessed:

> MESSENGER. When the children, those two boys of yours,
>   arrived with their father at the palace,
>   they found it all decorated for the wedding.
>   And us servants, who used to take your side,
>   we were delighted. Word had got around, you see,
>   that you and your husband had been reconciled.
>   People shook the boys' hands or patted their golden hair.
>   I was so excited I followed them to the women's rooms.
>   The princess – she has our allegiance now, not you –
>   she turned her gaze on Jason lovingly
>   until she caught sight of the two children,
>   then turned away and wouldn't look at them,
>   white as a sheet, furious to find them there.
>   Your husband tried to placate her, saying,
>   'Don't be angry. Look. They only want to love you.
>   Your husband's friends must be your friends too.
>   They've brought presents. Accept them.
>   and ask your father to reprieve them. For me?'
>   The moment she saw the finery, she couldn't resist,
>   and gave in to all he asked.
>   Father and sons were barely out the door
>   before she snatched the gorgeous dress and put it on,
>   then the gold coronet, checking in the mirror,
>   giggling at the reflection of herself,
>   as she arranged her curls round the tiara.
>   Up she jumped from her dressing-table
>   and prinked around the room on her little white feet,
>   glorying in her presents, again and again,
>   posing, checking from head to heel.
>
>   Then, all of a sudden, something dreadful.
>   She changed colour, staggered,
>   started to shiver, managed, just,
>   to fall on the bed, not on the floor.
>   An old servant mumbled a prayer,
>   assuming some god-frenzy or a fit.
>   But one look at her mouth –
>   froth was bubbling from her lips,

eyes rolling, colour drained.
No prayer then but a howl.
Someone ran for her father,
Someone else for the new husband,
to tell them what was happening to the bride,
the corridors echoing with running feet.
For the time it takes a runner to complete a lap
she lay mute, poor woman,
then started up with a scream, eyes tight shut,
ravaged by a double torture.
From the golden crown about her hair,
flames shot, burning, ghastly.
But on her body so soft, the soft dress
that the children brought began to feed.
She rose, ran, on fire,
tossing her head every which way,
to shake off that halo. But it clung.
The more she shook, the more it flared.
Seared to the bone, at last she fell to the ground.
A father might recognise her, only a father.
You couldn't pick out her eyes,
her features. Just blood dripping
from her head onto the flickering flames,
while her flesh, gorged on by the poison,
dribbled off her like gum from a pine.
Horrible. I can see it. No one dared touch her.
We were witnesses. We'd learned.

But her poor father knew nothing of this.
Rushing in he threw himself on her body,
weeping, clinging to her, crying
'Child, poor child, who or what has destroyed you?
Who has turned this old man into a gravestone?
Oh child, let me die too.'
Eventually his sobbing began to subside
and he started to try to get up.
But as he'd clung to her, so she clung to him,
like ivy clings to the laurel.
And with her dress he began a ghastly wrestling-match.
As he scrabbled to get to his knees,
she seemed to reach and grab him.
He fought her off and the flesh stripped from his bones.
At last – it took time – the wretched man
succumbed to his fate and gave up the ghost.

173

The corpses lie together, child and father, close.
'Let me die too.' The release of tears he craved.

And your part in this? I've said nothing.
You'll have secured your own escape.
'Walking shadows', that's all we are.
And so-called clever men, the silver-tongued –
I'm not afraid to admit it – pay too. They pay.
Call no man happy. That's what I say.
You might be luckier than your neighbour,
be more prosperous. But happy? Not a chance.

The Princess never appears in the play, nor is the audience given much of an impression of her beyond Jason's claim to be marrying her simply to help his career prospects. What the Messenger implies is someone very young, perhaps a little vain and shallow. Her father Creon though, in his single scene with Medea has demonstrated a ruthlessness, tempered only by his fatal mistake of allowing Medea a day's leeway before retiring into exile. His own death, as horrible as that of his daughter, presents the Messenger with having to cap the first death with an account of the second. The 'ghastly wrestling-match' offers the most graphic of images. Messengers in Greek tragedy (see also 10 below) report on events. They have seldom been directly involved. To try and top the awfulness through an emotive presentation of what they have seen will usually countermand the dramatic shape of the play. The shocked witness is often far more dramatically effective than the weeping carpet-chewer.

3. Admetus to the Chorus after Alcestis' funeral, Alcestis, ll. 935–61

The play's opening on the very day when Admetus was destined to die gives immediate impact to Alcestis' agreement to take his place. During her deathbed scene her husband seems unduly concerned about his own welfare, while she is preoccupied with what will happen to the children once she's gone. Heracles arrives and is cordially welcomed, though kept in the dark about Alcestis' death. The funeral scene with Admetus' father, Pheres, which dissolves into fierce recrimination over whether or not she should have been allowed to die on Admetus' behalf, gives way to Heracles discovering the truth and racing to the rescue. This comparatively brief speech from Admetus on his return from the grave appears to mark a change in him, a genuine awareness, perhaps, of what his wife's death will mean:

ADMETUS. Friends, dear friends, this may seem strange to say.
My wife is luckier in her fate than me, I think.
No pain can touch her any more.
She has a blessed release from all her troubles.
It is I who should not be alive, I who live on time,
less borrowed than ransacked, the bitterer for that.
Till now I never realised, never knew till now.
How can I face the world indoors?
What conversation could I ever again enjoy?
Where am I to turn?
In there lives only loneliness to drive me out.
No one in her chair. Her bed empty.
Cobwebs under the eaves.
The children falling down and crying for their mother.
Servants tearful for the mistress they have lost.

That's indoors. And in public?
There'll be weddings in Thessaly. Crowds of women.
And I'll suddenly see one who reminds me of Alcestis.
Enemies will sneer 'There goes the man who's still alive,
the coward without the nerve to die:
who sold his wife and chased her off to Hell.
Do you call that a man? Condemns his parents
when he couldn't die himself.'
To crown it all, I've lost my name.
Is there anything else to live for, friends,
when I've branded myself a coward?

Though there is still an element of self-pity here, there are also indications that Admetus is beginning to face up to what has happened. The various small instances he cites of what the future holds carry a genuine touch of the true nature of bereavement. If, as seems possible, this is meant to appear a turning point from which Admetus will begin to deserve his wife back, then it is in the detail. The fractured nature of what he says here owes something to translator's licence, though the tone, I hope, is appropriate. What cannot be doubted is that some of the earlier accusations of his father, Pheres, for all their heartlessness, have struck home, and he is beginning, though still egotistical, to see himself and his actions as others may see them.

4. *Heracles to Amphitryon and Theseus*, Heracles, *ll. 1255–1310*

Heracles is a surprisingly underrated play, dismissed too often because of a structure that has been described as 'broken-backed'. The first half involving Heracles' wife and children and their persecution by the usurper, Lycus, gives little indication of what is to come. After 500 lines Heracles arrives at the critical moment and deals with the tyrant. An ode of celebration from the relieved Chorus is interrupted by the sudden epiphany of Iris and Madness. In a bare 150 lines since the death cries of Lycus a Messenger has appeared to describe how Heracles, driven insane on the instructions of Hera, has murdered his family. Heracles, restored to sanity, has an extended scene with his father Amphitryon and Theseus who offer sympathy, Theseus in particular trying to prevent him committing suicide. Unusually, Heracles has two extended speeches in quick succession. Either might merit a place here. The first has been chosen, being longer and because it reviews his whole life as a hero:

> HERACLES. Hear me, now. I have listened to your advice
>   and need to make a proper response. I need
>   to make you understand how pointless my life is,
>   how pointless it has always been, from birth.
>   I was born to bloodshed. Amphitryon,
>   the man known as my father, was blood-guilty
>   at the time he married, killer of Alcmena's father.
>   A house constructed on warped foundations
>   condemns its descendants to adversity for all time.
>   And Zeus, whoever Zeus may be, my actual sire,
>   spawned in me a lifelong object of hatred to Hera.
>   Please, old Amphitryon, don't take this amiss.
>   You have always been my proper father.
>   I was still a baby fed on mother's milk
>   when a fearsome, evil-looking snake
>   was sent to throttle me in my cot. Hera sent it.
>   Then there were those many ordeals I had to face
>   when first I grew to manhood. Need I spell them out?
>   All those lions, monstrous Typhons, Giants,
>   Centaurs, half-horse! What about all that fighting?
>   I dispatched a hydra, with two heads, that grew two extra
>   for each I severed. So many labours and dozens more.
>   Finally, when all else had been accomplished,
>   I descended to the very depths of hell,
>   down among the dead, to fetch the guardian of its gate.
>   I brought back to the light Cerberus, the three-headed dog,

to complete my obligation to Eurystheus.
But there was one more mission for me to endure,
a hideous one, to cap the horrid history of our house.
Infanticide. The point of no return.

I cannot live a decent life in Thebes, my beloved Thebes.
Were I to stay, what shrine would welcome me,
what circle of friends? The blackness of my crime
brooks no excuse. Should I leave for Argos?
Argos would be exile. Some other city, then?
Everywhere I will be recognised and singled out,
the target for wagging tongues. Could I face that?
'Isn't that the son of Zeus? Killed his wife, you know,
and all the children. We don't want his sort here.'
A change of circumstance is harder to bear
for the man who was somebody: nobodies are immune.
I can see the day when the very earth would cry out
against my step, sea and rivers forbid my passage.
I'll be like Ixion, for eternity broken on the wheel.
No Greek who knew my good times would approach.
Why live, then? What's the use of a life devoid of purpose,
devoid of dignity? She wins, Hera, wife of Zeus.
Let her dance her triumph, tapping heaven's floor with her shoe.
Her ambition is fulfilled. Is this a goddess to revere?
A husband's lapse, his love for a mortal woman,
provokes her to single out a hero of Greece,
innocent though he was, and annihilate him.

The blend of mythological background and introspection is carefully judged. The challenge to the actor, in the context of the play as a whole, is to manage an abrupt transition from superhero to social pariah. The playwright helps by bringing him onstage, complete with the bodies of his children and his wife. He has been tied up and recovers from his mania only gradually. His attention is drawn to the bodies before Amphitryon lets him know that he is the one responsible. He then sits for some time, face covered, in total silence. Only when there has been sufficient occasion for the horror of the situation to sink in does he reach the conclusion that killing himself too is his only option. The last twenty or so lines of the speech take it out of the specific and mythical circumstances into the despairing world of the fallen and the disgraced.

5. *Phaedra to the Chorus,* Hippolytus, *ll. 373–430*

Phaedra's confession of love for her stepson, Hippolytus, comes only after prolonged questioning by the Nurse. Aphrodite opens the play, claiming responsibility for Phaedra's passion. In the first scene proper Hippolytus, the devotee of Artemis, enters after hunting. Only when he and his servants have gone indoors does news arrive of Phaedra's sickness, so grave that the Chorus of local women and the Nurse fear for her life. When she reveals the cause, the Nurse is initially aghast and may have left the scene.[1] It is to the sympathetic Chorus that Phaedra addresses her first and only major speech, a much more balanced and considered account of her condition, now that her secret is out, than her earlier state of mind might herald:

> PHAEDRA. Women of Trozen, you are residents here,
>   in this extreme outpost of the land of Pelops.
>   Elsewhere, in other times, I have often mused,
>   through the dark reaches of my wakeful nights,
>   on how so many lives end up in ruin.
>   Catastrophe is not inbred in human nature,
>   I'm sure of that. There are plenty of sensible people.
>   We need to consider this in a different light.
>   We're taught how to behave. We know what's proper.
>   Failure to follow such a path is shiftlessness in some,
>   in others flawed priorities, pleasure preferred to virtue.
>   Life holds its many diversions, conversation,
>   taking it easy: but guilty pleasures too. A sense of shame.
>   Shame can work two ways: to the benefit of the family,
>   or as a burden round its neck. In a simple world,
>   the same word would not have more than one meaning.
>   I happen to have the strongest views on this,
>   which no drug could affect or make me change my mind.
>   I want to tell you how I reached this conclusion.
>
> When passion struck my immediate reaction was
>   to endure as best I could. To put up with it,
>   keep everything secret and suffer in silence.
>   The tongue cannot be trusted, quick to condemn
>   the behaviour of others, but liable to create
>   nothing but trouble on its own account.

---

[1] Who is present and who off stage is less clear than usual in this play. Apart from the uncertainty in the present scene, Phaedra may hear all, or part, or nothing at all, of Hippolytus' subsequent tirade against the female sex. One reason may be that there was an earlier version of the play, rejected as being too explicit. Some of the present text may have incorporated elements of the earlier and confused the issue.

My next approach was self-discipline: have the sense
to confront my madness and get rid of it.
When neither approach proved able to master
such passion, my final answer was suicide,
by far the best solution, you'll not deny.
As I would choose to have my virtues known,
I would not wish my imperfections public.
That my situation itself, and even desiring it,
are dishonourable, I'm all too well aware.
I'm a woman, an object of hatred to men, I know.
I curse whoever first disgraced her marriage
by taking strangers to her bed, a contagion
fostered among the upper classes.
And once the nobility condone such behaviour,
ordinary people will quickly follow their betters.
I deplore even more those who parade their virtue,
but secretly enjoy a vicious double life.
Goddess of Love, how can such women
bear to look their husband in the eye?
How can they not live in fear that the darkness
or the walls themselves will not cry out their crimes?

And this, dear friends, is why I have made my decision
to kill myself: to avoid shaming my husband
and my children. I want them to return to Athens,
glorious Athens, free to speak their minds,
and free of scandal from their famous mother.
Awareness of a parent's crimes becomes a prison
for a man, however confident he seem.
One thing alone competes with life itself,
or so they say, and that's an honest heart.
Sooner or later wickedness comes to light,
reflecting the evildoer – as to a young girl
Time will hold a glass. I won't be of that number.

This is another suicide speech, but very different from that of Heracles.
Phaedra's icy control here needs to be seen in the light of seeming close to
death, when wheeled in on her first entrance. Then she confesses her love
for Hippolytus, a declaration which initially shocks the Nurse provoking
Phaedra's decision to kill herself. Her apparent calm in the ensuing speech
conceals the most harrowing emotions and demands a full sense of
subtext in the playing. The threat to her own life is no idle one. After the
pitiless reaction of Hippolytus she will also find she has it in her to accuse
the object of her love of rape and, as a result, will cause his death. There

is a great deal below the surface of what at first reading may seem a remote and almost dispassionate assessment of her situation.

6. *Clytemnestra to Agamemnon,* Iphigeneia at Aulis, *ll. 1146–1208*

The portrait of Clytemnestra found in Aeschylus' *Oresteia* is unremittingly hostile. In *Agamemnon* she is the prime mover in the murder of her husband Agamemnon, the conqueror of Troy, on his return home. The help of Aegisthus seems hardly necessary except to threaten the Chorus when they start to cut up rough. Her excuses, the sacrifice of their daughter at Aulis and his arriving with Cassandra, intent on establishing her in his bed, are stressed less than they might be if a real defence was intended. In *Libation-Bearers*, the second play of the trilogy, Orestes on his return from exile, instructed by Apollo to avenge his father's murder, sees her and her lover as fair targets, though Orestes has a moment of doubt when confronted with the reality of what he means to do. The Furies that arise in protest at the act of matricide continue into the final play and are egged on by Clytemnestra's vengeful ghost, only to lose a court case on the dubious grounds that the father is the only true parent. The Clytemnestra of Sophocles' *Electra* is just as ruthless, though her execution precedes and is less important than that of Aegisthus.

Only Euripides is prepared to offer some sort of defence for her, first in *Electra* where she feels some remorse for her past and, when she is informed that she has become a grandmother, at least tries to help her estranged daughter: more so in *Iphigeneia at Aulis* which is set in and around the sacrifice of Iphigeneia that heralds the inauspicious expedition to Troy. Clytemnestra has been tricked into bringing Iphigeneia to Aulis where the Greek fleet is waiting to set out for Troy, on the pretext of a marriage to Achilles. She suffers a series of humiliations, not least greeting the greatest of the Greek warriors as a potential son-in-law, the first that Achilles has heard of any such arrangement. Even when the Old Man has told them everything Agamemnon tries to bluff it out and the blameless Clytemnestra responds:

> CLYTEMNESTRA. Now, you take heed! I don't intend to mince my words.
> The time for subterfuge is over.
> First things first. You married me against my will:
> murdered Tantalus, my husband, and raped me.
> You snatched my baby from my breast
> and smashed his head on the ground.

My half-brothers, the Dioscuri, sons of Zeus,
raised an expedition against you, on horseback.
And when they brought you grovelling before Tyndareus,
my elderly father, he handed me back to you, as a bride.
I learnt to live with this, and in your household,
you'll not deny it, I was a 'good' wife to you,
attentive in bed and bearing your children.
You were glad to come home to me. The house prospered.
You'll not find many wives as virtuous as I was,
though there are plenty of bad ones around.
I bore you a son, here, this son, Orestes,
and three daughters. And my reward for this?
You're proposing to kill one of them.
So, if anyone happens to ask you why
you mean to do this, what's your answer going to be?
Let me guess what your reply will be, shall I?
'So that brother Menelaus can get his Helen back.'
Fine! What's the going rate for the return
of a wayward whore? A loving daughter, apparently.
Now you'll be off on your war-games,
how do you think I'll be feeling, back at home,
when I look at my daughter's chair, and it's empty?
When I go to her bedroom? And it's empty.
While I sit at home, in tears. Grieving. Alone.
Still talking to her. 'Oh, my dear, killed by your father.
By his own hand. No one else's.' There'll be such hatred here.
Is that what you'll look forward to on your return?
A small excuse we'd need, her sisters and I,
to prepare the reception you deserve.

Please don't. Please don't make me.
Don't do this and force me to become as bad as you.
That's it, is it? Your daughter, a human sacrifice?
Do you know the right prayers for such an occasion?
A personal blessing as you slit her throat?
For a homecoming to match your sickening farewell?
Might I ask, perhaps, for a benediction for me?
Always assuming, that is, that the gods are so stupid
as to smile kindly on child-killers.
When you come home to Argos, do you mean
to give your children a hug? I wouldn't, if I were you.
They won't meet your eye, in case they're next.
Has any of this ever occurred to you?
Or are you so busy playing at being a general?
There's one thing only you should ask the Greeks. Just one.

181

'You want to sail for Troy, do you, you Greeks?
Right. Let's draw lots. Short straw kills his child.'
That would be fairer, wouldn't it, than you
offering your daughter? Or Menelaus, of course.
His daughter Hermione in exchange for Helen.
After all, it is his business. Whereas, as things now stand,
the faithful wife loses her child, the whore's
stays safe at home in Sparta. Lucky Helen!
Any of you. I ask you, am I right?
Change your mind. She's our daughter. Do not murder her.

The mixture of sarcasm, rage and desperation is finely judged. There is an immediacy in Clytemnestra's speech that is appropriate to the occasion, but also presages a future of which the entire audience will be aware. The opening revelations are a real shock, especially as this is such a public occasion. Though most of what she says is aimed directly at her husband, both Iphigeneia and Orestes are present. The appeal at the end is less to them than to the Chorus who are the first to respond before Iphigeneia makes her own appeal.

7. *Hecuba to Agamemnon*, Hecuba, *ll. 787–845*

Hecuba's ordeal in the immediate aftermath of the fall of Troy takes a different path in this tragedy from in *Trojan Women*, though both pinpoint the suffering of the former queen and the loss of her children. Polydorus, whose ghost opens the play, had been sent to safety, as she hoped, with the Thracian Polymestor. But Polymestor has abused that trust, murdered the boy and thrown his corpse into the sea. Hecuba finds out her daughter Polyxena must die, to satisfy a different ghost, the ghost of Achilles. Confronted with a covered corpse she assumes it to be that of her daughter, only to discover it is her son whom she believed safe and with friends. Agamemnon, leader of the Greeks, enters, to tell her she should now make the burial arrangements for Polyxena. She confronts him with this new loss:

HECUBA. I am on my knees before you. Let me tell you why.
  If you decide what I have suffered would meet
  with the approval of the gods, then I'll put up with it.
  If not, accept the role of protector against the broken faith
  of the most treacherous of hosts, so treacherous
  as to outrage the powers above and powers below.
  This is a man who shared our table many times.
  He was our guest, among the most esteemed of friends,

always treated with respect. This man has murdered my son.
Worse than the killing, whatever the cause for that,
he denied him burial: deposited my boy's body in the sea.
I am a slave now. I'm insignificant.
But the gods are powerful: so is moral law,
which they respect, as we acknowledge them,
and can tell the difference between right and wrong.
If someone comes before you demanding Justice,
and is turned away, if murderers of guests,
or those who ransack temples, are condoned,
then it's Justice itself on trial. And Justice is the loser.
If you are outraged by such behaviour, accept my plea.
Stand back and, like a painter, dispassionately, pity me.
I have suffered, a queen once, now your slave.
I had wonderful children. In old age I have none.
No home. No friends. Nothing left.

Why do you turn away from me? I'm in despair.
Desperate maybe, but unconvincing too, it seems.
We'll sweat at learning anything, we humans.
So we should. But will not pay a thing
to learn about persuasion, the only art that rules
the minds of men. Why should that be when this is
the only way we have to win an argument?
What use is hope for a happy outcome?
The children that I had, they are no longer.
I must work my life away on demeaning chores,
a prisoner, as my city goes up in smoke.
That's how things are. It will probably be fruitless
to invoke Aphrodite now: I can but try.
Cassandra, my daughter, the visionary,
sleeps at your side. Will those nights of passion
count for anything to you, my lord?
What does she get out of it, my daughter,
for all those embraces: or I for her?
In the dark, when the lights are out,
that's the time of matchless pleasure.
So attend to what I say. You see this corpse, lying here?
He's a virtual brother-in-law to you.
You should do right by him as family.
My words lack something, I know that.
Would that the power of speech were implanted
in my arms, my hands, my feet and hair,
some miraculous means contrived
by Daedalus or a god, so that my every feature

could unite in tongue, my every limb
make plea in supplication at your knee.
My lord and master, beacon of the Greeks,
heed these words. Stretch out a hand. Grant an old woman,
a nobody and nothing though she be, satisfaction.
It is the duty of any decent man
to see the guilty punished: in the name of Justice.

For all she claims no skill in argument, this is an effective piece of rhetoric from Hecuba. It is also a crafted dramatic speech, with Agamemnon's unwillingness to comply with her request clearly planted, before she ups a gear. If the extravagance of her approach seems less convincing in the latter part, it can only be because Agamemnon has been so softened up by what she has to say about the nature of justice. She pleads the desperation of her plight, kinship and lack of ability as a speaker. But at the end it is a repetition of the demand for 'justice' on which she relies, and to which Agamemnon reluctantly concedes. The bigger challenge is to show how she has moved in this latter part of the play from acquiescence at her fate, however cruel, to hard vengeance on Polymestor, the man who has so betrayed her and murdered her son from sheer greed.

8. *Electra over the body of Aegisthus*, Electra, *ll. 907–56*

Electra's erratic behaviour in the early part of the play can be defended or downplayed. It is hard to ignore. The image that she has of her brother proves sorely misplaced when she is faced with the real thing. Her hatred of her mother and her stepfather may be justified, but her account of their behaviour seems at odds with what is said of them elsewhere and how Clytemnestra converses with her daughter. When the Messenger (probably Pylades) brings news of how Aegisthus died, he seems to be glossing over the unheroic nature of the deed as it was performed. Orestes and Pylades accepted an invitation to join in a sacred feast. Aegisthus handed over the weapon and Orestes cut him down from behind without warning. The body is brought in and this is how Electra responds to it:

ELECTRA. Very well. Where shall I begin, or end
my catalogue of your crimes? What will be the middle?
Every sleepless dawn, I've been going over and over
what I would say to your face if I were not afraid.
Now that's past, and I'm free to heap on you
the insults that I wanted to when you were alive.

When you deprived me of my father you ruined my life,
and you did this though I had done you no wrong.
You shamefully married my mother,
and killed the commander of the Greeks,
you who never even went to Troy.
You were so stupid you imagined
she would stay faithful,
though she'd betrayed my father's bed.
If a man seduces someone else's wife,
and finds he has to marry her,
he's in trouble if he thinks that she,
who has been unfaithful before,
will suddenly be faithful to him.
You were in hell, though you pretended it was fine.
You knew your marriage began in infamy,
and my mother saw what an evil husband she had.
You were each as bad as the other,
and infected each other's lives.

All the Argives said this about you.
'He's called the Queen's husband, she's called the Queen.'
It's a disgrace when a woman's head of the house
and not the man. I hate it when people talk of a child
as his mother's rather than his father's.
When a man marries above his station,
his wife is all-important, but he's a nobody.
Your biggest mistake was to think
you could do anything because you had money.
Money's nothing except a temporary friend.
It's character that lasts, not wealth.
Character stays with us through thick or thin.
Prosperity lives with fools who don't deserve it,
to hand one moment, till the flower's gone.

Then there's your women – no topic for a virgin,
so I'll keep quiet, but give you a hint.
You pursued women simply because
you lived in a palace and were so good-looking.
I'd always prefer a husband with rugged looks:
no pretty boy for me.
A real man's children will be fit to fight,
not just to dance in a chorus line.
So much for you then!
You may not know how Time found you out,
but at last you have paid for your crimes.

Criminals should realise that
completing the first lap isn't winning the race.

Though the idea of reviling a dead body is unpleasant in itself, Electra's opening is at least to the point. But from there on her assault leaps all over the place. She accuses her mother of being unfaithful, not to Agamemnon but to Aegisthus; she accuses Aegisthus of marrying Clytemnestra for her money; of pursuing other women; of being too good-looking; of not being rugged enough. The blunderbuss accusations are incoherent to the point of insanity, a model of anti-rhetoric. It is a really difficult speech for an actor – which is why it is included here.

9. *Helen to the Chorus,* Helen, *ll. 255–305*

Here is another 'suicide note', but in a very different mood from those of Heracles and Phaedra (4 and 5 above). Helen's prologue has already made it clear that this play defends a character who elsewhere receives a hostile reception. She has been the victim of a trick. Hera, again the villain of the piece, created an identical version of Helen, fashioned out of ether, and that is what Paris abducted to Troy and for which the ten years of the Trojan War were fought. She, meanwhile, was shanghaied to Egypt to the palace of Proteus where she has lived in unhappy, if comfortable, circumstances. This, her second diatribe against her fate, is provoked by the arrival of one of the Greek heroes who casts all the blame for the war on to Helen. He is in baleful mood and thinks he recognises her. She has the *nous* not to try to explain that she really is Helen, but an innocent Helen. Instead she pours out her heart to a somewhat sanguine Chorus, themselves Greek slaves:

> HELEN. Dear women, to what fate am I condemned?
>   Am I some freak my mother bore?
>   No other Greek woman, nor even a barbarian,
>   laid a big white egg. But that's what Leda did,
>   thanks to Zeus, with me inside it. So they say!
>   Yes, all my life, whatever I've done, a monstrosity!
>   Hera's fault, of course, but my beauty hasn't helped.
>   I wish my life could be erased like a chalk drawing,
>   and I could start again, not beautiful but plain,
>   so that the Greeks had no knowledge
>   of my reputation, but recalled only the good things,
>   none of the bad they now attribute to me.
>   A man pursuing a single-minded vision,
>   who suffers the worst of fortune from the gods,

must simply put up with it, however hard.
But look how many disasters have piled up on me.
To start with there's the terrible reputation
which I *don't* deserve: a groundless accusation
is worse than a valid one.

Then there are the divinities who uprooted me from my native
land and dumped me in this godforsaken spot.
Removed from my nearest and dearest, I'm just a slave,
me, freeborn as I am, and a queen! In a place like this,
this barbarian country where, the king apart, everyone's a slave.

Now the single anchor in the storms of fate,
the hope my husband would come to my rescue,
has been shattered by news of his death.
My mother no longer lives and I'm her murderer.
It's so unfair! But what in my life has ever been fair?
And the glory of my home, my daughter,
will never find a husband, condemned to die an old maid.
Castor and Pollux, my brothers also fathered by Zeus –
they're dead too. Cursed at every turn, I too am dead,
in my life's course and circumstance, if not in actual fact.
And here's the final straw. Should I ever reach home,
the door would be slammed in my face, all men believing
that after Troy, Helen died with her husband, Menelaus.
Had he survived, I might be recognised by virtue of secrets
only the two of us could know. Hopeless, now he is no more.

Why do I stay alive? To what future can I look forward?
Escape into marriage with some wealthy barbarian?
But when a woman is saddled with a husband she despises,
her own body becomes hateful to her. Better off dead.
But how to do it, with decorum? Hanging's so undignified:
even for a slave, that's always been true. The sword
has something noble, something glorious about it.
But you have to find the exact spot so as not to botch the job.
I really have reached the depths of despair.
Other women find beauty makes them happy.
For me it has been the cause of my downfall.

This is a delightful speech, which offers much more than the 'moan'
which it may first appear to be. Helen does grumble on and off throughout the opening scenes, here contemplating her prospects with
understandable pessimism, believing her husband, her last hope of rescue,
is now dead. She speculates on marriage to someone you cannot care for,
laments her beauty and decides that the only response is to kill herself.

The comedy comes when she reviews the ways of doing so and finds them all disagreeable. Here is none of the stoical resolve of Phaedra or Heracles, or of Sophocles' Ajax, or most of the suicides in Greek drama for that matter. Here the sticking point is simply the method. The Chorus, in their subsequent reaction, give the impression that they have heard this all before: often probably. The Helen that emerges later in the play, tactful, resourceful and far cleverer than the other characters, may also be hinted at within the speech. After all, she has had seventeen years of frustration.

10. *The Messenger to the Chorus*, Bacchae, *ll. 1043–1152*

Pentheus' departure, dressed as a Bacchant and carrying a thyrsus, the Bacchic wand, is as ominous as any in Greek tragedy. His opposition to the Dionysiac religion has been a lost cause since before his entrance, thanks to the prologue from the god Dionysus who reveals his intention of taking revenge for the way he has been ignored. The Chorus, supporters of Dionysus, anticipate Pentheus' downfall in the short time between his exit and the arrival of the Messenger. When they hear he is indeed dead, their reaction is to celebrate. The shocked Messenger is taken aback, but proceeds to give the gruesome details of Pentheus' last moments:

> MESSENGER. We left the last cottages of Thebes behind,
> then crossed the Asopus heading for Cithaeron.
> Just Pentheus, me following my master,
> and that foreigner to show us the way.
> As soon as we got there, we crouched down
> in a grassy hollow to watch, silent and unseen.
> There's a rift between tall cliffs,
> waterfalls running down them,
> all shaded by pinetrees.
> That's where we saw the Maenads, hard at work, but content.
> Some were decorating thyrsi with sprigs of new ivy.
> Others sang Bacchic songs to one another,
> frisking, free as colts.
> Pentheus couldn't see the whole company
> so he said, poor man,
> 'I cannot get a proper view from here
> at these self-styled Maenads.
> If I could climb up higher,
> in one of those pines perhaps,
> I could get a decent look at this debauchery of theirs.'

Then I saw the foreigner do a remarkable thing.
He took hold of a soaring branch from one of the pines,
and he pulled it, pulled it right down to the dark earth.
Bent over like a bow or the curved felloe on a wheel,
just so did this strange man take that tree
in his two hands, and bend it to the ground.
No ordinary man could have done it.
His strength was superhuman. He sat Pentheus astride the branches,
before letting the tree slowly straighten,
taking care not to unseat him.
Up it went, up towards the sky, my master on its back,
for all the Maenads to see, plainer than he saw them.
No sooner was Pentheus up there in full view
than the foreigner disappeared and a voice
came out of the air, as it were the voice of Dionysus.
'Ladies,' he cried, 'here is the man
who would make mock of us and our mysteries.
I offer him to you for punishment.'
He spoke and a blinding flash of fire
struck earth from heaven.
Everything went quite still, air, trees, animals even.
Quite still.

The Maenads got to their feet,
some having missed his words,
staring about them. He called again.
This time Cadmus' daughters knew what he required.
And they ran!
They ran, swift as birds,
Agave, her sisters, all of them,
over river and rock, mad,
for the god had breathed on them.
When they saw my master perched in his tree,
they hurled stones at first and sticks,
climbing the cliff opposite.
Some threw thyrsi at their wretched target.
He was too high even for their frenzy,
but could only sit there appalled.
They snatched off branches from the oaks
to lever up his pine, but their efforts bore no fruit.
Then Agave spoke.
'Circle the trunk, Maenads, grasp it.
We need to catch this clamberer
before he reveals god's dances.'
Dozens of hands hauled at the tree,

then heaved it out of the earth.
Down fell Pentheus,
down to the ground with an awful cry.
He knew now what was happening.

His mother started it, the ritual slaughter.
Desperate Agave. As she fell upon him,
he tore off the headdress so she would recognise him
and grabbed her cheek.
'Mother, it's me. It's Pentheus, your son.
Pity me. I've done no wrong.
Don't kill me.'
But her eyes were rolling.
She was frothing, imagining god knows what
in her Dionysiac frenzy.
She ignored his words, and took his left hand in hers,
planted a foot in his ribs.
And ripped off his arm at the shoulder.
Her strength was supernatural.
Ino set to work on the other side,
Tearing out handfuls of flesh,
then Autonoe and the whole mob of Bacchants.
A single terrible scream,
Pentheus' agony, their exultation.
One ran off with an arm, another a foot still in its shoe.
His ribs were stripped to the bone.
Bright red hands toyed with lumps of flesh.

The remains are strewn about,
by the rocks, in the undergrowth, anywhere.
We'll never find them.
But the head, the poor head –
his mother chanced to snatch it up,
and jammed it on her thyrsus.
She left her sisters dancing away
and set off across Cithaeron,
brandishing the head as though it were a mountain lion's.
She arrived in the city glorying in her frightful trophy,
shrieking about her splendid Dionysus,
fellow-huntsman, victorious.
A victory of tears.
I can't stay to see this sight,
not Agave's homecoming.
Balance. Reason. That's all we can aim for.
Honour the gods and stick to that.

Many of the deaths in Greek tragedy are gruesome. Dismemberment of a young man by his mother and his aunts is, perhaps, the worst. As in the messenger speech from *Medea* (2 above) there is little point in trying to match the graphic description with over-emotive playing. One difference between the two speeches does reside in the reaction of the Choruses. The Chorus in *Medea* are local women of Corinth who have declared an allegiance to Medea. In *Bacchae* they have an ethereal quality, figurative almost, as an embodiment of the religion. What the speeches share is that, however horrifying, they are only a prelude to even greater horrors, the death of the children in *Medea*; in *Bacchae* the arrival of Pentheus' mother, Agave, with her son's head on her thyrsus, believing it belongs to a lion. Messenger speeches are usually isolated, delivered by characters who have no involvement with the plot except as eyewitnesses. We are more squeamish today than the Greeks of Euripides' time and less used to listening to an extended narrative in the theatre. The challenges that this offers to today's actor are ones that need addressing in any lengthy speech, but they are surmountable by trusting the playwright and working out his structure. Like the greatest playwrights of any period the Greeks appreciate and explore that most engaging of relationships between actor and audience.

11 HEIRS TO THE LEGACY

Shaw, Strindberg, Brecht, Pirandello, Anouilh, Sondheim, Frisch

Go into most sizeable bookshops and you will find that the drama section is where to look for plays: that is if, by plays, you mean dramatic material written in the last few hundred years. If you want to find anything Greek or Roman, in translation, you will have to go to a separate section, probably labelled 'Classics'. The same is true of classification in most academic libraries. The purpose of this last chapter is to remind those guardians of ancient Greek and Roman literature that Aeschylus, Sophocles, Euripides, Aristophanes, Menander, Plautus and Terence were makers of plays first, anything else second.[1] So the Greek and Roman playwrights deserve a place on the shelves, not only with Thucydides and Tacitus, but also alongside Marlowe, Shakespeare, Molière, Sheridan, Chekhov, Wilde, Coward, Beckett, Stoppard, Pinter, Hare and Churchill, with Euripides, probably flanked alphabetically, for better or worse, by Eliot, T. S. and Feydeau, Georges.

If Euripides is everything that has been claimed for him in previous chapters, as the most adventurous and resilient pioneer in stage presentation, it should be possible to trace something of a legacy in the best playwrights of the modern era. It should also be possible to identify where such analogies break down. This living, breathing art form of drama, now well into its third millennium, was less than a hundred years old when Euripides threw his cap into the ring and simultaneously threw down the gauntlet to the true founder, Aeschylus, and his own near-contemporary, Sophocles. The Greek tragedians do have plenty in common with one another, but Euripides sought to forge new paths.

Tracing the influence of classical Athens on later times is no new undertaking. It was a regular pastime for critics of past centuries. When F. L. Lucas' readable and erudite *Euripides and His Influence* was published in 1924, the final two pages of the edition could be devoted to no fewer than fifty others in the same series, published by George G. Harrap and Sons under the blanket title of 'Our Debt to Greece and

---

[1] Seneca is a special case, being the only surviving dramatist of the ancient world who also published prose treatises and letters.

Rome'. Subjects ranged from Mathematics, Biology and Engineering to Astronomy and Astrology, Music and Warfare. All the major literary figures from Greece and Rome were covered with the exception of Menander, none of whose complete plays had yet surfaced. Apart from this series there have been a number of volumes devoted to the subject.[1]

Three years before Lucas' *Euripides and His Influence*, Gilbert Norwood's leading essay, in a volume of three, had been entitled 'Euripides and Shaw: A Comparison'.[2] Norwood confessed that finding similarities between these two playwrights, one long dead, the other very much alive, had even by then been made on several occasions: nor could it be that surprising when two of the most influential figures in and around the innovative Vedrennne-Barker management at the Court Theatre in the first years of the twentieth century were also close friends, George Bernard Shaw and Gilbert Murray. Granville Barker directed four of Murray's translations of Euripides at the Court (*Hippolytus* in 1904, *Trojan Women*, 1905, *Electra*, 1906 and *Medea*, 1907) and William Poel another (*Bacchae*, 1908). Fifty years later when Stephen Sondheim wrote his musical version of Aristophanes' *Frogs*, first performed by the Yale Repertory Theatre in 1974, he replaced the character of Aeschylus with Shakespeare, Euripides with Shaw.

By the late nineteenth century Greek drama had been represented for hundreds of years on the public stage by a mass of more or less loose 'versions', from Seneca onwards, which may have taken their inspiration from Greek mythology, though more often from Roman, but owed little to Aeschylus, Sophocles, Euripides or Aristophanes. The classical world still held a fascination in the Renaissance. Shakespeare's own plays have settings that include Troy, Athens, Ephesus, Sicily and Cyprus, but it was not until the return of some of Euripides' plays to the stage four hundred years later that the modern era of European drama could properly be said to begin, sparked off by Henrik Ibsen.

The conceit of trying to identify Euripides' influence through the playwrights of the late nineteenth and twentieth centuries is one I have ventured upon before.[3] In that first version of my parlour-game, all five extant Greek playwrights were targeted. Little attempt was made to discover who might have best copied the external aspect of Greek drama. It was not an exercise in reviewing translations or versions of Greek

---

[1] Prominent among such collections have been Livingston, ed. (1921), Highet (1949 and 1967), Bolgar (1954), Belli (1969), Finley, ed. (1984).

[2] Norwood (1921).

[3] Walton (2007 a) in a tribute to Walter Puchner, who will, I hope, excuse my reworking of an idea that was originally developed as a gift to him.

tragedy: nor did it involve comparing dramatic structure, where the Greeks turn out not to be better or worse than, but simply different from, playmakers of more recent times. Philosophical and theological issues were a factor, but primarily as a means of identifying which of Aristotle's formulae make sense in a modern world, and which gods transcend the gulf between Olympian pantheism and subsequent religions.

Finding the true heir of Aeschylus had not been difficult. Ibsen, though sometimes compared to Euripides in his own lifetime – the 'Greek Ibsen' and the 'Attic Shaw'[1] – seemed in retrospect to be a very different kind of dramatic pioneer. It was Ibsen, who, like Aeschylus, combined huge themes with the exploration of human behaviour through complex stage image in such plays as *The Master Builder*, *Little Eyolf* and *Ghosts*. There is surely something of Prometheus in the inflexible Brandt, both overwhelmed as they defy their god on the mountain-top. Many of Ibsen's early plays from *Cataline* to *The Vikings of Helgeland* and *The Pretenders* evoke that sense of a past where myth and history blend, where monumental characters are defined in the broader strokes, but are betrayed by massive human failings. Yet what stands out in Aeschylus is the grasp of one of the great fundamentals of theatre, that it combines and balances verbal and visual image, intertwined with and enhanced by *mousikê* and by *choros* (music and dance). Aeschylus is supreme in the moments when words fail and music expresses the emotions that cannot be spoken; or when language is overtaken by action; or silence speaks volumes: the slow countdown of heroes in *Seven Against Thebes*, the Chorus of *Suppliants* threatening mass-suicide, the figure of Prometheus, pinned out on his rock, unrepentant in the face of every elemental power.

The only possible rival to Ibsen was Eugene O'Neill, less for his introspective *Mourning Becomes Electra* than for the sheer range of dramatic device from mask to the supernatural with which he experimented in plays as diverse as *The Great God Brown*, *The Emperor Jones* or *Lazarus Laughed*. Surviving Aeschylus suggests a similar sense of adventure in style: what we have lost of Aeschylus must have contained more.

Sophocles too was comparatively easy. Arthur Miller was likely to feature somewhere among the heirs, despite Miller's sometimes eccentric interpretations of Greek tragedy. The doom-laden central figures from *The Man Who Had All the Luck*, *Death of a Salesman* or *A View from the Bridge* match, perhaps consciously, the tormented outcasts of Sophocles. What Miller replicated in Sophocles was that sense of impend-

[1] Hall and Macintosh (2005), p. 490.

ing disaster to be found in *Antigone, Oedipus Tyrannus, Ajax* or *Women of Trachis*, all plays that contain the act of suicide. In Sophocles a world dominated by superhuman figures from the past melds with a new society view which focuses on individual responsibility. The mistakes that are made and which lead to catastrophe are compounded by human error – the jealousy of Ajax, the stubbornness of Creon, the gullibility of Deianira. What is left for his damaged Electra when the focus of her hatred is removed? *Oedipus Tyrannus* is more than one man's search for the truth of his birthright in the face of circumstances for which he is not responsible: it is a compound built from a web of small deceptions and evasions, by commoners as much as by kings, which do not so much serve to provoke parricide and incest as to account for them. Sophocles' two late plays, *Philoctetes* and *Oedipus at Colonus*, suggest some sort of coming to terms with the slings and arrows, but only the most forced of reconciliations.

Aristophanes has attracted few disciples who could combine the wildness of his imagination with the seriousness of his purpose. The best of the Victorian masters of burlesque, James Robinson Planché or W. S. Gilbert, lacked solemnity amid their anarchies. The mix of speculative fiction and dangerous immediacy were truly reborn in the work of Vladimir Mayakovsky, both in his circus plays such as *Moscow's Burning*, with the Czar played by a dwarf clown and Kerensky literally jumping through hoops outside the door of the Czarina's bedroom, and in the three full-length pieces for which he is better known. The scatology may have been somewhat toned down in *Mystery-Bouffe, The Bedbug* and *The Bathhouse*, but not the sense of the subversive. This was Stalin's USSR and Mayakovsky shot himself soon after the opening of *The Bathhouse* in 1931. A more modern Aristophanic might be Dario Fo, Nobel Laureate and comfortably within a southern Mediterranean ethos. The politics are there, so is the farce and the satire, especially in plays such as *Accidental Death of an Anarchist* and *Trumpets and Raspberries*, but surprisingly little of his output has been translated into English, apart from the short pieces often co-written with and performed by his wife Franca Rame.

Menander, so close in several ways to Euripides in more familial mode, is sparsely represented, even since the publication of the Bodmer manuscripts less than fifty years ago. His ability to walk carefully, within the confines of everyday life, the tightrope between the ridiculous and the pathetic can today be found in the plays of Alan Ayckbourn, where audiences reach the point at which it is difficult to know where laughter has to stop. The best of the television sit-coms, British and American, from *Steptoe and Son* to *Frasier* may perhaps claim Menander as their spiritual father.

What then of Euripides, whose modern successor ought to encompass the extraordinary range identified in preceding chapters? Here, surely, no single figure can embrace so many facets. This, my second shot at Euripides, concerns the nuts and bolts of dramatic playmaking and the theatrical devices that underline the peculiar nature of his approach to performance. Who, then, from the collective of 'modern' writers for the theatre best pinpointed thematic, dramatic or theatrical essences that originated with Euripides? Who is the true heir? It is in the form more than in the content that the quest for an answer begins.

Seven possible candidates have been earmarked from which others may pick a preferred candidate or substitute their own. Only one of these seven is still alive at the time of writing, which may either be a reflection on the fact that playwrights no longer wish to learn from the past, or see no need for it. The claims of these seven will not necessarily be considered in chronological order from the birth-date of the playwrights (though those born in the nineteenth century precede those from the twentieth) but through a different sort of progression, the logic behind which will hopefully reveal itself.

As the ante-post favourite, GEORGE BERNARD SHAW has to come first. He is one of four potential 'beneficiaries' who were born in the nineteenth century and, of all, probably the most conscious of Euripides and his shared status as an iconoclast. Indeed, Shaw's enthusiasm for playing the part of *enfant terrible* marks his card as the playwright who might most have cultivated a comparison had there not been plenty of others to do the marking for him. The most compelling of these, though not the first, as suggested above, was Gilbert Norwood with his 'Euripides and Shaw: A Comparison'. In 1921 Shaw was already sixty-five, but was still to complete the massive *Back to Methuselah* (1921), *St Joan* (1924), *The Apple Cart* (1929), *The Millionairess* (1936) and *Geneva* (1938 and 1940). None of these was especially Euripidean, though the juxtaposition of Old Testament mythology with contemporary politics to be found in the five plays of *Methuselah*, or the portrait of Joan as a blunt country girl taking on the authorities, might have appealed to the Athenian were not Christian mythology to prove even more baffling than Greek. Shaw's awareness of Euripides surfaces frequently in his writings, notably in *Major Barbara* with its portrait of Murray in the character of Adolphus Cusins. There is even an exchange in *Major Barbara* where Professor of

Greek Cusins confronts Undershaft, the arms manufacturer whose son-in-law he hopes to become:

CUSINS. You remember what Euripides says about your money and
   gunpowder?
UNDERSHAFT. No.
CUSINS [*declaiming*].   One and another
      In money and guns may outpass his brother;
      And men in their millions float and flow
      And seethe with a million hopes as leaven;
      And they win their will; or they miss their will;
      And their hopes are dead or are pined for still;
      But who'er can know
      As the long days go
      That to live is happy, has found his heaven.

   My translation: what do you think of it?
UNDERSHAFT. I think, my friend, that if you wish to know, as the long
   days go, that to live is happy, you must first acquire money enough for a
   decent life, and power enough to be your own master.
CUSINS. You are damnably discouraging. (*He resumes his declamation.*)

      Is it so hard a thing to see
      That the spirit of God – whate'er it be –
      The law that abides and changes not, ages long,
      The Eternal and Nature-born: these things be strong?
      What else is Wisdom? What of Man's endeavor,
      Or God's high grace so lovely and so great?
      To stand from fear set free? to breathe and wait?
      To hold a hand uplifted over Fate? (*Major Barbara*, Act Two)

Shaw even includes a note before his Preface to the published text:

N.B. the Euripidean verses in the second act of *Major Barbara* are not by me,
nor even directly by Euripides. They are by Professor Gilbert Murray, whose
English version of *The Bacchae* came into our dramatic literature with all the
impulsive power of an original work shortly before *Major Barbara* was
begun. The play, indeed, stands indebted to him in more ways than one.[1]

Norwood's comparison of the two playwrights in 'Euripides and Shaw'
may be taken seriously because he knows a great deal about the theatre
of the past as well as that of his own time, not something by which all
other critics of classical theatre are distinguished. His first and, perhaps,
central point is that Euripides was writing, as was Shaw, at a time of

[1] Bernard Shaw, *John Bull's Other Island with How He Lied to Her Husband and Major
Barbara*, London: Constable, 1907, rev. in Standard Edition, 1931, p. 202.

'moral and intellectual bankruptcy'. The times were not really similar, of course. Euripides' plays are mostly set against a background of an Athens hurtling towards the disaster that was the outcome of the Peloponnesian War with Sparta. The final defeat of Athens came less than two years after the playwright's death. Shaw's playwriting may have framed the carnage of the First World War and, indeed, the Second, but political or social comparisons between classical Athens and early twentieth-century Britain or Ireland can only be taken so far.[1]

Nonetheless, Norwood's association between the two recognises a number of features that link craft to intellectual outlook and are undeniably to be found in both dramatists. The challenge to accepted beliefs, though hardly exclusive to either period – surely the governing aspect of any serious drama with a broad political message – is certainly a dominating feature of the work of both Euripides and Shaw. The treatment and behaviour of women and the lower classes (in Euripides' case, slaves) comes under scrutiny, along with a wide debate over the nature of morality. Each in his own way could confront and diminish perceived reputation, frequently for comic effect. Admetus, Achilles, Menelaus, Jason, Orestes and Electra are subjected to the treatment Shaw dishes out to men of the cloth, soldiers, doctors and self-appointed liberals in *Candida*, *The Doctor's Dilemma*, *The Man of Destiny* and *Arms and the Man*. Unsurprisingly, both Euripides and Shaw attracted attention and opprobrium during their own lifetimes, principally from the targets of their scorn.[2]

For all this, if part of the reason for looking beyond Shaw resides in a case having already been made on his behalf eighty years ago, that is not the whole story. There is a major reservation. Euripides does not appear so conscious of himself. How often Shaw seems a little too knowing, a little too sure of his prime comic weapon, the paradox. Maybe this is no more than Aristotle's *peripeteia*, 'reversal of expectation'. But there is also in Shaw something self-important, absent in Euripides, that lurks midway between mischief and sheer childishness, often to be found in those with such an exceptional gift of the gab they will argue anything that may permit them to lay claim to the mantel of Socrates.[3] In addition, Shaw's theatrical vision is surprisingly earthbound. There is little of Euripides' quest for means of dramatic expression. Shaw, the master wordsmith, is the arch-literary dramatist of his own lifetime. At home as much as critic

---

[1] See McDonald and Walton (2002).

[2] The extent to which Shaw knew his classics can be found in Albert (2003), pp. 167–80.

[3] Socrates, the philosopher known from Plato's record of his disputations in dialogue form, was put to death in 399 BC, six years after the death of Euripides, for 'introducing new gods, corrupting the youth and making the worse cause appear the better'.

and commentator as he is in a theatre, it is difficult to escape the cartoon version of Shaw as a master-marionettist, none of whose characters has independent life beyond the strings he pulls. Euripides is more than that.

Seven years younger than Shaw, AUGUST STRINDBERG died in 1912, but he always seems much less the last gasp of the Victorian and Edwardian twilight than a true harbinger of modernism. Many of his plays, especially those from his post-naturalistic phase of writing, were quite unlike anything seen previously, notably *A Dream Play* (1902) and *The Ghost Sonata* (1907) where the action swirls and shudders in a style more akin to experimental film than a piece of theatre. At first glance Strindberg's range seems parallel to that of Ibsen, historical dramas, naturalistic pieces and what have been termed 'Pilgrimage Plays'. But where Ibsen chose to deal with broad social issues in the dramas for which he is best remembered (*An Enemy of the People*, *Ghosts*, *A Doll's House*, *Rosmersholm* and even *Hedda Gabler*), Strindberg homed in on the blood-curdling nature of the battle of the sexes in such works as *The Father* (1887), *Miss Julie* (1888) and *The Dance of Death* (1901). There he most closely resembles the savage Euripides of *Hippolytus* or *Medea*, where the intensity of human existence finds its most wrenching stage exposé, though for the most part, unlike Euripides, any sympathy for women is strictly conditional.

While Ibsen looks backwards to the nineteenth century, as Aeschylus looks back to the earliest period of Greek tragedy, Strindberg looks forward to the twentieth, both in his themes and stage treatments. Like Euripides, he broke boundaries stylistically and viscerally. Of all the playwrights from the last hundred years Strindberg seems to have his emotional nerves most close to the surface. There may even be a parallel between their unhappy relationships with women: Strindberg three times married, disastrously on each occasion, Euripides too having more than one unsatisfactory marriage, if we can read anything reliable into the smatterings of gossip that filter into the later biographies. The reputation of both playwrights as misogynists may be equally unjustified, in that Euripides, as shown earlier (see Chapter 3, pp. 44–61) frequently displays sympathy with women reduced to desperation by the behaviour of men. It is doubtful how far Strindberg does that, but what does link the two is the fascination of both with the battle of the sexes which may first raise its dramatic head in Aeschylus' *Agamemnon* or Sophocles' *Women of Trachis*, but never takes flight until Euripides' Phaedra and Medea make their first entrance and Alcestis, Hecuba, Andromache and Creusa make bids to have their voices heard. In Euripides there are pre-echoes as much of the pity of Strindberg's Daughter of Indra in *A Dream Play* as of the unleashed wilfulness of Alice or Laura in *Dance of Death* and *The Father*, or the iconic and eponymous heroine of *Miss Julie*, all plays where Strindberg's apparent naturalism overlaps with a new stage method. In such a way does Euripides home in on 'real' people and 'real' human reactions while still working through the medium of myth and a drama of mask, dance and music.

So little is known of Greek music – a fragment from *Orestes* is one of the few examples to survive in any annotated form – that we are on uncertain ground here. What has often been noted is Strindberg's experiment in musical structure in his Chamber Plays for the Intimate Theatre in Stockholm. Something that he initiated, perhaps, in *Miss Julie* as early as 1888, led to the subtitle of 'Opus' for some of the plays, the best known of which is *The Ghost Sonata*. The playwrights share a freedom of form which their work made their own. What separates them is that Euripides extended the possibilities of Greek tragedy (at what was in any case a major turning point in Greek political history) so that it had nowhere else to go, except towards the social comedy of Menander. In Strindberg's case he may be claimed as the forerunner, not only of dramatic expressionism, but of surrealism and the matching intensity of the theatre pioneer Antonin Artaud.

Strindberg prided himself on his progressiveness and in the renowned Preface to *Miss Julie* unwittingly underlined his kinship to Euripides when he wrote of his characters:

> I congratulate myself on this multiplicity of motives as being up-to-date, and, if others have done the same thing before me, then I congratulate myself in not being alone in my belief in my 'paradoxes', as all innovations are called [. . .] My souls (characters) are conglomerations of past and present stages of civilisation, bits from books and newspapers, scraps of humanity, rags and tatters of fine clothing, patched together, as is the human soul.[1]

And so for Euripides, give or take the books and newspapers.

What Strindberg lacks by comparison with Euripides is not the dimension of paradox but the dimensions of paradigm, parable and parody. Euripides surely had a mean streak, but he also had a lightness of touch. Despite the historical dimension to some of his work Strindberg does not obviously rework the past in order to dissect the

---

[1] from the Preface to *Miss Julie*, trans. Elizabeth Sprigge, New York: Doubleday, 1955, pp. 64–5.

present. Their work may from time to time run parallel but Strindberg, despite his claimed 'conglomerations of past and present', does not appear influenced by any other past than his own. Others are, as we shall see.

A book, or at least a major part of a book, was written on Euripides and Shaw eighty years ago. There is a book waiting to be written on Euripides and BERTOLT BRECHT. Brecht died in 1956, only six years after Shaw. The briefest look at the settings of Brecht's plays identifies one of the major features he can offer to the current debate. *The Good Person of Szechwan* and *The Caucasian Chalk Circle* are set in China, the latter through the medium of a tale told by villagers in the Caucasus; *The Life of Galileo* in seventeenth-century Padua; *Mother Courage* in and around the battlefields of the Thirty Years War; others in Chicago, fourteenth-century and eighteenth-century London, Rome and ancient Thebes. The stage for Brecht was where the action of a play takes place, as it was for Euripides, and frequently Shakespeare, whatever the notional setting. Who better than Brecht, since the Greeks, has explored the stage mileage to be won from creating a mythical world, to both distance the audience from an issue and focus them in on it? His manufactured worlds of Szechwan, the Caucasus, Padua or Chicago are surely the scenographic equivalents of Corinth, Trozen, Pharsalus or Thebes. Brecht's theatre, like that of Euripides is a theatre of music, song and masks. There is a similar appreciation of the emblematic power of stage props, and of children as stage props.

Both created stage worlds wherever it was convenient to offer a frame for a fable, or 'parable', as several of Brecht's dramas are subtitled. As John Willett put it: 'It's more important nowadays for the set to tell the spectator he's in a theatre than to tell him he's in, say, Aulis' (Willett, 1966, p. 233). The freedom that this bestows from any requirement for historical accuracy is a dominant feature of all Greek tragedy and comedy, though in modern staging terms such freedom probably owes as much to Meyerhold and the great Russian directors of the late Czarist and early Soviet periods as to the specific originality of Piscator or Brecht.

Through his use of alienation devices Brecht returned to a sense and awareness of dramatic form found originally in the Greek tragedians and comedians, using that form to enhance rather than to diminish content. His espousal of an epic theatre to contrast with the dramatic theatre rooted, as he saw it, in Aristotle might suggest that Euripides and Brecht were opposites rather than equivalents. Both have suffered from some misreading, especially over emotional commitment. Brecht's Philosopher in *The Messingkauf Dialogues* can state categorically that 'Neither the public nor the actor must be stopped from taking part emotionally' (Brecht, 1965, p. 57). Aristotle's appreciation of Euripides only as 'the most tragic' seems handicapped by his being a philosopher rather than a drama critic, demonstrating little understanding of what later generations have deciphered as Euripides' dramatic shape-changing.

In advocating a theatre which extolled thought in place of emotional indulgence, Brecht was only one of a number of early twentieth-century dramatists and practitioners to break free from the restrictions of the past. The same was true, in the fifth century BC, of Euripides, whom some critics have judged a prisoner of his time because of the conventions of the Greek theatre within which he worked: he was nothing of the sort. The chorus, masks, dance and song, which Brecht too was to employ, may have been aimed at distancing his audience from 'realism' but served as a new way to draw an audience into the process of telling a story. Euripides kept the devices of the theatre of his time, but expanded and renewed them in the same cause.

When Brecht turned directly to the Greeks, it was not Euripides but Sophocles that he took as his inspiration, with his take on *Antigone* (1948). He was later to write:

> The old masterpieces become as it were dustier and dustier with neglect, and the copyists more or less conscientiously include the dust in their replica. What gets lost above all is the classics' original freshness, the element of surprise (in terms of their period), of newness, of productive stimulus that is the hallmark of such works.[1]

Such an endorsement of *peripeteia* and *anagnorisis* ('reversal' and 'recognition' or 'awareness') is, as it happens, far more fundamental to Aristotle's analysis of tragedy in the *Poetics* than his comments on *katharsis* ('purgation of emotion'). Brecht's *Antigone*, however, was not a great success. In Switzerland in 1948 any *Antigone* could hardly fail to resonate, but the four performances at Chur and one in Zurich suggested in the staging, by the few eyewitness accounts, little more than a return to the Reinhardt Sophoclean tradition of the early part of the century.[2] Ultimately, it would seem that Marxist reduction to economics as the source of all conflict was simply incompatible with anything the Greeks could have understood. Of all the possible inheritors of Euripides' legacy, Brecht is the only one known as much for his work as director as play-

---

[1] 'Classical Status as an Inhibiting Factor', Willett (1966), p. 272.
[2] Hofmannstahl's adaptations *Electra* (1903) and *Oedipus Rex* (1910).

wright. Brecht's emphasis on properties may be found to some extent in all the Greek tragedians: his concern over stage objects has a real place in Sophocles (especially *Ajax* and *Philoctetes*), but less in Euripides except among those characters, as in *Trojan Women*, for whom dispossession becomes a theme in its own right.

Where Euripides and Brecht stand on common ground is in the moral paradox of those who do the right thing for the wrong reason, or the wrong thing for the right reason. When the gods come down to earth to reward virtue in *The Good Person of Szechwan* (1943) and give financial assistance to Shen Teh, she finds herself unable to survive in business unless she dons a mask and submerges herself in the ruthless alternative personality of Shui Tah. Pope Urban VIII (*The Life of Galileo*, 1943), Azdak (*The Caucasian Chalk Circle*, 1948) and Ui (*The Resistible Rise of Arturo Ui*, 1958), all find that they change according to the emblems of office. Brecht sees political circumstance as the trigger for change; Euripides had no such illusions. The gods may interfere in people's lives, but ultimately they turn out to be more personifications than deities. In the final analysis, Brecht moves further in the direction of classical staging than almost any playwright since Euripides. Remarkable dramatic manipulator though he was, gifted with stage sense and sensibility, there are many occasions, in contrast to Euripides, where it is Brecht's agenda which dictates events rather than the characters. Every situation is either promoted, or demoted, depending on your own perspective, to being explicable primarily in economic terms. Euripides had less of a sense that the world was remediable.

From the Marxist Brecht straight to the Fascist LUIGI PIRANDELLO may seem an abrupt transition, but there are certainly Euripidean echoes to be found in some of Pirandello's perceptions, not least the deep sense of his own unpopularity. Euripides managed only four first prizes in Athens in a working career that spanned half a century. There are no later stories of his plays being hissed off the stage, but his taste for speaking the uncomfortable in all sorts of areas, from the conduct of war to the treatment of women, ensured, at the very least, that a mention of his name, or appearance as a caricature, guaranteed a laugh for Aristophanes.

Pirandello's dramatic experimentation in his own time provoked hostility beyond what seems reasonable, especially in a writer who was to be awarded a Nobel Prize in 1934. Unhappy man though he was, it must have been more than paranoia that inclined him to write, after the uncomfortable première of his highly experimental *Tonight We Improvise* in 1930, 'Everywhere I am pursued by hatred. Perhaps it is only right that this should be so, that I should die this way, annihilated by the hatred of triumphant cowards, by the incomprehension of idiots. After all they are in the majority.' This comes from a personal letter to Marta Abba (in her own translation) published in the Introduction to his remarkable final and unfinished play (another Euripidean echo), *The Mountain Giants* (New York: Crown, 1958). A strange piece, it is set among a group of lunatics led by an illusionist. A young playwright, Ilse, agrees to present the poetic play she has written at a wedding celebration and is torn to pieces by her audience. Though Euripides' *Bacchae* is nowhere directly invoked, it requires no great leap of the imagination to start a search for further parallels.

The seeds of Euripides' awareness of the stage as a place where what is real and what is not come under scrutiny are sown in *Alcestis* or *Helen*, never mind *Bacchae* where little is what it seems on the surface. Pirandello's investigations into the nature of truth, of reality, of theatre itself, form the backbone of his most successful and lasting group of plays: *The Rules of the Game* (1919), *Six Characters in Search of an Author* (1921) and *Henry IV* (reputedly completed only a fortnight after *Six Characters*), where the audience is constantly invited to speculate on their own role within the theatre experience. More than with most playwrights, the task of deciphering what is real and what is staged reality transcends the 'game' of theatre, where the rules are set out by the dramatist, and reaches into the territory of metaphysics through metatheatre. In all three plays the characters play roles as the actors play characters. Theirs is a world of masks, both figurative and literal, as, in the half-masks Pirandello suggested within the stage directions for the Six Characters at their entrance, 'designed to give the impression of figures constructed by art, each one fixed in its own fundamental emotion'. The confusion of Euripides' Ion when trying to sort out the circumstances of his birth – 'Couldn't it have been some youthful indiscretion, Mother, and you decided, as girls do, to blame a god?' (*Ion*, ll. 1522–5) – seems echoed in Pirandello's Producer pleading 'Tell me what really happened' when the conjured characters, now seven, start to play out their own unfulfilled drama. The four-year-old girl is drowned, her brother shoots himself. 'What do you mean, dead?' laughs the Leading Man, one of the acting company, not one of the Six. 'It's all make-believe. It's all a pretence.' 'What do you mean, pretence?' responds the Father whom the Leading Man had singularly failed adequately to play. 'Reality, ladies and gentlemen, reality! Reality!'

In *Henry IV* the leading character has no other name but that of the medieval king Henry IV, into whose personality he has become frozen after an accident while playing him in a masquerade. Several of the other characters feel sceptical about this 'madness', including the woman he loved and her present lover, Belcredi. 'Henry' has in fact returned to sanity and stabs Belcredi to death, an act which guarantees he must retreat for ever into his historical role as madman. Though way beyond anything in Euripides, these challenges, both to the nature of theatre and to what happens to those who are cast within the expectation of their mythical prototype are the stuff of a whole series of Euripides dramas, for characters as diverse as Helen, Heracles, Clytemnestra and Achilles: what Susan Bassnett-McGuire described in Pirandello as 'the investigation of theatre form through use of that form' (Bassnett-McGuire, 1983, p. 8).

It may be added, and not simply as a coda, that the Sicilian Pirandello, born close to where the fifth-century BC Greek philosopher and scientist Empedocles had lived, translated Euripides' satyr play *Cyclops* into the Sicilian dialect, this being the only surviving ancient Greek play set in Sicily. Pirandello had at least some knowledge of the classical playwright.[1]

JEAN ANOUILH (1910–87) was one of a group of twentieth-century French writers who consciously returned to Greek myth for much of their dramatic material. Though others may seem to have latched on to the Greek tragedians and manipulated them to their own agendas, Anouilh shows more respect for the originals, though re-working them within a modern context. Two, *Antigone* (1942) and *Oedipe: ou Le Roi boiteux* (1986), are closely based on Sophocles originals, though with a personal slant. *Antigone* acquired the reputation of being a Resistance play for occupied Paris, an interpretation over which Anouilh himself remained coy, perhaps because his Creon has an answer to all Antigone's objections and is portrayed with real sympathy.

The charmingly titled *Tu étais si gentil quand tu étais petit* (1972) is Anouilh's take on the story of Orestes and Electra, versions of which survive from all three of the Greeks, as well as from Giraudoux, Cocteau and Sartre. Anouilh's play about the return of the exiled Orestes to avenge the death of his father Agamemnon, by killing his mother Clytemnestra and her lover Aegisthus, is the most idiosyncratic of all his classical pieces. The action is accompanied by a quartet of musicians (piano, violin, cello, double-bass) whose own issues counterpoint the Aeschylean version of the story with a diversionary outcome and

---

[1] *U ciclopu* was first performed at the Teatro Argentina in Rome in 1919.

conclusion which has the pianist rescuing Orestes from the Furies (the other musicians) and leaves the queen and her consort alive. There is a Pirandellian touch too in the manner in which Anouilh juggles theatre and reality.

Medea (1937) is a one-act *pièce noire*, whose central theme is the destructive power of a love that was based exclusively on physical passion and, when burnt out, can only turn to hate. This is the play's most obviously Euripidean aspect. It ends, not with Medea's escape to Athens in a winged chariot after the act of matricide, but downbeat. Medea does kill the children, but then commits suicide inside a burning wagon, her last words 'I am your little brother and your wife, I, the horrible Medea! And now, try to forget her!' And Jason, drained of all emotion, responds 'Yes, I will forget you. Yes, I will live.' He leaves the stage, the last words of the play belonging to the Nurse and a Guard, who calmly discuss the weather and the prospects for the harvest. It is an unexpected ending, subdued and muted, but marking the extent to which the relationship between Medea and Jason had been wholly self-absorbed.

This version of one of Euripides' most memorable plays is not the whole reason for including Anouilh here. What is truly Euripidean about Anouilh is an emotional range and compass played out with an immaculate theatrical flair over a wide range of material. He chose to link his work under a number of headings, *pièces baroque*, *pièces grinçantes* ('teeth-grinding' or 'black comedy'), *pièces brillantes*, *pièces secrètes* (the category which includes *Tu étais si gentil quand tu étais petit*), *pièces costumées*, *pièces roses* and *pièces noires* (including *Medea*). Few playwrights of the modern era have encompassed such a range, from romantic fantasies such as *Time Remembered* or *Ring Round the Moon* – the most familiar English titles for *Léocadia* (1940) and *L'Invitation au château* (1947) – to the 'teeth-grinding' cruelty of *Ardèle* (1948) in which the ludicrous (and horribly funny) family of General St Pé hound a hunchback aunt into suicide when they discover she has a hunchback lover. The same leading characters, General St Pé and his neurotic wife reoccur in later plays, one of them, *The Waltz of the Toreadors* (1952), which moves from pure farce to a finale close to *grand guignol*. Then again, there is *The Lark* (1953), Anouilh's St Joan play which many find more satisfying than Shaw's; and *Becket* which these days comes rather well out of any comparison with Eliot's *Murder in the Cathedral*. Anouilh had a knack of making figures from the past, even the past as long ago as Oedipus and Antigone, seem to speak as though they live in the present. He had a distinctive approach to Greek myth and its ability to reincarnate, phoenix-like, in a world where its decodings are inexhaustible. In his plays which have no direct contact with any Greek forebears, Anouilh shows a peculiarly twentieth-century capacity for dark farce, testing an audience's boundaries between the comic and the tragic. Like those of Euripides, Anouilh's bleakest plays always contain a touch of absurdity, the sunniest a murky undercurrent.

Such apparent cynicism over human relationships is often condemned as coldness: one part of his dramatic method, it is true, is to have a character or characters introduce or comment on the action as though it has already happened and is being reviewed in retrospect. But then Euripides too is criticised for cynicism by most of those who prefer the heroics to be found in Aeschylus or Sophocles as best reflecting classicism proper. Euripides has returned to the stage in this our cynical age: maybe Anouilh will too, and introduce a new generation to his combination of dazzling theatrical surprise and diversity of mood. 'He has the greatest natural genius for the stage of any man living,' wrote *Sunday Times* critic, Harold Hobson, reviewing the first British production of *The Cavern* in 1965. Here surely is an original playwright who could appreciate the shifting shapes of *Heracles, Helen, Phoenician Women, Iphigeneia Among the Taurians* or *Andromache*. No playwright in antiquity was such a manipulator of the theatrical moment as was Euripides. Few in the modern period, if any, stand as real rivals in this respect to Jean Anouilh.

In Aristophanes' *Frogs* (405 BC), Dionysus goes to Hades to bring back Euripides to 'save' the city. As a result of a competition between Aeschylus and Euripides, it is Aeschylus whom Dionysus decides to resurrect, on political grounds. When the two playwrights compete over their respective techniques, music is one of the central areas of disagreement, both choral and solo. 'You', complains the infuriated Aeschylus, 'have the nerve to criticise songs of mine, you who turn out musical tricks like some stripper!' (l. 1330). Because our access to the original music of Greek tragedy is so limited it is all too often forgotten that all Greek drama was highly dependent on music, almost to the level of opera.[1] STEPHEN SONDHEIM, as mentioned above, turned Aeschylus and Euripides into Shakespeare and Shaw in his *Frogs*. He lays claim to inclusion here as a composer who excites equally enthusiasts and detractors, and for the innovation of his theatrical techniques.

Sondheim's accomplishment in music theatre may serve as a reminder that Euripides too was a worker in 'synthetic theatre', to use Alexander

[1] See McDonald (2001) for a comprehensive study of Greek myth in opera.

Tairov's term, theatre as a synthesis of the other arts. Some of Sondheim's worlds have the domestic context of New York, as some Euripides explores the social *mores* of his Athens, but Sondheim can equally take off into the sub-cultures of kabuki, sensation melodrama, neo-impressionism or fairy-tale. *Into the Woods* (1987) takes as its starting point a familiar fairy-story, that of the baker who must lift a curse, if he and his wife are to have a child, by bringing to the witch four objects, 'a cow as white as milk, a cape as red as blood, a lock of hair as yellow as corn and a slipper as pure as gold'. The successful search involves the baker becoming involved with characters from other fairy-tales and the second half follows the consequences of this. It is hardly stretching genres to see a parallel here with Euripides' adjusting characters such as Helen or Heracles according to the varying contexts into which he places them. The mythical past impinges on the present and the perception of other cultures involves for Sondheim a move into those other cultures, as in the various settings in *Assassins* (1991) or the old and new Japans of *Pacific Overtures* (1975), to interrogate imperialism and, on occasions, the after-math of invasion. The *Boston Times* had found the music 'always complex and extremely irritating'. By the time it arrived on Broadway after rewrites, the *New York Times* still found *Pacific Overtures* 'an irritating bore', but for the *Daily News* 'it breaks new ground in the theater and leaves the audience shaken and breathless with excitement and beauty'.

There is a risk, of course, in all such comparisons. Almost any play by any playwright can be made to look like any other if you try hard enough. The revenge of Sweeney in *Sweeney Todd, the Demon Barber of Fleet Street* (1979) can be made to appear like every other revenge drama or melodrama, give or take the odd meat pie, but where there is a real parallel is in the sheer intensity of both Euripides and Sondheim, perhaps reflected in their music – we cannot know – but certainly present in all Euripides' bitter post-war plays (*Trojan Women*, *Hecuba* and *Andromache*), as well as in the destructive passion of Electra, Medea and Phaedra. 'A god should not show passion like a man,' howls the desperate Cadmus at the end of the *Bacchae*.

Passion (1994) is one of Sondheim's most intense and surprising works. An extraordinary dramatic tale, potentially it is as destructive as *Hippolytus*. The sickly leech-like Fosca whose obsession for young Captain Giorgio comes to dominate her existence initially provokes him to sing:

Is this what you call love?
This endless and insatiable
Smothering

Pursuit of me,
You think this is love?

Fosca's calm response in the next scene:

Loving you
Is not a choice.
It's who I am.

eventually engulfs the young captain and forces him to abandon the
woman to whom he has sworn undying love, knowing only that a love
like Fosca's is more powerful than any emotion he believed could exist.
Such obsession transcends her death and can only be expressed in music.
Such passion is exclusive, unconditional, perhaps deadly. Sondheim
attends through music the extremes of human sentiment where few
playwrights dare to tread.

A similar intensity governs Sondheim's *Assassins* which brings
together nine of those who tried to murder an American President, four
of them successful, and dares to investigate the impulse that drove them
to behave as they did. The carnival setting – stage direction '*a sign lights
up:* HIT THE "PREZ" AND WIN A PRIZE' – may be more Aristophanic than
Euripidean, but it is hard to resist a sense that here are two dramatists
who travel to the outer limits of historical behaviour. It may be
Sophocles of the Greek tragedians who identifies the outsiders (Ajax,
Philoctetes, Antigone, Deianira) brought to mind by Jim Lovenseimer in
his 'Stephen Sondheim and the Musical of the Outsider' (Everett and
Laird, 2002, pp. 181–96), rather than Euripides, but where Euripides
and Sondheim do coincide is in the risks they will take in exploring
human feeling.

I originally homed in on eight contenders for Euripides' crown, but
ultimately there could not be room for both FRIEDRICH DÜRRENMATT and
MAX FRISCH. For much of their careers critics lumped them in the same
basket, though they are perhaps only as alike as Sophocles and Euripides.
What both do is create strange situations, stranger than any in Brecht or
Sondheim, and have their characters react within such situations as
though they were real. The monstrous Claire Zachanassian of
Dürrenmatt's *The Visit* is one of the twentieth century's most trenchant
icons, buying a man's life through a consciousness of how greed works.
An Angel Comes to Babylon features the radiant Kurrubi brought to
earth to be given to the most deprived man in the world. The situation

seems to echo Strindberg's *A Dream Play* but Dürrenmatt's treatment is wholly ironic. By chance, Nebuchadnezzar, king of Babylon, has chosen this very day to disguise himself and show the unreconstructed beggar Akki the error of his ways. In a begging competition witnessed by Kurrubi, Nebuchadnezzar is beaten hands down by Akki, and Kurrubi, therefore, bestows herself on the king.

Dürrenmatt did write a Hercules play set in antiquity, *Hercules and the Augean Stables*, in which, much as the usurper Lycus tries to do in Euripides' *Children of Heracles*, the twelve labours are derided as failures. There is also something decidedly Euripidean in the turning on its head of a received story, but irony alone is not quite enough and, though *The Visit* is perhaps the best play written by either of them, Dürrenmatt loses out here to Frisch.[1]

Max Frisch explores, as do Jean Anouilh and Friedrich Dürrenmatt, how to devise new dimensions in which their characters may function. Something similar can be found in several of Frisch's novels, *Homo Faber* (based on the Oedipus story) and *My Name is Gantenbein* where questions of identity and levels of perception are consciously infiltrated by classical myth. From his dramatic output the immobilised firemen of the 1958 *Biedermann und die Brandstifter* (variously translated as *The Fire Raisers*, *The Firebugs* and, in 2007, *The Arsonists*[2]) parody the powerlessness of a tragic chorus trying to avert disaster. But it is in none of these that Frisch most truly reveals his Euripideanism. That resides in two recurrent theatrical ideas.[3]

In several of Frisch's mature plays someone, often a fringe character, performs the physical action of removing and polishing spectacles to find a new perspective on the situation as it unfolds. The concept can be found in *The Fire Raisers*, but is a major theme in *Count Oederland* (1951), *Don Juan or The Love of Geometry* (1953 and 1962), and *Andorra* (1961). Characters in Frisch who cannot lengthen their vision by polishing their glasses tend to discover, often in front of a mirror, that they amount to no more than the product of what others believe them to be. For Helen, Andromache, Clytemnestra, Ion, all of these and more,

---

[1] Dürrenmatt's own views on Greek tragedy and comedy are anyway laid out in his essay 'Problems of the Theatre', originally a lecture delivered in Germany in 1954 and, translated by Gerhard Nellhaus, published as a Preface to *Dürrenmatt: Four Plays, 1957–62*, London: Jonathan Cape, 1964, pp. 9–41.

[2] 'Frisch's dazzling 1958 parable gains extra resonance in this age of anxiety', 'Critics' Picks', *Guardian*, 3 December 2007.

[3] Excerpts from Max Frisch's *Tagebuch* [*Diary* or *Sketchbook*] 1946–1949, translated by Carl Richard Mueller, were published in *The Tulane Drama Review*, 6.3 (March 1962), pp. 3–13.

Euripides poses a similar dilemma, subject every one to the expectations of myth.

A linked feature of Frisch's dramaturgy which marks him out as a latterday Euripides is his ability to play with biographies, and biographies, in particular, as an extension of the self. From *Santa Cruz* (1946) to *Triptych* (1979), Frisch's dramatic personae dress and undress their personalities as circumstances require. *Biography* (1967) opens with a note from the author that:

> The play takes place on the stage [...] What is being presented is what can only be shown in a game, the different course events might have taken in someone's life. The subject of the play is not Herr Kürrman's biography, which is banal, but his relationship to the fact that with the passage of time one inevitably acquires a biography. The events are not portrayed illusionistically as taking place in the present, but are reflected upon – as in chess, when we reconstruct the decisive moves of a lost game, curious to find out whether the game could have been played differently.

Frisch also cites Vershinin's speech in Chekhov's *Three Sisters* about living a second life as a 'fair copy' (which is what the present biographical game proposes for Euripides as a playwright).

Frisch and Euripides share with Anouilh and Pirandello a sense of black comedy which approaches the macabre. In *The Fire Raisers*, which most consciously adopts and parodies the form of a Greek tragedy, impotent chorus and all, the millionaire Biedermann allows his house to be invaded by two strangers, Schmitz and Eisenring, even though he knows that there are arsonists in the town. Eisenring, who possesses more than a passing resemblance to Dionysus, toys with Biedermann as Dionysus toys with Pentheus, both he and Schmitz second-guessing every reaction of their simple dupe. Eventually Biedermann's house goes up in smoke, the whole town with it. The sting in the tail, however, comes in an afterpiece which is not always performed. Schmitz and Eisenring, as Biedermann and his wife discover, are indeed Beelzebub and the Devil, but have decided to close down Hell. All the potential newcomers are being pardoned because they were wearing uniforms when they committed their atrocities. Biedermann catches a glimpse of the Earth, rising again from the ashes and declares that his giving the matches to the arsonists was 'a positive blessing from a town-planning point of view'. Schmitz and Eisenring return to the Earth to wreak their havoc all over again.

So there we have it: seven contenders for Euripides' Chair of Modern Drama, one Irish, a Swede, a German, an Italian, a Frenchman, an

American and a Swiss: two writing in English, but none of them British. Should room have been found for John Galsworthy, Brian Friel, Edward Bond, David Hare or even Howard Barker? I think not. Euripides could be, and can be, both shocking and satirical, iconoclastic and ironic, absurdist, modernist and post-modernist. Pick an 'ism' (realism, impressionism, symbolism, modernism, absurdism) and Euripides will show us that there are few new discoveries in theatre.

What all the featured seven share with Euripides is a sense that the world of theatre is a game, reflecting the larger game of life. Their comedy is often bitter – the world is a bitter place, differently now from in classical times, but no less threatening, bleak and absurd, in the Camus sense of 'without meaning'. For the most part the European experience predominates, and rightly so. Euripides was, after all, a Greek. Television has so distorted traditional drama that today's stage playwright has been forced to seek new means of expression. Sometime this involves going back to a world of choral dance, music and mask. More often it has been a search forward to where Dionysus will manifest himself next. If one thing is sure it is that the live theatre will not die. It will simply emerge through new guises, on new sites, in new manifestations. And Euripides will be there somewhere.

Searching for disciples of Euripides has been no more than a pastime, but one with point if it makes it possible to see Euripides, not as a limited example of a primitive and dead culture, but as the master among the Athenian playwrights for his ability to speak to subsequent generations and, more than any other, to show us to ourselves, two thousand years on, warts and all. Not today's playwright, Euripides is still a playwright for today.

APPENDIX

This is a brief résumé in alphabetical order of the plots of all nineteen surviving plays of Euripides for those who may be unfamiliar with some and need a broader context in the earlier chapters.

Alcestis

The god Apollo opens the play, explaining in a prologue how and why he rewarded Admetus, king of Pherae, for treating him so well during a period Apollo spent in his service. This had been imposed by Zeus for Apollo's killing the Cyclopes, makers of Zeus' thunderbolts. Apollo's gift to Admetus was to grant that, when his time came to die, he could cheat the Fates by finding a member of his family to take his place. His wife Alcestis was the only one willing to replace him and this is the fatal day. Death now appears, incensed at Apollo's attempt to rob him of his victim by saving Alcestis too. Apollo predicts the arrival of someone who will save Alcestis from Death's clutches.

The two immortals leave and the Chorus arrive, local townspeople, aware of Alcestis' impending death, but unsure whether or not she is still alive. One of Alcestis' servants gives an emotional account of her mistress bidding farewell to her house and home. Alcestis is now wheeled out, too weak to stand, accompanied by Admetus and their young son and daughter. She instructs her husband to protect the children, but before entrusting them to his care, makes him promise never to marry again. Admetus agrees and she dies. Her son sings a lament and the family return to the palace with the dead queen.

The Chorus are offering their tribute when they are interrupted by the entry of Heracles, on his way to complete one of his twelve labours, and seeking hospitality. Admetus returns to greet him, but when Heracles notes the signs of mourning, tells him that it is only a distant relation who has died, and that Heracles is welcome to stay. Heracles reluctantly agrees, but after he has gone indoors to the guest rooms, the Chorus show concern that Admetus has deceived him in this way. Admetus pleads the demands of hospitality and goes to prepare for the funeral. The cortège enters and Admetus' father, Pheres, turns up to offer sympathy and gifts. Admetus rejects both, pointing to the refusal of his father and his mother to sacrifice their lives on his behalf. A full-scale row breaks out over the body, during which Pheres blames his son for accepting Apollo's gift in the first place. Admetus disowns his parents and the procession proceeds, without Pheres.

A second servant comes from the palace, complaining of Heracles' drunken behaviour. When Heracles follows him onstage, the servant is goaded into revealing that it is Alcestis who has died. A chastened Heracles sobers up fast and leaves the scene, vowing to go and challenge Death. Admetus returns, overcome with grief at the prospect of life without his wife. After another choral ode, Heracles comes back, accompanied by a veiled woman he claims to have won in an athletics competition. He reproves Admetus for not telling him about Alcestis and asks him to take this woman into his house while he is away on his mission. Admetus is reluctant, but finally agrees, only for Heracles to reveal the woman as Alcestis, whom he has brought back from the grave after wrestling for her with Death. The family is reunited and Heracles departs.

Andromache

Andromache was the wife of the Trojan hero Hector, killed by Achilles during the defence of Troy. After the fall of the city, their baby son was thrown from the city walls (see *Trojan Women* and *Hecuba*) and Andromache 'allocated' to Achilles' son, Neoptolemus, who lives in Pharsalus. She has had another son, by Neoptolemus, but is still a war-slave and suffering persecution from Neoptolemus' new wife, Hermione. Hermione is the daughter of Menelaus and Helen, but is childless and holds Andromache responsible. She means to have her revenge while her husband is away attempting to appease Apollo at Delphi.

All this is revealed by Andromache in the prologue, which she delivers from the sanctuary of a shrine to the sea-goddess Thetis – former wife of Peleus and mother of Achilles – where she and her son have taken refuge. A Servant arrives to tell Andromache that Menelaus is on his way to offer support to his daughter. The Chorus of local women of Thessaly arrive set on effecting a reconciliation between Hermione and Andromache, whom they advise to leave her refuge. Their mission seems unlikely to succeed. They are followed shortly by Hermione herself who has no such ambition. A furious row ensues between the two women, with Hermione flaunting her wealth and current position, contrasting it with that of the former princess, now a slave. Andromache responds equally forcefully, despite her precarious situation. Menelaus arrives to support his daughter and tricks Andromache into giving herself up, in the belief that this will be a way to save her boy. The Chorus sing a choral ode about how two women with one man is a recipe for disaster and Andromache enjoys a brief farewell with her young son. Menelaus returns, but his machinations are thwarted by the sudden entrance of Peleus, mortal father of Achilles and grandfather of Neoptolemus. Old as he is, Peleus sees off Menelaus who has no stomach for a fight and who heads for Sparta, abandoning Hermione.

The boot is now on the other foot and it is the deserted Hermione who finds herself so friendless that she threatens suicide. The arrival out of the blue of Orestes, son of Agamemnon and Clytemnestra, provides another twist. He has been waiting nearby to see how events proceed and has arranged for Neoptolemus to be assassinated at Delphi, so that he can run off with Hermione, his cousin, whom he had previously been expecting to marry. The two depart for Sparta. Peleus, meanwhile, receives news from a Messenger of how his grandson has indeed been murdered in Delphi. The body is brought in for him to mourn. His future as a lonely old man, deprived of all family, is unexpectedly averted by the arrival of Thetis *ex machina*. She decrees a future for Andromache and her son with Helenus, a brother-in-law who managed to survive the fall of Troy. She also offers Peleus immortality, once he has arranged for a suitable burial for their grandson, and the chance to live with her for the rest of time in the house of her father Nereus, a god with his goddess. Peleus is happy to agree.

Bacchae

The god Dionysus delivers the prologue, informing the audience that he has returned to Thebes, the city of his birth, in disguise as a human being. His mother, Semele, was one of the four daughters of Cadmus, king of Thebes. When she became pregnant by Zeus a jealous Hera suggested to the girl that she should persuade Zeus to appear to her in his true guise. This he did, at her insistence, but Semele was incinerated, the god's real form being a thunderbolt. The embryo was saved and placed in Zeus' thigh from which, in due time, Dionysus was born. Semele's father, Cadmus, and her sisters refused to acknowledge what had happened and now Dionysus has returned to exact his revenge. He has already driven the women of Thebes mad and they now roam the mountains, instigating miraculous happenings, entranced by the Bacchic religion. Pentheus, king of Thebes after the abdication of Cadmus, his grandfather, has heard about their activities and is determined to stamp out the religion as subversive and dangerous.

At the end of his opening speech, Dionysus summons the Chorus, a group of followers who have accompanied him from Asia. After their entrance song, Teiresias the blind prophet appears, wearing the paraphernalia of a Bacchant, a wreath and fawnskin, and carrying a thyrsus, the Bacchic wand with a pine-cone fixed to the top. He has come to the palace to go with Cadmus to the mountains where they can celebrate this new religion. Pentheus arrives, infuriated to find the old men so dressed. He gives orders for the 'stranger' to be apprehended – at this stage not even the Chorus know Dionysus' true identity.

Cadmus and Teiresias leave. The Chorus remain openly hostile to the king and sing of the benefits the religion can bring. A Servant arrives with Dionysus who has allowed himself to be arrested. Dionysus and Pentheus confront one another and, after losing the argument, Pentheus orders the stranger to be locked up in the palace dungeon. They leave the stage, but a few moments later the Chorus experience what appears to be an earthquake. Dionysus re-enters, informing them how Dionysus used his powers to derange the king.

When Pentheus emerges, Dionysus invites him to witness the Bacchic rites for himself, persuading the king that he must dress up as a woman if the women are not to discover his identity. The infatuated Pentheus does so and Dionysus leads him away. A short ode later and a Messenger arrives with news of the horrific death of Pentheus, torn to pieces by his mother, Agave, his aunts and the other ecstatic women. The Chorus are exultant. Agave now enters, still under the Bacchic influence and carrying on her thyrsus the head of her own son. Cadmus comes back soon after, with a stretcher on which are the remains of his grandson. Agave is slowly restored to sanity by her father and realises what she has done. When Dionysus appears above the action, this time in his true form as the god, Cadmus criticises him for wreaking such vengeance. The god is unmoved, but the human family which had disowned him as one of their own has been utterly destroyed. Cadmus and Agave must be parted and leave Thebes.

Children of Heracles

Heracles was the son of Alcmena and Zeus, who seduced her during her husband Amphitryon's absence by making himself look exactly like him. As a result Heracles incurred the lifelong enmity of Zeus' wife Hera and was forced to serve Eurystheus, king of Tiryns and Mycenae (see also *Heracles*). He successfully completed twelve labours for Eurystheus, only to fall victim to a poisoned robe which his second wife Deianira had impregnated with what she thought was a love-charm. After the hero's death, Eurystheus continued to persecute the family. *Children of Heracles* opens in Marathon, at a shrine in front of the temple of Zeus to which Alcmena has fled for sanctuary along with Iolaus, Heracles' old friend and helper, and with his children from the second marriage. The girls are inside the temple with Alcmena: Hyllus, Heracles' eldest son, has gone to seek help. Iolaus remains with the younger boys.

Copreus, Eurystheus' herald, arrives, threatening the children and attacking Iolaus when he tries to protect them. The Chorus, old men of Marathon, arrive in response to Iolaus' cries for help and, soon after, Demophon, son of Theseus, now king of Athens. Copreus claims the right to exercise the laws of Argos beyond the boundaries of his country. The children have been condemned to death and he has come to fetch them. Any opposition from Athens will result in unconditional war. Iolaus makes a spirited defence of his situation and that of the children, citing Athens' reputation as a protector of refugees.

Demophon considers the case made by both parties, deciding in favour of protecting Iolaus. Copreus makes more threatening noises, but is sent packing by Demophon. Iolaus expresses his gratitude and Demophon departs to prepare against attack. He returns with bad news. Oracles have suggested that a child sacrifice to Persephone is necessary if Athens is to succeed. He is not prepared to propose his own daughter or that of a fellow-countryman. Heracles' daughter, Macaria, enters from the temple and volunteers to die on behalf of the family. In an uncomfortable scene she reviews the alternatives and Iolaus finally concurs.

News arrives from Hyllus that he has found troops who will fight their cause. Iolaus calls Alcmena from the temple, declaring he wants to take part in the battle. Despite the reluctance of Hyllus' servant to assist him, Iolaus takes up arms and totters off. After a choral interlude a Messenger returns with news of a miraculous transformation: Iolaus has taken part in the successful engagement with the Argives and succeeded in capturing Eurystheus, having been transformed, so the Messenger was told, into a muscled young man. Soon after, Eurystheus is brought in in chains. Alcmena wants to have him killed, despite the resistance of the Chorus to murdering a prisoner-of-war. Her solution is to do the job herself, thus absolving Athens from responsibility. Eurystheus says that his body buried in front of Athena's shrine will ensure prosperity for Athens and Alcmena orders the guards to take him away and kill him.

Cyclops

The satyr play was a comic afterpiece to a tragic submission. Each playwright in the fifth century BC submitted a group of four plays as a festival entry at the Great Dionysia, the last of which was usually (though not always – *Alcestis* was a fourth play) a short comic take on an aspect of the story already dealt with in the three tragedies. Satyrs were semi-human, semi-animal creatures, with the head and tail of a horse, and usually sporting a phallus. Led by Silenus, they serve as the Chorus, often in search of their god Dionysus with whom they have lost touch during one of his escapades.

Euripides' *Cyclops* is the only satyr play to have survived in its entirety. The plot comes from Book IX of Homer's *Odyssey*, though the satyrs are not part of the Homeric story. The play opens with the Chorus of satyrs driving a flock of sheep back to the cave of the giant Polyphemus, the one-eyed Cyclops who has enslaved them. Silenus catches sight of a ship on the beach: soon after, Odysseus arrives with some of his men. They need provisions and ask for hospitality. Silenus warns them not to expect anything from the Cyclops when he returns from hunting. He is a cannibal. Odysseus gives Silenus a drink of special wine in return for meat and cheese; the satyrs are more interested in hearing about the recovery of Helen from Troy.

Silenus spots the Cyclops heading for home. When he enters Odysseus tells him that he and his crew are from Ithaca and on the way back from defeating Troy. The Cyclops is unimpressed and offers his own philosophy of life, amoral and anarchic, with no respect for Zeus or any god except himself. He drives Odysseus and his companions into the cave. After a brief song and dance from the satyrs, Odysseus returns, having crept out from a cleft in the cave wall. He tells of the slaughter and cooking of two of his plumpest men, after which Odysseus began to ply him with the special wine. The Cyclops is now well on the way to being drunk and Odysseus wants revenge. He asks the satyrs to assist him in blinding the giant with a heated olive branch. The satyrs think it a grand idea, but the Cyclops now emerges. Odysseus tells him his name is 'Nobody' and offers more and more drink until Polyphemus grabs an appalled Silenus and drags him off into the cave to have sex with him.

Faced with having to do something to help Odysseus the Chorus now find all sorts of excuses not to go into the cave and assist him to put out the giant's eye, confining themselves to shouting support from outside. Odysseus is successful and the blinded Cyclops emerges to be roundly mocked by the satyrs for being maimed by 'Nobody'. Odysseus admits who he really is and departs with his remaining men. The Chorus go with him leaving the Cyclops threatening vengeance.

Electra

For those who know the Aeschylus or Sophocles versions of the same story, Euripides has plenty of surprises. The play opens close to the border of Argos, in front of the cottage of a local Farmer. In the prologue he tells the audience that Electra was married off to him by Aegisthus to prevent her having a son who might prove dangerous, but that the marriage has not been consummated. Electra enters, on her way to the well to fetch water. He leaves for the fields, she for the well.

Her brother Orestes arrives with Pylades whose family have brought him up since his escape from Argos as a child. Orestes has heard rumours about his sister and has come to find out how things are. They see someone they take to be a slave and hide, but it is Electra returning and quickly revealing who she is. The Chorus now arrive, local girls offering to take Electra to a festival, an offer she rejects. Orestes and Pylades confront her, but without admitting who they are. Electra tells them about her unhappy life until the Farmer returns, concerned to find his wife talking to strangers. She tells him they have news of Orestes and he offers hospitality before Electra sends him off to ask for provisions from the old servant of Agamemnon's who had originally saved Orestes.

When the Old Man arrives, he believes that Orestes may already be in Argos. Electra rejects his suggestions for recognising her brother (the tokens used by Aeschylus in *Libation-Bearers*) and any idea that Orestes would have arrived in secret, but when the two visitors emerge from the cottage, the Old Man identifies Orestes by a scar. Brother and sister are reunited. Plans are then made to kill Aegisthus, into which the Old Man enters with enthusiasm. Aegisthus is currently at a sacred feast not far away. Electra volunteers to see to their mother, who is not with him: they decide to tell Clytemnestra that Electra needs help after the birth of a child. They leave on their various missions.

Cries are heard from far away and Electra fears the worst, but a Messenger (? Pylades) arrives with news of the successful killing of Aegisthus whose remains Orestes brings back. Electra reviles the corpse and, when Clytemnestra's chariot is sighted, Orestes takes the body inside. Mother and daughter justify their past behaviour at length, Clytemnestra showing some remorse. She is persuaded to go indoors where she too is killed. Orestes and Electra return with their mother's body. Both are distraught and the account of the killing is gruesome. Their recriminations are interrupted by the arrival *ex machina* of Clytemnestra's twin brothers, Castor and Pollux. Castor appears to blame Apollo for what has happened, but forecasts the future for brother and sister. Pylades is to marry Electra (the Farmer having been suitably rewarded). Orestes is to go to Athens, hunted down by the Furies, there to stand trial and be acquitted at the Court of the Areopagus. The locals will bury Aegisthus. Menelaus and Helen, who never really went to Troy (see *Helen*) are already on their way to bury Clytemnestra.

Hecuba

In the unusual opening to *Hecuba* the prologue is delivered by the ghost of Polydorus, a son of Hecuba and Priam who was sent away from Troy for safe keeping at the beginning of the war against the Greeks. After the defeat of Troy and the death of Hector, Polymestor, king of Thrace, betrayed his trust as a host, murdered Polydorus for his gold and threw his body into the sea. Now Polydorus' ghost has been hovering over Hecuba for three days and forecasts the death of his sister Polyxena, and that his mother is about to mourn the deaths of two of her children.

The ghost departs and Hecuba enters, now a prisoner of the Greeks. She has had a dream and fears for the safety of her remaining children. The Chorus of her fellow-slaves come to tell her the result of a debate about another ghost, this time that of the Greek warrior Achilles who is apparently claiming Polyxena as a human sacrifice at his tomb. Polyxena enters to be told that the Greeks mean to kill her. Odysseus arrives advising submission to what has been decided, but Hecuba reminds him of an occasion, earlier in the war, when he went on a spying mission into Troy, was recognised and saved only by Hecuba's merciful refusal to give him away. Odysseus acknowledges that he owes Hecuba his life, but will not relent. Hecuba and her daughter bid one another farewell and Polyxena leaves with Odysseus.

After an ode from the Chorus, Talthybius, the Greek herald, brings news of Polyxena's brave death. Hecuba prepares to lay out her dead daughter. When a body is carried in on a stretcher, its head covered, she assumes it to be Polyxena, only to discover beneath the coverlet her murdered son Polydorus. Now she understands her dream. When Agamemnon appears, she reminds him that his chosen concubine is another of her daughters, Cassandra, the prophetess cursed by Apollo to know the future, but never to be believed. Hecuba tells Agamemnon of the treachery of Polymestor and asks him, from his obligation to Cassandra, to support her in her revenge. Agamemnon does not wish to be seen to be involved, but agrees that a message be sent to Polymestor inviting him to visit Hecuba and to bring with him his two young sons.

When Polymestor arrives, Hecuba asks after her own son and is assured that he is well. She responds by telling him of Trojan treasure hidden from the Greeks, including some inside the tent that she is sharing with the other captives. Polymestor goes inside with his boys, soon to return blinded, both children killed by the women. He calls for help from Agamemnon, who rejects him, claiming he has received the punishment his deceit deserves. The blind Polymestor, turned prophet now, predicts Hecuba's future: when he does the same for Agamemnon, the Greek commander-in-chief orders him to be abandoned on a desert island while he and Hecuba leave to face their respective futures.

Helen

Helen opens the play, appearing not from the palace in the background, but from a shrine where she has taken refuge. She identifies herself as the wife of Menelaus and, by general account, the cause of the Trojan War. This, she tells the audience, is completely wrong. Zeus had wanted a major war in order to reduce the population, but it was an image of her, fashioned by the gods from mist, which Paris took to Troy: she was spirited away to Egypt where she has remained for the ten years of the war and another seven since its end. While Proteus, the former pharaoh, was alive she lived safely, but his son Theoclymenus is now keen on marrying her. That is why she has taken refuge at the old man's tomb.

Teucer enters, a Greek soldier at Troy, who recognises her, but then assumes he must have made a mistake. She is in no mood to admit who she is. He gives her news of her own family, including Menelaus who is missing presumed drowned in a storm, and of other Greeks who fought at Troy. He himself has been banished by his father for failing to prevent the suicide of his brother Ajax, and is here seeking directions to Cyprus from Theonoe, the sister of Theoclymenus and a prophetess. When Helen tells him that Greeks in Egypt face death, he quickly departs. The Chorus arrive, Greek prisoners who serve as Helen's attendants, and they all exit into the palace to consult Theonoe.

Menelaus now arrives, shipwrecked and dressed in rags, but far from dead. He tries to gain entrance to the palace, but is dismissed by a female doorkeeper who assumes he is a beggar. He hides in the shrine when

Helen and the Chorus return but is discovered. Husband and wife are startled to recognise one another, though Menelaus finds it hard to believe Helen's story. The arrival of one of his crew from the beach to inform him that the phantom Helen has disappeared convinces him and they start to make plans for escape. The all-knowing sister of Theoclymenus is the big problem, but when she enters, they plead for her help. Theonoe agrees not to give them away and Helen concocts a plan. She will dress in mourning clothes and tell Theoclymenus that Menelaus has brought news of her husband's death. She is now prepared to marry the pharaoh, if he first allows her to perform funeral rites out at sea for Menelaus.

Theoclymenus finally agrees and gives Menelaus provisions and weapons as well as the fastest ship in his navy. In due course a Messenger arrives with a report of the massacre of the Egyptian crew by the Greeks and the escape of Helen with the man who they now realise was Menelaus. The pharaoh threatens everybody with repercussions, but is prevented from murdering his sister by the arrival *ex machina* of Castor and Pollux, Helen's celestial brothers, who convince him that this was all ordained by Zeus.

Heracles

The play is set in Thebes where Heracles married his first wife, Megara, daughter of Creon. A prologue is delivered by Amphitryon, Heracles' earthly father – he seems ambivalent over whether he or Zeus was Heracles' real father – who gives his account of Eurystheus and the Twelve Labours, an arrangement entered into voluntarily by Heracles to absolve Amphitryon for the murder of the king of Argos (the version in *Children of Heracles* is rather different). Heracles is now engaged on the last and most dangerous task, the bringing back from Hades of the three-headed dog, Cerberus. The hero has been away for a considerable time. Lycus has usurped the throne of Thebes and means to kill the sons of Heracles and Megara. Heracles' father, Amphitryon, and the boys have sought sanctuary at an altar of Zeus.

Megara enters and speaks what amounts to a second prologue in which she describes how much the children miss their father and look forward to his return. Amphitryon tries to comfort her and the Chorus of old men join them, sympathetic but too feeble to be much practical use. Lycus now arrives, the epitome of a bullying tyrant. He debunks Heracles' heroic exploits and justifies his own actions before ordering kindling to be fetched so that he can burn them to death in their place of refuge. The Chorus threaten resistance, but Megara has reconciled herself to their fate and asks only that they be permitted to dress in ceremonial clothes. Lycus agrees and leaves while the children, Megara and Amphitryon depart into the house. After the Chorus sing an ode celebrating Heracles' real accomplishments the family return, prepared for death.

This is the moment when Heracles makes his appearance. His wife and Amphitryon quickly put him in the picture and he goes indoors with the children to wait for Lycus. Getting rid of the tyrant does not take long, but, when all seems to have turned out happily, the play takes a different direction. Two figures appear above the action, Iris, the messenger of the gods and Madness, whom Iris instructs to afflict Heracles and make him kill his own children. The justification is that the vengeful Hera can attack him openly, the twelve labours being now completed. Madness reluctantly agrees. Soon a Messenger arrives from indoors with news of the shocking massacre, which has included Megara, and is cut short only by Athena's knocking Heracles unconscious.

A tableau reveals the full horror of the scene and Amphitryon brings his son back to his senses as gently as he can. Theseus now arrives, Heracles' companion on the trip to Hades, and manages to persuade him not to commit suicide. Inconsolable though he is, and in self-imposed exile from Thebes, Heracles agrees to go with Theseus to Athens. There he will try, though not responsible for his actions, to come to terms with their appalling consequences.

Hippolytus

The goddess Aphrodite introduces the play. She enters in vengeful mood. Theseus is currently living in exile for a year in Trozen with his wife Phaedra and Hippolytus, his son by the Amazon warrior queen, Hippolyta. Hippolytus is the only man in the land who refuses to pay respect to Aphrodite as the goddess of sexual love. Instead he is a follower of Artemis and spends his time hunting. Aphrodite has as a result made Phaedra fall in love with Hippolytus, knowing that when Theseus finds out, he will curse the boy: both Hippolytus and Phaedra must die, Aphrodite admits, so that her honour can be protected.

As soon as the goddess has left, Hippolytus arrives with a secondary Chorus of huntsmen and pays his respects to Artemis, despite the advice of an Old Man that he acknowledge Aphrodite too. Hippolytus goes into the palace and the main Chorus of local women arrive, having heard that

Phaedra seems mortally ill. When she enters, walking only with the help of a Nurse, she refuses at first to identify the nature of her sickness. When the Nurse finally persuades her to confess her love for her stepson, the Nurse is at first deeply shocked but then offers to find a love potion which will win Hippolytus round. Satisfying her lust will be the only way to control it. Phaedra's protestations over revealing her passion to Hippolytus are proved justified when Hippolytus reacts with revulsion to the mere idea, and turns his attack on to the whole female sex. He promises, however, not to reveal what has happened to his father.

The humiliated Phaedra blames the Nurse for giving away her secret and retreats indoors where she hangs herself. When Theseus returns home he finds the household in mourning. Confronted with the body of his wife, he sees a letter in her hand in which she accuses Hippolytus of trying to rape her. Theseus instantly curses his son, though he knows that in the past Poseidon granted him three curses all of which would be fulfilled. Confronted by Phaedra's suicide, Hippolytus sticks to his oath not to reveal the real truth, simply swearing his innocence. The furious Theseus disowns his son and exiles him. Hippolytus departs, but, after a choral ode, a Messenger arrives with news of what has happened to Hippolytus. The curse has worked. Poseidon has sent a bull from the sea which terrified Hippolytus' horses so that they bolted. Hippolytus fell from the chariot, his feet caught in the traces, and is mortally hurt.

Hippolytus is brought on, dying. Theseus still refuses to believe that Phaedra was at fault until Artemis arrives *ex machina* to tell him what really happened. She refuses to blame Aphrodite – gods are seldom openly critical of one another's actions – but holds Theseus responsible for the death of his son. She exits hastily, unwilling to be present at a death, leaving time for a reconciliation between father and son before Hippolytus dies.

Ion

A great deal happens in this play. The god Hermes sets the scene, informing the audience of the setting, Delphi, and the circumstances which have contributed to the present situation. Years ago Creusa was raped by Apollo in a cave near the Acropolis in Athens. When the child was born, Creusa told no one and abandoned him in the same cave in a basket, with a necklace and wrapped in a shawl she had woven herself. Apollo intervened at this point and told Hermes to rescue the child and bring it to Delphi. This Hermes did and left the baby on the steps of the temple, where he was discovered by the Priestess. Now grown up, the young man Ion, though he will not be given this name until late in the play, serves as a temple attendant. His mother, meanwhile, has married King Xuthus in Athens.

When Hermes exits Ion enters, sweeping the steps and trying to discourage the birds which are fouling the roof and trying to build nests in the cornices. The Chorus arrive. Fresh from Athens, they have accompanied Creusa who has come with her husband, Xuthus, to consult the oracle over their childlessness. The Chorus are impressed by everything they see and Ion explains the oracle procedures. Creusa enters and Ion tells her he is a foundling while she admits to some secret in her past that she wants to sort out with Apollo. Xuthus enters, heading for his consultation in the temple. After a choral ode he re-emerges and embraces a startled Ion before informing him that Apollo has told him that the first person he meets outside the oracle will be his son: and this is Ion.

Xuthus and Ion are happy with the arrangement, but it does not meet with Creusa's approval when she hears. An Old Man, who has accompanied her, persuades Creusa it is all a plot against her and offers to kill Ion. Creusa tells him everything that has happened and gives him a bottle of poison to put in Ion's cup at the celebration he is holding with Xuthus. The plot fails when a drop is spilt and a pigeon drinks it and falls dead. The townspeople are now out to lynch Creusa for attempted murder. Ion and Creusa confront one another, but the sudden arrival from the temple of the Priestess changes everything. She has brought the cradle, necklace and shawl which were found with Ion: Creusa recognises them. She now claims Ion as her lost son, explaining that Xuthus was not his father after all.

The young man is confused and unconvinced, though she can describe the trinkets in detail. His problem is with believing that Apollo could ever behave in so disgraceful a fashion. Ion is heading for the temple to find the real truth when Athena arrives *ex machina*. She explains Apollo's reluctance to appear in person, but suggests that Ion accept what has happened, which will suit everybody very well. Creusa and Ion depart with the Chorus to return home to Athens with Xuthus.

Iphigeneia Among the Taurians

Though this looks like a sequel to *Iphigeneia at Aulis*, it was written earlier and is set many years later, after the ten-year war against Troy is over. It does take as its starting-point that Iphigeneia was indeed rescued by Artemis and taken to the land of the Taurians in the Crimea where she is now a priestess whose function, on the orders of King Thoas, is to sacrifice any Greeks found in the country. Iphigeneia delivers the prologue, outlining the circumstances of the Trojan War and how she came to be where she is. She has had a dream of her home back in Argos being destroyed by an earthquake which she interprets as meaning that her brother Orestes is dead. She retreats into the temple of Artemis to pray for him.

No sooner has she left than Orestes enters with Pylades. He is still afflicted by a rogue element of Furies who refused to accept the verdict of the court in Athens which acquitted him of murdering his mother Clytemnestra. As a part of his expiation Apollo has instructed him to find a statue of Artemis which fell here from the sky and is now lodged in the temple. He must steal it and take it back to Athens. Looking at the temple they realise it will not be easy to break in. They decide to wait until it is dark and depart. The Chorus, consisting of Greek slaves who serve Iphigeneia, enter and Iphigeneia tells them of the death of her brother. A Herdsman arrives who has seen two men on the beach, one of them called Pylades by the other who seems to be suffering some sort of a fit. Iphigeneia tells him to fetch the men and Orestes and Pylades are brought in under guard.

A long scene ensues during which Iphigeneia quizzes her brother about his background without either discovering their relationship. Iphigeneia decides to offer one of the two men the chance to escape if he will take back a letter to Argos for her. In case Pylades loses it on the way she reads the letter out loud and it becomes clear to all that the other man and the priestess are indeed brother and sister. After an extended reunion, during which Orestes tells Iphigeneia everything that has happened to him, they start to plan their escape. Iphigeneia will tell Thoas that Orestes has defiled the statue by his presence and that she must take it out to sea for purification. Thoas now arrives and is easily persuaded to provide a ship. He volunteers to join Iphigeneia, but she tells him to remain at the shrine. The procession duly sets out and, a choral ode later, a Messenger turns up to inform Thoas that the Greeks have all escaped and taken his statue with them. The furious king threatens to murder the entire Chorus for colluding in what has happened, and is about to set out in pursuit when Athena appears *ex machina*. She instructs Thoas to let the fugitives go, to free the Chorus and send them back to Greece into the bargain. Thoas quickly bows to the inevitable.

Iphigeneia at Aulis

This play, first performed posthumously in 405 BC along with *Bacchae* and two others now lost, shows signs of a lack of revision but is certainly playable in the form that has survived.[1] It opens, not with a prologue, but with Agamemnon, commander-in-chief of the Greek forces assembled to bring Helen back from Troy, summoning an old slave from his tent at Aulis where the Greek fleet is at present becalmed. There is an almost Shakespearean discussion between the two about the burdens of high office, leading to Agamemnon's entrusting the Old Man with a letter to take to his wife, Clytemnestra. The prophet Calchas has told Agamemnon that he must sacrifice his daughter to Artemis or the expedition will never be able to leave for Troy. Agamemnon has already sent a first letter to his wife telling her to bring Iphigeneia to Aulis on the pretext that she is to marry Achilles. Now he has had a change of heart and is sending a second letter countermanding the first, though not giving the real reason.

The Old Man leaves, but soon after the entry of the Chorus, local girls who have arrived excitedly to see the troops, the Old Man is hauled back by an angry Menelaus who has intercepted the letter. The two brothers argue bitterly about the contrasting obligations of authority but are interrupted by a Messenger who says that the wedding party has turned up. Menelaus now has a change of heart and tells his brother that no other obligation is worth the sacrifice of a daughter. Agamemnon, however, realises that the power of the army may already have grown too great to defy. Menelaus leaves to try to prevent Clytemnestra discovering what has been happening.

Clytemnestra now arrives, prepared for the marriage, with Iphigeneia and the baby Orestes. Iphigeneia's greeting of her father is full of affection and he cannot bring himself to confess either to her or to her mother what he intends to do. He and Clytemnestra exit with Iphigeneia and, after a choral ode, Achilles enters. He knows nothing of Agamemnon's subterfuge and is embarrassed by an effusive welcome from Clytemnestra who thinks she is greeting her future son-in-law. The Old Man reveals the truth to the two of them. An angry Achilles leaves to tackle the troops. Clytemnestra calls in Iphigeneia with the baby Orestes and then confronts her husband, forcing him to confess. Iphigeneia pleads for her life and Agamemnon tries to justify himself before leaving the scene.

Achilles now returns, appalled to find that the army have refused to

---

[1] Diggle's Oxford text identifies passages which seem to him doubtful or completed by a later hand. Scholars are particularly suspicious about the final scene.

listen and shouted him down. Iphigeneia decides that, if she must die, she will do so voluntarily and with dignity. She departs to her death. A Messenger arrives to tell of a miraculous intervention by Artemis who at the last minute has substituted a stag for the victim. Clytemnestra is unconvinced of the truth of this, but the fleet can now prepare to leave for Troy.

Medea

The Nurse to Medea's children delivers the prologue, giving the background to the story. Jason, Medea's husband (though their marital status is a little uncertain), sailed some years ago to the far end of the Black Sea to fetch the Golden Fleece. He was assisted in his task by Medea, the king's daughter in Colchis who fell in love with him. She accompanied him back to his home in Iolcus where she contrived the death of Jason's uncle who had usurped the throne. For this she and Jason were exiled together with their two young boys. They now live in Corinth. Jason has decided it is in his own interests to marry the daughter of Creon (no relation to the Theban Creon), king of Corinth. The Nurse is fearful for the children's future as Medea, deranged with grief at her husband's rejection, seems intent on revenge.

The Tutor enters with the boys. He has heard a rumour that Creon means to send Medea and the children away from Corinth. Medea's voice is heard lamenting off stage. She continues to do so when the Chorus of local women arrive. After the Nurse and Tutor take the children away, Medea appears, apparently calm and rational as she persuades the Chorus to keep quiet about any plans she may make. Creon enters, confirming his decision to exile Medea because he is afraid of what she might do. She persuades him to concede her one day to prepare for departure and begins to work out what to do in the time she has. Jason arrives and justifies his new marriage, in the teeth of Medea's accusations, as best for all of them. After he leaves, he is replaced by Aegeus, king of Athens, who has been visiting Delphi. Medea offers to help him over his childlessness if he offers her a refuge whatever may happen. Aegeus agrees and Medea, her escape route guaranteed, firms up her course of action which now includes the murder of her children as the only way to hurt her husband.

She sends the Nurse to call Jason back, pretends to make peace and sends him off to the palace with the Tutor and the children, to take a dress and a tiara for the princess which she has imbued with poison. Tutor and children return and go indoors: the gifts have been accepted. A Messenger arrives from the palace describing the horrific deaths of both the princess and of her father, Creon, who has tried to help free her from the clinging robe. Medea delivers a farewell speech to the boys, twice changing her mind, but then steeling herself to what she must do. She sends the children inside and follows them in. Their death cries soon resonate from off stage.

Jason returns, shocked at what has happened at the palace, only to find a worse situation inside his own home. Medea appears above the action (like a god *ex machina*) in a dragon chariot supplied by her grandfather, the Sun, the dead children draped over the side. The stricken father begs to be able to touch his children, but Medea departs, implacable as ever, and leaves Jason to face his grim future.

Orestes

It is Electra who opens *Orestes*, though her brother is present, lying asleep on a couch. Orestes has been in a state of delirium for the last six days since the murder of their mother Clytemnestra, for which Electra claims equal responsibility. She gives an account of what happened and why. The people of Argos have now passed a decree outlawing them and are about to vote on whether they should be stoned to death or allowed to commit suicide. The only hope she can see resides with Menelaus who has arrived with Helen and their daughter Hermione.

Helen now enters, saddened by the death of her sister, but inclined to hold Apollo responsible rather than Electra or Orestes. Helen asks Electra to take an offering for her to Clytemnestra's tomb, being uncomfortable about appearing in public. Electra refuses, so Helen calls her daughter Hermione and sends her instead. The Chorus of local women now enter. Electra is concerned that they will awaken Orestes, sleeping at last for the first time since the murder. Eventually they do wake him. He is still afflicted by the Furies, though when Menelaus enters Orestes attributes his condition to conscience over what he has done. Orestes asks Menelaus to intercede on their behalf, but then Tyndareus turns up, Helen and Clytemnestra's earthly father and Orestes' grandfather. Orestes tries to defend his actions. Tyndareus will have none of it and warns off Menelaus from offering any assistance. He then leaves. Menelaus points out to Orestes the difficulty of opposing the will of the people, but when he too departs help appears in the person of Pylades, exiled from his home for his part in the killing of Clytemnestra. The two men decide to face the court.

Electra returns and an elderly Messenger reports on what happened when Orestes tried to make his case. The best he could win was the right for brother and sister to kill themselves rather than be stoned. It is Pylades who comes up with a plan. They should win approval with the people by murdering Helen. Orestes has doubts, but Electra suggests seizing Hermione to use as a bargaining card with Menelaus. Orestes and Pylades go indoors and Helen's death cries are heard. Hermione arrives soon after and is dragged into the palace. A Trojan slave enters, giving an account in broken Greek of what has been happening indoors. Orestes comes out after him, but lets him escape before returning inside. Menelaus runs in with his soldiers to find Electra and Pylades on the roof with Orestes holding a knife at Hermione's throat. Orestes threatens to set the palace on fire if Menelaus tries to break in.

To this scene of mayhem Apollo appears *ex machina*. Helen is with him, not killed but rescued at the order of Zeus and granted immortality. Electra is to leave and marry Pylades, Orestes to stay and marry Hermione, after which he will become king of Argos: and with these pronouncements peace breaks out and the play ends.

Phoenician Women

Jocasta, wife and mother of Oedipus, delivers the prologue. She supplies a history of the events that led up to her giving birth to a son who would grow up to kill his father, Laius, though warned by the oracle not to have a child. Laius exposed the baby who was saved and brought up abroad. In due course the oracle was fulfilled and Jocasta married her own son and had four children with him. When Oedipus discovered the truth he blinded himself. Now the two boys, Eteocles and Polyneices, are engaged in civil war for the throne while the infirm Oedipus remains shut up inside the palace.

When Jocasta leaves, Antigone and her Tutor replace her and review from the roof the Argive army – who are supporting Polyneices – identifying individual warriors. The Chorus make their entrance, distant relations on their way from Phoenicia to Delphi, but caught up in the war. They are alone when Polyneices arrives. He is the brother trying to take his place as king, as promised by Eteocles, a promise on which Eteocles has reneged. Jocasta returns. She wants to negotiate a reconciliation between her two sons. When Eteocles arrives, the brothers discuss the nature of power and it soon becomes clear that only bloodshed will resolve their dispute. Polyneices leaves, and Eteocles and Creon, Jocasta's brother, plan their tactics. The enemy have chosen one hero to fight at each of the seven gates of the city. Eteocles' only interest is at which he will be able to find his brother.

Thebes' blind prophet Teiresias now enters with Menoeceus, Creon's son, and reluctantly forecasts that the city cannot be saved unless Creon sacrifices the boy. Creon makes plans for Menoeceus to escape but, when his father leaves, Menoeceus admits that he only pretended to go along with his father's suggestion. He cannot betray his city and exits, resolved to kill himself. After an ode where the Chorus rehearse the encounter between Oedipus and the Sphinx, a Messenger arrives to tell Jocasta of Menoeceus' suicide and to give a lengthy and graphic account of the engagement in the field. The battle has turned in favour of the defenders, but Eteocles and Polyneices have agreed to single combat.

Jocasta rushes off with Antigone to try and prevent their duel and Creon, aware now of his son's death, is faced with another Messenger. The two brothers have killed one another. Jocasta arrived too late and has added to the carnage by putting a sword through her own throat. But Thebes has been saved. A procession arrives bringing in the three dead bodies, mother and two sons, with Antigone to mourn them. Only then does Oedipus make his entrance. Despite Antigone's protestations Creon decrees that, in accordance with Eteocles' wishes, Polyneices' corpse remain unburied, though Eteocles will be granted full honours. Antigone prepares to leave Thebes with Oedipus, but means to return secretly before they go to see that her brother Polyneices too receives a proper burial.

Rhesus

There is no prologue in this play which opens with the agitated arrival of the Chorus, Trojan sentries on night duty. The action of the entire drama, it transpires, will take place during hours of darkness. They have come to bring urgent news to Hector, the commander-in-chief of the Trojan army. Something major seems to be taking place among the Greek forces on the shore which is alight with bonfires. Hector surmises that the Greeks are planning a withdrawal and tells the sentries to wake the whole Trojan army and prepare to attack. Aeneas arrives to find out what is going on, but agrees with the Chorus that Hector is being impetuous: better to send a spy in case it is a trick. Dolon volunteers, as long as his reward will be the horses of Achilles if the Trojans manage to capture them. Hector reluctantly agrees, fancying the horses himself, and Dolon prepares to leave.

A Messenger now arrives with news from a different quarter. A shepherd has caught sight of the Thracian king, Rhesus, arriving, if belatedly, with a large contingent to fight as allies of the Trojans. Rhesus enters and meets with a grudging response from Hector for not having been there sooner. Rhesus has his excuses and Hector departs to show him where he and his troops may set up camp. The Chorus now start to complain about not having been relieved at the end of their watch, exiting eventually to go and look for their replacements. This gives the opportunity for the two Greek heroes, Odysseus and Diomedes, to sneak into the Trojan camp intent on assassinating Hector. They are stopped by the arrival *ex machina* of Athena who tells them that their target ought to be Rhesus, not Hector or Paris. Athena hears Paris coming, the son of King Priam who abducted Helen in the first place. The Greeks leave and the goddess distracts Paris by pretending to be Aphrodite and telling him that all is well.

As soon as she and Paris have departed, the Chorus are back, hot in pursuit of the two Greeks who have succeeded in their mission. Confusion in the darkness and Odysseus' knowledge of the password (which he has earlier tortured from Dolon before killing him), ensure that the Greeks escape. The Chorus realise they have been tricked and probably by Odysseus. Rhesus' Charioteer now staggers in, wounded and full of recrimination for the treacherous killing of his master which he blames on Hector. Hector is furious at what the Greeks have managed to pull off. He orders the Charioteer to be taken to his own tent. The Muse, mother of Rhesus, now appears *ex machina* with her son's body and laments his death. She leaves the scene and, as dawn begins to break, Hector orders an attack on the Greek fleet and the play comes to an end.

Suppliants

One of the less familiar characters from Greek mythology opens this play, Theseus' mother, Aethra. She has come from Athens, where her son is king, to Eleusis to offer support to the Chorus who are suppliants at the temple of Demeter. They are then identified as the mothers of the seven heroes on the Argive side who died in the ill-fated attack on Thebes which ended with the two sons of Oedipus and Jocasta, Eteocles and Polyneices, killing one another in single combat. The Thebans have refused burial to the seven and Adrastus, king of Argos, who is sitting with the women, his head covered, seeks backing from the Athenians.

Theseus arrives, surprised to see his own mother with this group of women. When Aethra tells him who the man is wrapped in a cloak, Theseus addresses him. Adrastus is contrite, confessing to having made a drastic error of judgement over the war, but believing that Athens, the home of compassion, should now support the mission of the mothers. Aethra is more forthright, telling her son that he will be accused of cowardice if he refuses. Theseus agrees to let Adrastus address the Assembly in Athens in person.

When they return, after a favourable reception, Theseus is instructing his own Herald to take a message to Creon, king of Thebes, politely requesting that the bodies be buried, when a Theban Herald arrives. This man is full of scorn for the idea of democracy which Theseus strongly debates with him. The Theban Herald's message is unambiguous. Send Adrastus away and stop this agitation for the burial, or it is war between Athens and Thebes. Unimpressed by such threats, Theseus responds with dignity but firmness. The Theban Herald angrily departs and Theseus leaves to prepare for battle. The Chorus sing an ode about the outcome, but a Messenger soon arrives to give Adrastus a vivid account of what happened when the two armies met. The Athenians were victorious, but Theseus declined to press home his advantage and attack the city of Thebes. They are now bringing home the bodies about whom the dispute arose.

The remains are carried in and Adrastus and the Chorus offer lamentations for their dead. Theseus arrives back and asks Adrastus to identify the heroes, but prevents the women from seeing the disfigured corpses, most of whom will be cremated on a single pyre. The Chorus accept this, but suddenly catch sight of Evadne, the wife of Capaneus, one of the seven, on the roof of the temple. Intent on suicide, she gives an impassioned speech. Her father Iphis enters, but is unable to dissuade her from hurling herself into the flames. In another unexpected twist, the sons of the seven enter to join in the mourning. Another coda sees the arrival of Athena, *ex machina*, who looks forward to the boys growing up and marching on Thebes to avenge their fathers. Theseus thanks the goddess for her protection and the play comes to an end.

Trojan Women

The play begins with the god Poseidon, a supporter of Troy in the war to liberate Helen, lamenting the destruction of the city and the fate of all those who fell trying to defend it. He is not alone, however, and points out Hecuba, the wife of the king of Troy, lying on the ground below, waiting to discover what is to happen to herself and the remaining prisoners. Athena, who took the side of the victorious Greeks, now enters offering Poseidon an alliance. She is angry that the Greeks declined to punish Ajax for defiling her temple when he dragged Cassandra, Hecuba's daughter, from sanctuary. She wants Poseidon's help to ensure that the voyage home is accompanied by storms and shipwreck. Poseidon quickly agrees and the gods exit. They may have been on opposite sides in the war, but are united that sacrilege must be punished.

Hecuba speaks at last. Most of her family are dead and she awaits further news of her own fate. The Chorus of Greek fellow-prisoners join her, fearful for what the future may bring. Hecuba is especially concerned about her daughter Cassandra, the prophetess cursed by Apollo never to be believed. The Greek herald Talthybius arrives with news (compare *Hecuba*). Agamemnon is to take Cassandra as his concubine. Talthybius is less forthcoming about the fate of another daughter, Polyxena, who he says is to serve Achilles at his tomb. Hector's wife, Andromache, is awarded to Achilles' son Neoptolemus and Hecuba herself as a slave to the hated Odysseus. Cassandra bursts in, deranged and carrying a torch. She forecasts Agamemnon's death and further disasters for the Greek army, especially Odysseus and his men, before being taken away by the soldiers.

Hecuba and the Chorus grieve over their homes and families until Andromache and Astyanax, her young son by Hector, are wheeled in on the top of a cart of looted treasure. Andromache tells her mother-in-law what Talthybius really meant. Polyxena has been sacrificed at Achilles' tomb, while she must sleep with Achilles' son. Talthybius returns, reluctantly revealing that Astyanax, as a potential future threat, is to be thrown from the battlements of Troy. Andromache is dragged off in one direction, Astyanax carried off in the other. Following a choral ode Menelaus arrives in cheerful mood. He is about to have his wife Helen returned to him, to kill when he gets back to Sparta. Helen is brought in and tries to justify herself as best she may. Hecuba fiercely disputes Helen's version of events, advising Menelaus not to return home on the same ship, but Helen and Menelaus leave together.

The Chorus lament the fate of the children from whom they have been parted for ever, and Talthybius comes back with the body of Andromache's dead baby carried in on his father's shield, for Hecuba to mourn. The women do what they can to dress and honour the tiny corpse from whatever they have managed to salvage. In the background Troy burns. Hecuba is physically restrained from throwing herself into the flames. The Chorus and their former queen are finally removed to the last of the Greek ships.

SELECT BIBLIOGRAPHY

Among the large number of translations and 'versions' of the nineteen Euripides plays, there is considerable variety, from the more literal Loeb editions and those from Aris and Phillips, with the Greek alongside the English, to other major collections, or individual plays, published by, alphabetically, rather than in any order of preference: Cambridge University Press, Methuen Drama, Nick Hern Books, Oxford University Press, Penguin Books, The University of Chicago Press.

Much of the most valuable and accessible discussion of individual plays is to be found in the Introductions to the above, or in other published editions and translations, too many to detail here.[1] Inclusion of all the modern plays referred to in Chapter 11 was also impractical, though a small number of critical works on the individual playwrights are included in the general bibliography.

The identification of commentaries on the plays of Euripides is certainly not comprehensive. There have been over four hundred individual articles, books or series of notes on *Bacchae* alone. The bibliography is aimed for the most part at those who wish to look further at any of the issues raised in connection with any single play, or group of plays, but who have no knowledge of ancient Greek. It also covers a range of approaches to Euripidean dramaturgy. Where several relevant articles or chapters occur in the same compilation, at the risk of alienating individual contributors, I have included volume details only. These are identified with an asterisk. Publications dealing primarily with the social and historical background to Euripides' work, or to original staging conditions in Athens, have been excluded.

Albert, S. P., 'G.B.S. in Hellas: A Resource for Classicists', *Annual of Bernard Shaw Studies* 223 (2003), 167–80

Allan, W., *The 'Andromache' and Euripidean Tragedy*, Oxford: OUP, 2000

Appleton, R. B., *Euripides the Idealist*, New York: Dutton, 1927

Aristotle, *The Poetics*, trans. M. E. Hubbard, *Classical Literary Criticism*, Oxford: OUP, 1972

[1] For a more complete listing of translations from the Greek into English (up to 2005) see the Appendix to my *Found in Translation: Greek Drama in English* (2006). For the many plays based on Euripidean originals see Hall and Macintosh (2005).

Arnott, P. D., *Public and Performance in the Greek Theatre*, London: Routledge, 1989

Arnott, W. G., 'Parody and Ambiguity in Euripides' *Cyclops*', *Antidosis: Festschrift für Walter Kraus zum 70. Geburtstag*, Vienna: Boehlau, 1972

Arrowsmith, W., 'Euripides and the Dramaturgy of Crisis', *Literary Imagination: The Review of the Association of Literary Scholars and Critics* 1.2 (1999), 201–26

— 'A Greek Theater of Ideas', *Ideas in the Drama* (ed. J. Gassner), New York: Columbia University Press, 1964, reprinted as 'Euripides' Theater of Ideas' in E. Segal (1968), 13–33

— and R. Shattuck (eds.), *The Craft and Context of Translation*, Austin: University of Texas Press, 1961

Banfield, S., *Sondheim's Broadway Musicals*, Ann Arbor: University of Michigan Press, 1993

Barlow, S. A., *The Imagery of Euripides*, London: Methuen, 1971

— 'Structure and Dramatic Realism in Euripides' *Heracles*', *Greece and Rome* 29 (1982), 115–25

Bassnett-McGuire, S., *Luigi Pirandello*, London: Macmillan, 1983

— *Translation Studies*, London: Methuen, 1980, rev. ed. (as Bassnett), London: Routledge, 1991

Bates, W. N., *Euripides: A Student of Human Nature*, Philadelphia: University of Pennsylvania Press, 1930

Belli, A., *Ancient Greek Myths and Modern Drama*, New York: New York University Press, 1969

Blaiklock, E. M., *The Male Characters of Euripides: A Study in Realism*, Wellington: New Zealand University Press, 1952

Bolgar, R. R., *The Classical Legacy and its Beneficiaries*, Cambridge: CUP, 1954

Brecht, B., *The Messingkauf Dialogues*, trans. J. Willett, London: Methuen, 1965

Burian, P. (ed.), *Directions in Euripidean Criticism*, Durham, NC: Duke University Press, 1985*

— 'Euripides and the Dramaturg of Crisis: Notes and Commentary on Arrowsmith', *Literary Imagination: The Review of the Association of Literary Scholars and Critics* 1.2 (1999), 227–35

— 'Euripides' *Heraclidae*: An Interpretation', *Classical Philology* 72 (1976), 4–26

Burnett, S. P., *Catastrophe Survived*, Oxford: Clarendon Press, 1971

— 'Virtues of Admetus', *Classical Philology* LX (October 1965), 240–55

Carpenter, T. H. and C. A. Faraone (eds.), *Masks of Dionysus*, Ithaca: Cornell University Press, 1993*

Castellani, V., 'That Troubled House of Pentheus in Euripides' *Bacchae*', *Transactions of the American Philological Association* 106 (1976), 61–84

Clauss, J. J. and S. I. Johnston (eds.), *'Medea': Essays on 'Medea' in Myth, Literature, Philosophy, and Art*, Princeton: Princeton University Press, 1997*

Collard, C., *Euripides*, Greece and Rome Surveys in the Classics 14, Oxford: Clarendon Press (for The Classical Association), 1981

— (ed.), *Tragedy, Euripides and Euripideans*, Exeter: Bristol Phoenix Press, 2007

Conacher, D. J., *Euripidean Drama: Myth, Theme and Structure*, Oxford: OUP, 1967

Croally, N. T., *Euripidean Polemic*, Cambridge: CUP, 1994

Cropp, M. E. Fantham and S. E. Scully (eds.), *Greek Tragedy and its Legacy: Essays presented to D. J. Conacher*, Calgary: University of Calgary Press, 1986*

Decharme, P., *Euripides and the Spirit of his Dramas*, trans. J. Loeb, London: Macmillan, 2006

Dillon, J. and S. E. Wilmer (eds.), *Rebel Women: Staging Greek Drama Today*, London: Methuen Drama, 2005*

Dodds, E. R., *The Greeks and the Irrational*, Berkeley and Los Angeles: University of California Press, 1951

Dunn, F., *Tragedy's End: Closure and Innovation*, Oxford: OUP, 1996

Easterling P. E., 'Anachronism in Greek Tragedy', *Journal of Hellenic Studies* 105 (1985), 1–10

— (ed.), *The Cambridge Companion to Greek Tragedy*, Cambridge: CUP, 1997*

— 'The Infanticide in Euripides' *Medea*', *Yale Classical Studies* 25 (1977), 177–91

Eliot, T. S., 'Euripides and Professor Murray', *Selected Essays: 1917–1932*, London: Faber (1932), pp. 59–64

Evreinoff, N., *The Theatre in Life*, trans. O. Sayler, New York: Brentano, 1927

Finley, M. I. (ed.), *The Legacy of Greece*, Oxford: OUP, 1984

Foley, H. P., 'Anodos Drama: Euripides' *Alcestis* and *Helen*', *Innovations in Antiquity*, R. Hexter and D. Sedden (eds.), London and New York: Routledge (1980), 133–60

— *Female Acts in Greek Tragedy*, Princeton: Princeton University Press, 2001

— 'The Masque of Dionysus', *Transactions of the American Philological Association* 110 (1980), 107–33

— *Ritual Irony: Poetry and Sacrifice in Euripides*, Ithaca: Cornell University Press, 1985

Fuegi, J., *Bertolt Brecht: Chaos According to Plan*, Cambridge: CUP, 1987

Gill, C., 'The Question of Character and Personality in Greek Tragedy', *Poetics Today* 7 (1986), 251–73

Goldhill, S. and R. Osborne (eds.), *Performance Culture and Athenian Democracy*, Cambridge: CUP, 1999*

Greenwood, L. H. G., *Aspects of Euripidean Tragedy*, Cambridge: CUP, 1953

Gregory, J. (ed.), *A Companion to Greek Tragedy*, Oxford: Blackwell, 2005*

— 'Euripides' *Alcestis*', *Hermes* 107 (1979), 259–70

— *Euripides and the Instruction of the Athenians*, Ann Arbor: University of Michigan Press, 1991

— 'Euripides' *Heracles*', *Yale Classical Studies* 25 (1977), 259–75

— 'Some Aspects of Seeing in Euripides' *Bacchae*', *Greece and Rome* 32 (1985), 23–31

Grube, G. M. A., *The Drama of Euripides*, London: Methuen, 1941

Hall, E., 'Medea and British Legislation Before the First World War', *Greece and Rome* 46.1 (1999), 42–77

— and F. Macintosh, *British Theatre and Greek Tragedy 1660–1914*, Oxford: OUP, 2005

— — and O. Taplin (eds.), '*Medea' in Performance 1500–2000*, Oxford: Legenda, 2000*

— — and A. Wrigley (eds.), *Dionysus Since 69: Greek Tragedy at the Dawn of the Third Millennium*, Oxford: OUP, 2004*

Halleran, M., *Stagecraft in Euripides*, London: Croom Helm, 1985

Hardwick, L., *Translating Words, Translating Cultures*, London: Duckworth, 2000

— and C. Stray (eds.), *A Companion to Classical Receptions*, Oxford: Blackwell, 2008*

Heath, M., *The Poetics of Greek Tragedy*, London: Duckworth, 1987

Hettick, E. L., *A Study in Ancient Naturalism: The Testimony of Euripides*, Williamsport, PA: Bayard, 1933

Highet, G., *The Classical Tradition: Greek and Roman Influences on Western Literature*, Oxford: OUP, 1949; reprinted with corrections, 1967

Hourmouziades, N. C., *Production and Imagination in Euripides*, Athens: Greek Society for Humanistic Studies, 1965

Hughes, B., *Helen of Troy*, London: Jonathan Cape, 2005

Huizinga, J., *Homo Ludens*, London: Routledge and Kegan Paul, 1949

— *The Waning of the Middle Ages*, London: Edward Arnold, 1924

Innes, C. (ed.), *The Cambridge Companion to George Bernard Shaw*, Cambridge: CUP, 1998*

Johnson, W., *August Strindberg*, Boston: Twayne, 1976

Johnston, D. (ed.), *Stages of Translation*, Bath: Absolute Classics, 1996*

Jones, P., *Ancient and Modern*, London: Duckworth, 1999

Kirk, G. S., *The 'Bacchae' of Euripides*, Englewood Cliffs NJ: Prentice-Hall, 1970

Kitto, H. D. F., *Greek Tragedy*, London: Methuen, 1939; 3rd ed. 1961

Klotsche, E. H., 'The Supernatural in Euripides as illustrated in Prayer, Curses, Oaths, Oracles, Prophesies, Dreams, and Visions', *Nebraska University Studies* XVIII (1918), 3–4

Knox, B., *Word and Action: Essays on the Ancient Theater*, Baltimore: Johns Hopkins University Press, 1979

Kolve, V. A., *The Play Called 'Corpus Christi'*, London: Edward Arnold, 1966

Kott, J., *The Eating of the Gods: An Interpretation of Greek Tragedy*, trans. Boleslaw Taborski and E. J. Czerwinski from *Ziadanie Bogów*, New York: Random House, 1973; London: Eyre Methuen, 1974

— *Shakespeare Our Contemporary*, trans. Boleslaw Taborski from *Szekpirze wspólczesny*, London: Methuen, rev. ed. 1967

Kovacs, D., 'Gods and Men in Euripides' Trojan Trilogy', *Colby Quarterly* 33 (1997), 162–76

— *The Heroic Muse: Studies in the* 'Hippolytus' *and* 'Hecuba' *of Euripides*, Baltimore: Johns Hopkins University Press, 1987

Lee, K. H., 'The Iris–Lyssa Scene in Euripides' *Heracles*', *Antichthon* 16 (1982), 44–53

Lefkowitz, M. R., 'Impiety and "Atheism" in Euripides' Dramas', *Classical Quarterly* 39 (1989), 70–82

— 'Vita Euripidis', *The Lives of the Greek Poets*, Appendix 5, London: Duckworth (1981), 163–9

— *Women in Greek Myth*, Baltimore: Johns Hopkins University Press, 1986

Livingstone, R. W. (ed.), *The Legacy of Greece*, Oxford: Clarendon Press, 1921*

Lloyd, M., 'The Helen Scene in Euripides' *Trojan Women'*, *Classical Quarterly* 34 (1984), 303–13

Lovenseimer, J., 'Stephen Sondheim and the Musical of the Outsider', W. A. Everett and P. R. Laird (eds.), *The Cambridge Companion to the Musical*, Cambridge: CUP (2002), 181–96

Lucas, D. W., *The Greek Tragic Poets*, London: Harrap, 1950

Lucas, F. L., *Euripides and his Influence*, London: Harrap, 1924

Macintosh, F., '*Alcestis* in Britain', *Cahiers du GITA* 14 (2001), 281–308

— *Dying Acts: Death in Ancient Greek and Irish Tragedy*, Cork: Cork University Press, 1994

— 'The Shavian Murray and the Euripidean Shaw: *Major Barbara* and *The Bacchae'*, *Classics Ireland* 5 (1998), 64–84

McDonald. M., *Ancient Sun: Modern Light*, New York: Columbia University Press, 1992

— *Euripides in Cinema: The Heart Made Visible*, Philadelphia: Centrum, 1983

— 'Iphigeneia's Philia: Motivation in Euripides' *Iphigeneia at Aulis'*, *Quaderni Urbinati di Cultura Classica* 63 (1990), 69–84

— *The Living Art of Greek Tragedy*, Bloomington: Indiana University Press, 2003

— *Sing Sorrow: Classics, History, and Heroines in Opera*, Westport: Greenwood, 2001

— *Terms for Happiness in Euripides*, Göttingen: Vandenhoeck and Ruprecht, 1978

— 'War Then and Now: The Legacy of Ancient Greek Tragedy', *Hermathena* 181 (Winter 2006), 83–104

— and J. M. Walton (eds.), *Amid Our Troubles: Irish Versions of Greek Tragedy*, London: Methuen, 2002*

— — *The Cambridge Companion to Greek and Roman Theatre*, Cambridge: CUP, 2007*

McIntyre, H. G., *The Theatre of Jean Anouilh*, London: Harrap, 1981

Marker, F. J. and L-L. Marker, *Strindberg and Modernist Theatre*, Cambridge: CUP, 2002

Marshall, C. W., 'Theatrical References in Euripides' *Electra*', *Illinois Classical Studies* 24–25 (1999–2000), 325–441

Meridor, R., 'The Function of Polymestor's Crime in the *Hecuba* of Euripides', *Eranos* 81 (1983), 13–20

Meyer, M., *Strindberg: A Biography*, London: Secker and Warburg, 1985

Michelini, A. N., *Euripides and the Tragic Tradition*, Madison: University of Wisconsin Press, 1987

Mikalson, J., *Honor Thy Gods: Popular Religion in Greek Tragedy*, Chapel Hill: University of North Carolina Press, 1991

Mossman, J. (ed.), *Oxford Readings in Classical Studies: Euripides*, Oxford: OUP, 2003*

— *Wild Justice: A Study of Euripides' 'Hecuba'*, Oxford: Clarendon Press, 1995

Murray, G., *Euripides and His Age*, Oxford: OUP 1913; 2nd ed. 1946

Nietzsche, F., *The Birth of Tragedy and The Case for Wagner*, trans. W. Kaufmann, New York: Vintage Books, 1967

Norwood, G., *Essays on Euripidean Drama*, Berkeley and Los Angeles: University of California Press, 1954

— *Euripides and Shaw: with other essays*, London: Methuen, 1921

Oranje, H., *Euripides' 'Bacchae': The Play and its Audience*, Leiden: Brill, 1984

Padel, R., *Whom Gods Destroy: Elements of Greek and Tragic Madness*, Princeton: Princeton University Press, 1992

Patsalidis, S. and E. Sakellaridou (eds.), *(Dis)Placing Classical Greek Theatre*, Thessaloniki: University Studio Press, 1999*

Pelling, C. B. R. (ed.), *Characterisation and Individuality in Greek Literature*, Oxford: Clarendon Press, 1990*

— *Greek Tragedy and the Historian*, Oxford: Clarendon Press, 1997

Plato, *The Republic*, trans. H. D. P. Lee, Harmondsworth: Penguin, 1955

— *The Symposium*, trans. W. Hamilton, Harmondsworth: Penguin, 1951

Podlecki, A., 'Some Themes in Euripides' *Phoenissae*', *Transactions of the American Philological Association* 93 (1962), 355–73

Powell, A. (ed.), *Euripides, Women and Sexuality*, London: Routledge, 1990*

Probst, G. F. and J. F. Bodine (eds.), *Perspectives on Max Frisch*, Kentucky: Kentucky University Press, 1982

Pronko, L. C., *The World of Jean Anouilh*, Berkeley and Los Angeles: University of California Press, 1961

Rabinowitz, N. S., *Anxiety Veiled: Euripides and the Traffic in Women*, Ithaca: Cornell University Press, 1993

Ragusa, O., *Luigi Pirandello: An Approach to his Theatre*, Edinburgh: Edinburgh University Press, 1980

Rehm, R., 'Performing the Chorus: Choral Presence, Interaction and Absence in Euripides', *Arion* 3 (1996), 45–60

— *Radical Theatre: Greek Tragedy in the Modern World*, London: Duckworth, 2003

— 'The Staging of Suppliant Plays', *Greek, Roman, and Byzantine Studies* 29 (1988), 263–307

Riley, K., *The Reception and Performance of Euripides' 'Herakles': Reason in Madness*, Oxford: OUP, 2008

Ritchie, W., *The Authenticity of the 'Rhesus' of Euripides*, Cambridge: CUP, 1964

Rosenmeyer, T. G., 'Tragedy and Religion: The *Bacchae*' in E. Segal (1968), 370–89

Schechner, R., *Performance Studies: An Introduction*, London: Routledge, 2002

— *Performance Theory*, London and New York: Routledge, 1988; rev. ed. 2003

Schlesinger, A. C., 'Is Greek Drama Modern?', *Classical Journal* 62.8 (May 1967), 337–42

Segal, C. P., *Dionysiac Poetics and Euripides' 'Bacchae'*, Princeton: Princeton University Press, 1982

— 'Shame and Purity in Euripides' *Hippolytus*', *Hermes* 98 (1970), 278–99

— 'The Two Worlds of Euripides' *Helen*', *Transactions of the American Philological Society* 102 (1971), 553–614

Segal, E. (ed.), *Euripides: A Collection of Critical Essays*, Englewood Cliffs: Prentice-Hall, 1968*

— (ed.), *Oxford Readings in Greek Tragedy*, Oxford: OUP, 1983

Seidensticker, B., 'Comic Elements in Euripides' *Bacchae*', *American Journal of Philology* 99 (1978), 303–20

Silk, M. (ed.), *Tragedy and the Tragic*, Oxford: OUP, 1996*

Smith, J. and A. Toynbee (eds.), *Gilbert Murray: An Unfinished Autobiography (with contributions by his friends)*, London: George Allen and Unwin, 1960

Smith, W., 'The Ironic Structure in *Alcestis*', *Phoenix* 14 (1960), 126–45

SELECT BIBLIOGRAPHY

Snell, B., *Poetry and Society: The Role of Poetry in Ancient Greece*, Bloomington: Indiana University Press, 1961
— *Scenes from Greek Tragedy*, Berkeley and Los Angeles: University of California Press, 1964
Sourvinou-Inwood, C., *Tragedy and Athenian Religion*, Lanham: Lexington Books, 2003
Stray, C. (ed.), *Gilbert Murray Reassessed: Hellenism, Theatre, and International Politics*, Oxford: OUP, 2007

Taxidou, O., *Tragedy, Modernity and Mourning*, Edinburgh: Edinburgh University Press, 2004
Thomson, P. and G. Sacks (eds.), *The Cambridge Companion to Brecht*, Cambridge: CUP, 1993; 2nd ed., 2006

Urs, J., *Dürrenmatt: A Study of his Plays*, trans. K. Hamnett and H. Rorrison, London: Eyre Methuen, 1978

Vellacott, P., *Ironic Drama: A Study of Euripides' Method and Meaning*, Cambridge: CUP, 1975
Vernant, J-P. and P. Vidal-Nacquet (eds.), *Myth and Tragedy in Ancient Greece*, trans. J. Lloyd, New York: Zone Books, 1988
Verrall, A. W., *Essays on Four Plays of Euripides: 'Andromache', 'Helen', 'Heracles', 'Orestes'*, Cambridge: CUP, 1905
— *Euripides, the Rationalist*, Cambridge: CUP, 1913
Vittorini, D., *The Drama of Luigi Pirandello*, Philadelphia: University of Pennsylvania Press, 1935

Walton, J. M., *Found in Translation: Greek Drama in English*, Cambridge: CUP, 2006
— *Greek Theatre Practice*, Westport: Greenwood, 1980; 2nd ed., London: Methuen Drama, 1991
— *Living Greek Theatre: A Handbook of Classical Performance and Modern Production*, Westport: Greenwood, 1987
— 'Playing in the Dark: Masks and Euripides' *Rhesus*', *Helios* 21.2 (Fall 2000), 137–47
— *The Greek Sense of Theatre: Tragedy Reviewed*, London: Methuen, 1984; 2nd ed., Amsterdam: Harwood Academic, 1996
— 'Travelling in Theatre History', Iossif Viviliakis (ed.), *Stephanos: Tribute to Walter Puchner*, Athens: Ergo Editions (2007 a), 1359–66
— 'Vacuum or Agenda: The Translator's Dilemma', *Classical and Modern Literature* 27.1 (2007 b), 93–120

Webster, T. B. L., *The Tragedies of Euripides*, London: Methuen, 1967

Weisstein, U., *Max Frisch*, New York: Twayne, 1967

West, M. L., *Euripides: 'Orestes'*, Warminster: Aris and Phillips, 1987

Whitman, C. H., *Euripides and the Full Circle of Myth*, Cambridge, Mass.: Harvard University Press, 1974

Wiles, D., *Greek Theatre Performance*, Cambridge: CUP, 2000

Willett, J. (ed.), *Brecht on Theatre: The Development of an Aesthetic*, New York: Hill and Wang, 1966

Wilson, J. R. (ed.), *Twentieth-Century Interpretations of Euripides' 'Alcestis'*, Englewood Cliffs: Prentice-Hall, 1968*

Winnington-Ingram, R., *Euripides and Dionysus: An Interpretation of the 'Bacchae'*, Amsterdam: Hakkert, 1948

— 'Euripides: *poietes sophos*', *Arethusa* 2 (1969), 127–42

Yunis, H., *A New Creed: Fundamental Religious Beliefs in the Athenian Polis and Euripidean Drama*, Göttingen: Vandenhoeck and Ruprecht, 1988

Zadan, C., *Sondheim and Co.*, New York: Macmillan, 1974; 2nd ed. London: Nick Hern Books, 1990

Zimmermann, B., *Greek Tragedy: An Introduction*, trans. T. Marier, Baltimore: Johns Hopkins University Press, 1991

Zuntz, G., *The Political Plays of Euripides*, Cambridge: CUP, 1965

INDEX

References to characters or gods
within quoted passages have usually
been omitted, except in Chapter 10,
as have those in the Appendix
(pp. 213–34), which mostly duplicates
what has been said elsewhere.